The Other World of Richard Wright

The Other World of Richard Wright

PERSPECTIVES ON HIS HAIKU

Edited by Jianqing Zheng

University Press of Mississippi / Jackson

Margaret Walker Alexander Series
in African American Studies

www.upress.state.ms.us

The University Press of Mississippi is a member
of the Association of American University Presses.

Manufactured in the United States of America

First printing 2011

∞

Library of Congress Cataloging-in-Publication Data

The other world of Richard Wright : perspectives on his
haiku / edited by Jianqing Zheng.
p. cm. — (Margaret Walker Alexander series in African
American studies)
Includes bibliographical references and index.
ISBN 978-1-61703-022-2 (cloth : alk. paper) 1. Wright,
Richard, 1908–1960—Criticism and interpretation. 2. Haiku,
American—History and criticism. I. Zheng, Jianqing.
PS3545.R815Z79 2011
811'.52—dc22 2010040114

British Library Cataloging-in-Publication Data available

For June and Ben

Contents

Introduction

— JIANQING ZHENG —

Invited by the French government, Richard Wright and his family left New York for Paris on May 1, 1946. According to Margaret Walker, during his visit there, Wright found Paris "to be quaint and beautiful, a fascinating, almost beguiling place where he felt he could live and die."[1] The Wrights returned to New York in January 1947, but they soon found that "New York," as Jerry W. Ward, a noted Richard Wright scholar, states, "was no longer satisfactory."[2] So, in August 1947, Wright and his family moved back to Paris where Wright lived in voluntary exile for thirteen years and three months until his death on November 28, 1960. Whatever reasons he might have for him to sail across the ocean, Wright's expatriation in Paris in fact opened a window for him to see a world different from America, a world where he had a chance to be exposed to other cultures. Virginia Whatley Smith asserts that Wright "entered an arena of intellectual thought and humanistic challenges that transcend the narrow limits of his former American home" after his "intercontinental shift."[3] I agree with Smith that Wright's intellectual transcendence was a result of his "intercontinental shift." However, his shift did not come to an end after he arrived in Paris. Using France as a gateway, Wright began to travel to various other countries, mainly including his journeys to Ghana in 1953 to write *Black Power*, to Spain in 1954 and 1955 to write *Pagan Spain*, and to Indonesia in 1955 to write *The Color Curtain*. His shift, especially in the last two years of his life, became more poetical and intellectual than geographical. For instance, his fascination with haiku and Zen Buddhism surely shows his interest shifted to learning about the Japanese culture, and this new interest can be considered as Wright's global mindshift that reflects a significant aspect of his reception of and sensibility to other cultures.

Why did Wright suddenly make such a shift to haiku and Zen Buddhism at the time when he was very sick from amoebic dysentery and in a state of troubled mind? On August 22, 1959, Wright was hospitalized in the American Hospital in Neuilly. Hazel Rowley, in her biography of Richard Wright, mentions that amoebic dysentery "was a debilitating disease. The symptoms were intermittent fever, a tender and enlarged liver, abdominal cramps and discomfort, dehydration, and fatigue. The heavy medication was known to make patients weaker still. In addition to sulfa, penicillin, bismuth, and arsenic, Wright was given injections of emetine hydrochloride. The drug was potentially cardiotoxic, and patients were advised to remain in bed while under treatment. They hardly felt like doing anything else."[4] Rowley goes on to say that Wright began to write haiku since being in the hospital: "He was possessed by these tiny Japanese poems. He loved their fragility—'like spider webs.' A form of meditation, they gave Wright a modicum of inner peace in the worst period of despair and self-doubt he had ever known."[5] Wright's haiku 425 surely reflects his feelings in this period:[6]

An empty sickbed:
An indented white pillow
In weak winter sun.

This haiku creates a world where sickness or death is associated with nature; it is a world where Wright gains satori, enlightenment that is "defined as the state of *mu*, nothingness, which is absolutely free of any thought or emotion."[7] The association of the empty sickbed with the weak winter sun reveals the *mu* of personal emotion since death itself is *mu*. His daughter Julia believes that during his illness Wright began "breaking down words into syllables [that] matched the shortness of his breath, especially on the bad days when his inability to sit up at the typewriter restricted the very breadth of writing."[8] Thus, the fragility of haiku echoed the shortness of Wright's breath. Margaret Walker talks likewise about Wright's difficult period in *Daemonic Genius*, "The entire year of 1959 was one of increasing tension, dread, despair, and news of death. . . . [Wright] wondered if he could continue any longer to make his living as a writer."[9] She continues to say briefly that Wright's "interest in Haiku and Japan may have been the beginning of an interest in Eastern philosophy and religion . . . as Haiku is quite different from the kind of poetry with which Wright began his literary career."[10]

Both Rowley and Julia Wright suggest that Wright's haiku writing had a therapeutic effect while Walker does not suggest such. However, based upon their analyses, we can say that Wright's immersion in the minimal form of haiku and Zen Buddhism was a much-needed therapy for his illness as well as his troubled mind. He found peace, balance, harmony, and enlightenment from this different poetic form and "Eastern philosophy and religion." In other words, Wright's haiku writing should suggest a transcendent shift from the state of personal emotions to the realization of lonelilessness, selflessness, and egolessness that come to terms with the principles of Zen Buddhism. Read haiku 1, which must be Wright's favorite poem:

> I am nobody:
> The red sinking autumn sun
> Took my name away.

This haiku suggests that only when he was enlightened could Wright see a world—his other world—with his enlightened eye. It is evident that Wright's contact with the Japanese culture helped him address many issues that confronted him at the close of the 1950s, and the healing power of haiku, as best summarized by Julia Wright, "kept him spiritually afloat. Some of us will even find these deceptively simple patterns of syllables tap-dancing in our minds long after they are read. They are Richard Wright's poetry of loss and retrieval, of temperate joy and wistful humor, of exile and fragments of a dreamed return. They lie somewhere in that transitional twilight area between the loss for words and the few charmed syllables that can heal the loss."[11]

Wright learned to write haiku through the introduction of Sinclair Beiles, a young South African writer and painter who exiled in Paris. Beiles was born to English parents in Kampala, Uganda, in 1930 and educated in Johannesburg, South Africa. He talks about his friendship with Wright in an interview in 1994, "There was also a number of Americans I was friendly with, particularly Richard Wright, who wrote *Black Boy*. I was familiar with Jimmy Baldwin, but not as friendly with him as I was with Richard Wright."[12] About Wright's encounter with Beiles, Ollie W. Harrington recollects, "A few months earlier he had asked a young South African writer what was the book he was carrying under his arm. It was Dick's introduction to Hai-Kai."[13] So, Beiles was the first key person who helped Wright shift his interest to haiku.

Immediately after Beiles's introduction, there was an enthusiastic intensity of haiku writing in Wright's life in Paris. Wright was "completely incapable of stopping" his new obsession with haiku[14] though he was very sick at the time. He followed the strict 5-7-5 pattern of this Japanese poetic form, and his ardent enthusiasm urged him to write more than 4,000 haiku, from which 817 were selected and published in *Haiku: This Other World* in 1998, long after his death. This collection is truly an embodiment of the African American cultural treasure and heritage and a brilliant enactment of his poetic sensibility to nature he tried to be imbued with; it also demonstrates a keen awareness of his true sensibility to his inner life. Wright's 817 haiku thus project his new vision into the human world and its relationship with nature and offer readers an opportunity to see "a talent very different from that of the well-known vigorous novelist, but in perfect harmony with the deeper manifestations of his sensibility."[15] However, in comparison to the abundance of criticism his novels have received, his haiku collection has never received enough attention or criticism from literary historians or critics in the mainstream. It is, therefore, significant to recognize the poetic talent in Richard Wright and emphasize its importance in African American literature; it is also significant to examine the poetic values and sensibility in Wright's haiku through this anthology of criticism.

Haiku, a short Japanese poetic form, always challenges the reader to imagine and sense. Asataro Miyamori says that "an ideal haiku is one in which a natural event is described as it is, and the poet's emotion does not appear on the surface."[16] Because of its brevity, haiku focuses on a momentary impression or, let me borrow Robert Frost's phrase, a momentary stay against confusion. A good haiku with the qualities of brevity, ellipsis, and suggestiveness should have some space for readers to fill in their imagination so as to develop aesthetic appreciation. A haiku's images should moreover produce a montage effect for readers to associate nature with human ideas. Haiku 253 is a good example:

From a tenement,
The blue jazz of a trumpet
Weaving autumn mists.

Wright produces a picture with images that are interrelated and interacted between visual and auditory senses. The speaker not only literally hears the sound of a trumpet but sees it weaving autumn mists in his mind's eye as well. This interaction further creates an effect that brings out the speaker's feeling of loneliness or his memory of the South through the image of "blue" and the seasonal reference of autumn. However, through his lonely listening, the speaker attains a state of lonelilessness and forgetfulness of himself. The poet also challenges readers to gain an aesthetical appreciation based upon the awareness of their synesthetic perceptions of the sound of the jazz and its visual motion. Read another one, haiku 571:

From across the lake,
Past the black winter trees,
Faint sounds of a flute.

As far as the synesthetic perceptions are concerned, what does Wright want us to imagine in this haiku? What is the connection between nature (the visual images of lake, black winter trees) and sounds of a flute? What does the flute symbolize? To understand this haiku, let's first draw a sketch in the mind: someone is playing the flute and its sounds reach across the lake where someone else is listening. The listener's creative involvement surely reverberates with the musician's playing: The auditory image of the sound of a flute joins artfully the visual images of lake, blackness, winter, and trees. In fact, both the auditory and the visual images intensify each other. The flute symbolizes art created by humans, and its joining with those visual images implies an interrelationship with nature. It invites human involvement so that the speaker listens and observes attentively on the other side of the lake. In other words, he gains an aesthetical appreciation through listening and visual response. This terse, elliptic, and suggestive haiku thus creates a momentary impression through the synesthetic perceptions of visual and auditory images. It is a beautiful, evocative haiku.

Through the minimal form of haiku Wright rediscovered or renewed his poetic sensibility to nature. This sensibility reveals the "intercontinental shift" in him as a poet as well as the tenderness in him as a human being. In Michel Fabre's words, it "brings to light an often neglected aspect of the writer's personality: his intimate sense of the universal harmony, his wonder before life, his thirst for a natural existence, all these tendencies which nourished, as much as did any ideology or faith, his courageous and incessant battle against all that prevents an individual from fully belonging to the world."[17] The significance of his haiku is that they helped Wright rediscover his sensibility to nature or his "belonging to the world"; they also help readers see, through his poetic sensibility, the perfect harmony between nature and human nature. However, we should also realize that quite a few number of Wright's haiku offer us an opportunity to see the disharmony between nature and human nature, especially those haiku about the South. Thus said, some attention should be given to Wright as a haiku poet.

This anthology gathers a collection of available critical essays on Richard Wright's haiku. They address different issues and analyze different themes with a focus on Wright's poetic spirit. Their criticism and interpretations should function, more like Bashō's frog jumping into the quiet water, to provoke thinking about the poetic and cultural values of Wright's haiku and in turn to draw more literary criticism in the twenty-first century. The first essay, "Richard Wright's Haiku, Zen, and the African 'Primal Outlook upon Life'" by Yoshinobu Hakutani, is compelling in that it provides a comprehensive analysis of Wright's haiku and the influence of African philosophy and attitude toward life as an inspiration to his poetic sensibility. Hakutani states that the images of nature in Wright's haiku express the "primal outlook upon life" he acquired from his travel to Africa and that absent subjectivity in composing haiku is akin to Jacques Lacan's postmodern psychoanalytical concept of the subject. He also points out that most of Wright's haiku thrive on poignant images of nature. The author's profound research in Wright's haiku opens a new territory in the Wright Studies by tracing the development of Wright's poetic sensibility in his "Blueprint for Negro Writing" and its relationship to African and Japanese cultures.

Toru Kiuchi, in "Zen Buddhism in Richard Wright's Haiku," provides a new lens for gleaning fresh insights into Wright's haiku. It explores the strong influence of Zen Buddhism on Wright's haiku through R. H. Blyth's four volumes of *Haiku* that emphasize the importance of Zen in writing haiku and offers a detailed analysis of the historical development of Wright's haiku writing. Kiuchi also asserts that Wright studied Zen Buddhism through Daisetz Suzuki's *Essays in Zen Buddhism* with an endeavor to gain a full understanding of the practice of Zen. The author analyzes in a convincing way the characteristics of Zen and Wright's employment of them in his haiku with a comparison of his haiku to traditional Japanese haiku. Through Kiuchi's analysis, we witness the fascinating way Zen Buddhism impacted Wright's haiku.

In the essay, "Healing and Loss: Richard Wright's Haiku and the Southern Landscape," Meta L. Schettler argues that Wright's haiku, written in exile at a time when decolonization and independence swept the globe, could serve as part of an emerging body of postcolonial literature. It uses Homi Bhabha's *The Location of Culture* as a theoretical foundation to analyze Wright's haiku; it also focuses on African American culture, history, and race relations that shape Wright's haiku and his intellect and imagination. Schettler projects a clear vision into Wright's haiku that rehabilitate images of nature in the South and create a space of healing through this new genre to revive and reclaim the core images of African American and Southern history. This is an essay that fully engages race relations in Wright's haiku.

Shawnrece D. Campbell argues, in "Female Imagery, Exploitation, and Richard Wright's Journey to His Other World: Haiku," that Wright the poet was able to achieve a wholeness of vision that Wright the intellectual thinker could not because he realized that individual freedom and fulfillment in relation to organized human society was a lifelong issue he could not answer in his earlier works. Thinking that after haiku writing, Wright seemed to be more vehement than ever in his belief that materialism and greed were the twin culprits of racial discord and poverty, Campbell offers a focused examination of how Wright's haiku reveal a conflict between nature and culture and how women are exploited for labor and sex by their culture.

Richard A. Iadonisi, in the essay "'I Am Nobody': The Haiku of Richard Wright," renders an extensive explication of Wright's haiku. It provides an argument with other scholars on Wright's haiku. He believes that Wright loaded his haiku with a linguistic "bomb" that he dropped to remind his readers of social inequities, not of his flight from these concerns. Iadonisi underscores that Wright reinvented the haiku form, making of it a revolutionary poetry that undercuts the possibility of Zen oneness. He positions Wright's haiku as a vehicle to articulate his anticolonial and anti-imperialist attitude. With this attitude, Wright filled his haiku with an African American subjectivity.

Thomas L. Morgan's essay, "Inverting the Haiku Moment: Alienation, Objectification, and Mobility in Richard Wright's *Haiku: This Other World*," provides an excellent examination of Wright's conscious manipulation of haiku aesthetics, arguing that Wright's revision of the haiku moment gave him a new form with which to pursue the themes of alienation, inequality, and dehumanization that appear in his earlier works. Wright's reformulation functions as a continuation of his earlier works, allowing him to reengage the same cultural and social mores in a different generic context, one stripped of the pre-inscribed notions of identity that influence the critical reception of his prior works. In breaking apart the relationship between humanity and nature implied by the haiku moment, Wright redirects the universal truth it creates to examine the relationship that exists between the function of social forces and the experience of alienation in the construction of identity.

In the essay "Japanese Influence on Richard Wright in His Last Years: English Haiku as a New Genre," Sanehide Kodama discusses the Japanese influence on Wright as well as parallels other American poets' haiku with Wright's. It analyzes Wright's haiku that reveal personal feelings and stresses the impact of Blyth's *Haiku* on Wright. Even though the author does not suggest that Wright was converted to Zen Buddhism, he believes that Wright was deeply interested in the Zen teachings.

Sachi Nakachi, in "From *Japonisme* to Modernism: Richard Wright's African American Haiku," asserts that *Japonisme*, a Western aesthetic infatuation with Japan, is often considered to be terminated in the 1920s. American *Japonisme*, however, evolved into a new form in the 1930s and 1940s. It discusses how Wright contributed to the development of

Japonisme in the field of literature in the postwar era; it also argues that although some critics consider that Wright reserved haiku only for his personal and sentimental literary expression, it is important to note that they were written in the period when Wright had become interested in postcolonial struggles of the Third World. Thus Wright's adoption of haiku can be regarded as his literary challenge to bridge the Third World countries under the Western oppression.

In "Nature, the South, and Spain in *Haiku: This Other World*," Jianqing Zheng states that Wright's writings experienced a change after he moved to Paris as an American intellectual, but this change helped him switch his focus from America to other parts of the world and from the human world to nature where he found peace. It compares Wright's haiku with his other works such as *Black Boy*, *12 Million Black Voices*, and *Pagan Spain*; it also stresses the function of nature in Wright's haiku as a necessary means to present beauty in nature or to express human sensibility to nature. For instance, the South in Wright's haiku is a place full of dreams and memories through the images such as croaking frogs, magnolia trees, and hog killing; it is also a place full of hardships and loneliness through the images such as cotton, freight train, and his mother's sad eyes. Zheng believes that nature, which fulfilled Wright and made him an integrated part of it through his haiku, is a fundamental element in his works.

While most of the selected essays focus on the importance and themes of Richard Wright's haiku, the concluding essay, "Richard Wright's Place in American Haiku" by Lee Gurga, distinguishes itself by pointing out the weaknesses of Wright's haiku through an expert analysis of the haiku techniques, believing that his haiku "must stand or fall on their own merits in this poetic genre." The importance of Gurga's essay is that it comments on Wright's haiku in terms of late-twentieth-century and early-twenty-first-century haiku literature and criticism. Because of his active involvement in contemporary American haiku movement and his own excellence in haiku writing and editing, Gurga's essay is very informative, and he knows haiku as his essay attests to the fact. The author calls for a celebration of Wright's haiku although some of them are seriously flawed, but the best of them will serve as a doorway for people who will enter American haiku.

As I noted earlier in the introduction, it is unfortunate that, in comparison to the huge national acclaim and circulation *Native Son* and *Black Boy* enjoyed,[18] *Haiku: This Other World* has remained almost invisible to the public since its debut. However, it is also fortunate with the publication of this collection of critical essays, representing the best possible scholarship on Wright's haiku, though a long overdue one, that *Haiku: This Other World* will become more visible for readers to discover and rediscover how Wright integrated a Western mind into an Eastern poetic form to enlarge his or our sense of human complexity and human union or reunion with nature. A haiku by Bashō reads:

Such fragrance—
from where,
which tree?[19]

I believe that Wright's haiku have enriched contemporary American literature, and I hope this collection of criticism will lead readers to the fragrant tree of *Haiku: This Other World* to read for aesthetic appreciation and for more criticism as well.

I came to have the idea of editing a book of criticism on Richard Wright's haiku in 2005 when I received a research grant from Mississippi Valley State University's Delta Research and Cultural Institute and then buried myself for a week in Wright's haiku manuscripts in the Beinecke Rare Book and Manuscript Library at Yale University. Two years later, a grant received from the National Endowment for the Humanities (NEH) made me ponder over this project again. Now the slow work on this project is finally completed, and I begin to wonder whether the unpublished haiku by Wright will be unveiled someday so that readers and the literary world will be able to see a clearer picture of Wright's outlook on race, nature, human life, and the South. And criticism on his haiku will become more comprehensive and convincing.

Many people have lent their support during my years of research on Richard Wright's haiku. At Mississippi Valley State University, I especially thank Ms. Jannette Adams, director of Sponsored Programs, for her professional support in my research effort. Words of appreciation go to Dr. Thomas M. Adams at NEH for his advisement to my Wright project, Dr. Jerry W. Ward at Dillard University for his academic support and friendship,

Mrs. Carolyn Vance Smith, founder and co-chairman of the Natchez Literary and Cinema Celebration, for inviting me to present a workshop on Wright's haiku at the Nineteenth Natchez Conference on Richard Wright in 2008, and Mr. Charles Trumbull, editor of *Modern Haiku*, for his timely help in my preparation of the bibliography on Wright's haiku.

Special thanks go to the staff at the Beinecke Rare Book and Manuscript Library at Yale University for their impressive professionalism and excellent service during my visit there and to contributors for their enthusiastic support of this project. I am deeply grateful to the University Press of Mississippi that decided to publish this collection devoted to a Mississippi-born writer. I would like to thank, in particular, the anonymous reader for the University Press of Mississippi, who read part or whole of the manuscript and offered constructive suggestions, some of which I have adopted in this introduction. Finally, my deepest appreciation goes to my wife, June, and my son, Ben, for their patience, sacrifice, and understanding. Their support over the years has come to fruition.

Notes

1. Margaret Walker, *Richard Wright: Daemonic Genius* (New York: Amistad, 1988), 208.

2. Diane Williams and Jerry W. Ward, "A Conversation on Richard Wright," *Valley Voices: A Literary Review* 8, no. 2 (2008): 106.

3. Virginia Whatley Smith, introduction to *Richard Wright's Travel Writings: New Reflections*, ed. Virginia Whatley Smith (Jackson: University Press of Mississippi, 2001), xi.

4. Hazel Rowley, *Richard Wright: The Life and Times* (New York: Henry Holt, 2001), 501.

5. Ibid., 505.

6. The number here or in parentheses after each of Wright's haiku quoted in this book refers to that number in *Haiku: This Other World*, ed. Yoshinobu Hakutani and Robert L. Tener (New York: Arcade, 1998).

7. Yoshinobu Hakutani and Robert L. Tener, afterword to *Haiku: This Other World* (New York: Arcade, 1998), 250.

8. Julia Wright, introduction to *Haiku: This Other World* (New York: Arcade, 1998), viii.

9. Walker, *Daemonic Genius*, 308–9.

10. Ibid., 314.

11. Julia Wright, introduction, xi–xii.

12. Gary Cummiskey, "Interview with Sinclair Beiles, Yeoville, 1994." http://realitystudio.org/interviews/who-was-sinclair-beiles (accessed July 14, 2010).

13. Ollie W. Harrington, *Why I Left America and Other Essays* (Jackson: University Press of Mississippi, 1993), 14.

14. Ibid., 14.

15. Michel Fabre, *The World of Richard Wright* (Jackson: University Press of Mississippi, 1985), 54.

16. Asataro Miyamori, *An Anthology of Haiku: Ancient and Modern* (Westport, CT: Greenwood, 1970), 8.

17. Fabre, *The World of Richard Wright*, 54.

18. *Native Son* sold 215,000 copies in three weeks after its publication by Harper and Brothers on March 1, 1940. *Black Boy* received "enthusiastic reviews" after its publication by Harper and Brothers in March 1945 and "sold 195,000 copies in the Harper trade edition and 351,000 through the Book-of-the-Month Club." See "A Chronology of Richard Wright," *Black Power* by Richard Wright (New York: HarperPerrennial, 2008), 12, 17.

19. Bashō, *On Love and Barley: Haiku of Bashō*, trans. Lucien Stryk (New York: Penguin, 1985), 67.

The Other World of Richard Wright

Richard Wright's Haiku, Zen, and the African "Primal Outlook upon Life"

— YOSHINOBU HAKUTANI —

Richard Wright is acclaimed for his powerful prose in *Native Son* (1940) and *Black Boy* (1945), books that he wrote early in his career. But later in his life he became interested in poetry and especially in the haiku. In the 1950s he liked to work in the garden on his Normandy farm, an activity that supplied many themes for his haiku.[1] Of his other experiences in this period, Wright's travels to the newly independent Ghana in West Africa are also reflected in his haiku. The African philosophy of life Wright witnessed among the Ashanti, the "primal outlook upon life," as he called it, served as an inspiration for his poetic sensibility.[2]

By the spring of 1960, Wright informed his friend and Dutch translator Margrit de Sablonière that he had returned to poetry and added, "During my illness I experimented with the Japanese form of poetry called haiku; I wrote some 4,000 of them and am now sifting them out to see if they are any good."[3] In his discussion of this development, Michel Fabre notes that Wright's interest in haiku involved research into the great Japanese masters, Buson, Bashō, and Issa; he ignored the European and American forms that were then becoming popular. Fabre states further that "Wright made an effort to respect the exact form of the poem," but adds that it was curious for Wright to become interested in haiku at a time when he was fighting his

Previously published in *Modern Philology* 104, no. 4 (2007). Reprinted with permission of the author.

illness. As Fabre reasons, "Logically he should have been tempted to turn away from 'pure' literature and to use his pen instead as a weapon."[4]

Constance Webb says that Wright had lost his physical energy and that "while lying against the pillows one afternoon he picked up the small book of Japanese poetry and began to read it again."[5] Apparently, Wright had borrowed it from a friend, a South African poet.[6] Wright read and reread the classic haiku collected in the book. Webb comments that Wright "had to study it and study to find out why it struck his ear with such a modern note."[7] The haiku "seemed to answer the rawness he felt, which had, in turn, created a sensitivity that ached. Never had he been so sensitive, as if his nervous system had been exposed to rough air."[8] In a letter to Paul Reynolds, his friend and literary agent, Wright explained that he had sent to William Targ of the World Publishing Company an eighty-two-page manuscript of haiku entitled *This Other World: Projections in the Haiku Manner*. After a few comments about Targ, Wright went on to say, "These poems are the results of my being in bed a great deal and it is likely that they are bad. I don't know."[9]

That manuscript had not been published in its entirety until 1998.[10] We will never fully know the reasons why Wright turned to haiku during the last years of his life, but a reading of the haiku in *This Other World*, as well as the rest of his haiku, indicates that Wright turned away from the moral, intellectual, social, and political problems dealt with in his prose work and found in nature his latent poetic sensibility. Gwendolyn Brooks called Wright's haiku collected in *This Other World* "a clutch of strong flowers."[11] "These haiku," Wright's daughter remarks in her introduction, "not only helped him place the volcanic experience of mourning under the self-control of closely counted syllables, but also enabled him to come to terms with the difficult beauty of the earth in which his mother would be laid to rest."[12] Wright's discovery of haiku, as Fabre says, "brings to light an often neglected aspect of the writer's personality: his intimate sense of the universal harmony, his wonder before life, his thirst for a natural existence, all these tendencies which nourished, as much as did any ideology or faith, his courageous and incessant battle against all that prevents an individual from fully belonging to the world."[13]

The genesis of Wright's poetic sensibility can be glimpsed in his "Blueprint for Negro Writing" even though its theory is Marxist. An African

American writer's perspective, Wright states, "is that part of a poem, novel, or play which a writer never puts directly upon paper. It is that fixed point in intellectual space where a writer stands to view the struggles, hopes, and sufferings of his people."[14] Wright establishes this vantage point in the autobiographical prose of *Black Boy*, yet he also there consciously creates a poetic vision of nature through and against which racial conflict is depicted. The poetic passages in *Black Boy* demonstrate Wright's incipient interest in the exaltation of nature and show the congeniality of images from nature to his sensibility.

On the basis of J. B. Danquah's *The Akan Doctrine of God*,[15] Wright was persuaded of the African belief that spirits reside in inanimate objects like trees, stones, and rivers. Wright also adopted an African belief in ghosts and in the spirits of the dead, which meant that life and death are not diametrically opposed. "Life in the ghost world," he remarks, "is an exact duplicate of life in this world. A farmer in this world is a farmer there; a chief here is a chief there. It is, therefore, of decisive importance when one enters that world of ghostly shades to enter it in the right manner. For you can be snubbed there just as effectively and humiliatingly as you were snubbed here."[16] This African religion furthermore does not recognize the existence of hell and sin, nor does it distinguish in the abstract between good and evil. "When the family is the chief idea," Wright quotes Danquah as saying, "things that are dishonorable and undignified, actions that in disgracing you disgrace the family, are held to be vices, and the highest virtue is found in honor and dignity. Tradition is the determinant of what is right and just, what is good and done." Whereas the Akan religion and Christianity share the concept of life after death, the Akan religion also resembles other religions such as Buddhism and Hinduism in its belief in reincarnation. Unlike Christianity, the Akan religion, as do Buddhism and Hinduism, believes in the existence of soul in nonhuman beings. "Death," Wright observes, "does not round off life; it is not the end; it complements life." To him the African religion looks "terrifying" but not "primitive."[17]

One of the theoretical principles in "Blueprint" calls for African American writers to explore universal humanism, what is common among all cultures. "Every iota of gain in human thought and sensibility," Wright argues, "should be ready grist for his mill, no matter how far-fetched they may seem in their immediate implications."[18] After a journey into the Ashanti kingdom in West Africa in 1953, when he was forty-five, Wright asserted in *Black Power*: "The truth is that the question of how much of Africa has survived in the New World is misnamed when termed 'African survivals.' The African attitude toward life springs from a natural and poetic grasp of existence and all the emotional implications that such an attitude carries; it is clear, then, that what the anthropologists have been trying to explain are not 'African survivals' at all—they are but the retention of basic and primal attitudes toward life."[19] Wright's exploration of the Ashanti convinced him that the defense of African culture meant renewal of Africans' faith in themselves. He came to see African culture buttressed by traditional human values—awe of nature; family kinship and love; the sense of honor—that had made the African survivals possible.

When an African was transplanted to Europe or America, as Wright observed, that person identified himself or herself with the rational, urban, and economic way of life in the West but retained the traditional values. In particular, the transplanted African kept intact the awe of nature. That person, Wright argues, "remains black and becomes American, English, or French" but "to the degree that he fails to adjust, to absorb the new environment (and this will be mainly for racial and economic reasons!), he, to that degree, and of necessity, will retain much of his primal outlook upon life, his basically poetic apprehension of existence." The way in which the African sees nature, as Wright realizes, is humanistic and is not materialistic. "The tribal African's culture," Wright argues, "*is* primally human; that which *all* men once had as their warm, indigenous way of living, is his. . . . There is nothing mystical or biological about it. When one realizes that one is dealing with two distinct and separate worlds of psychological being, two conceptions of time even, the problem becomes clear; it is a clash between two systems of culture."[20]

If the African American, such as Wright himself, retained, in time or for a time, this "primal" outlook on life, it was because that person was unable to "see or feel or trust (at that moment in history) any other system of value or belief": "What the social scientist should seek for are not 'African survivals' at all, but the persistence and vitality of primal attitudes and the social causes thereof. And he would discover that the same primal attitudes exist among other people; after all, what are the basic promptings of artists, poets, and actors but primal attitudes consciously held?"[21] When Wright studied R. H. Blyth's four volumes on the art and history of haiku,[22] he was struck with a strong affinity between the world-view that underlies haiku and the African "primal outlook upon life" that buttresses Ashanti culture, one of the oldest in Africa. Unlike Western romantic poetry and even the earlier Japanese poetry called *waka*, haiku, as Blyth observes, "is as near to life and nature as possible, as far from literature and fine writing as may be, so that the asceticism is art and the art is asceticism."[23] Blyth's definition of haiku as an ascetic art means that classic haiku by such masters as Bashō, Buson, and Issa, which Wright emulated, strictly concern objects and phenomena in nature. In composing a haiku the poet must, at first, observe an object or phenomenon in nature from a perspective devoid of thoughts and feelings. Only after he attains that stance and vision will the poet be able to achieve a harmonious union with nature.

The haiku poet's perspective without egotism bears a strong resemblance to the African's view of nature and self. In African life, Wright saw a closer relationship between human beings and nature than that between human beings and their social and political environment: "Africa, with its high rain forest, with its stifling heat and lush vegetation, might well be mankind's queerest laboratory. Here instinct ruled and flowered without being concerned with the nature of the physical structure of the world; man lived without too much effort; there was nothing to distract him from concentrating upon the currents and countercurrents of his heart. He was thus free to project out of himself what he thought he was. Man has lived here in a waking dream, and, to some extent, he still lives here in that dream." Africa evokes in one "a total attitude toward life, calling into question the basic assumptions of existence."[24] Wright was moreover fascinated by the African reverence for the nonhuman living, a primal attitude that corresponds to the haiku poet's awe of nature. He thus observed: "The pre-Christian African was impressed with the littleness of himself and he walked the earth warily, lest he disturb the presence of invisible gods. When he wanted to disrupt the terrible majesty of the ocean in order to fish, he first made sacrifices to its crashing and rolling waves; he dared not cut down a tree without first propitiating its spirit so that it would not haunt him; he loved his fragile life and he was convinced that the tree loved its life also."[25] For Wright, not only do the African and the haiku poet share an intuitive, selfless worldview, they have the common belief that humankind does not occupy the central place in the world.

In studying Blyth's analysis and reading of classic haiku, Wright learned that haiku masters were able to present in direct statement the paradox of union with nature, expressing the desire to be a part of nature while simultaneously maintaining their separate identity. Born and trained in Western culture and tradition, Wright as an artist must have struggled to develop such a characteristic in his haiku. Classic haiku call for simplicity of language, thought, and image, a lack of complication often revealed in the spontaneous joy of union with nature. The joy, Blyth points out, comes from "the (apparent) re-union of ourselves with things," our being among others.[26] Austerity on the part of the poet is not only a lack of intellectualization; it is almost a wordlessness, a condition in which words are used not to externalize the poet's state of feeling, but to "clear away something that seems to stand between" the poet and things in the world. Because things in the world are not actually separate from the poet, they "are then perceived by self-knowledge."[27] Classic haiku, as Wright learned, remove as many words as possible, stressing nonintellectuality, for thought must depend upon and not substitute for intuition.

Another major characteristic of haiku Wright learned is a love of nature that is inseparable from the ordinary. For Blyth this characteristic is explained in terms of selflessness, meaning that the poet has identified with nature. The loss of the poet's individuality involves a generalized melancholy or loneliness as an underlying rhythm. It represents the state of Zen, of "absolute spiritual poverty in which, having nothing, we possess all."[28] In Zen-inspired haiku, the material or the concrete is emphasized without the expression of any general principles of abstract reasoning. Animate and inanimate lose their differences so that one might say haiku are not about human beings but about things. Zen teaches, as Blyth observes, that the ordinary thing and the love of nature are reduced to a detached love of life as it is without idealistic, moralistic, or ethical attachments. Things are equal to human beings; both exist through and because of each other.

The most famous haiku by the seventeenth-century Japanese poet Bashō, "The Old Pond," has served in haiku criticism as a model for the Zen-inspired haiku. To explain the poetics of nature, Yone Noguchi, a noted bilingual poet and critic, quoted "The Old Pond" in his criticism:

Furu ike ya	The old pond!
Kawazu tobikomu	A frog leapt into—
Mizu no oto.	List, the water sound!
	(Noguchi's translation)

One may think a frog an absurd poetic subject, but Bashō focused his vision on a scene of autumnal desolation, an image of nature. The pond was perhaps situated on the premises of an ancient temple whose silence was suddenly broken by a frog plunging into the deep water. As Noguchi conceived the experience, Bashō was "supposed to awaken into enlightenment now when he heard the voice bursting out of voicelessness, and the conception that life and death were mere change of condition was deepened into faith."[29]

Bashō was not suggesting in the haiku that the tranquility of the pond meant death or that the frog symbolized life. He had the sensation of hearing the sound bursting out of soundlessness. A haiku is not a representation of goodness, truth, or beauty; there is nothing particularly good, true, or beautiful about a frog's jumping into water. In Zen one is taught to annihilate one's thoughts or feelings before satori is attained: satori is the achievement of a state of *mu*, nothingness. The state of nothingness is free of subjectivity; it is so completely free of any thought or emotion that such a consciousness corresponds to the state of nature.

Directly concerned with objects and phenomena in nature, Bashō completely suppresses subjectivity. Wright attempts to do so as much as possible in many of his haiku. Wright's interest in this doctrine in Zen, the effacement of subjectivity, is reflected in haiku 508:

It is September,
The month in which I was born;
And I have no thoughts.

In the first haiku in *Haiku: This Other World*, Wright, as the subject as well as the narrator, describes himself deprived of his name and of his subjectivity:

I am nobody:
A red sinking autumn sun
Took my name away.

The state of nothingness, however, is not synonymous with a state of void, but is functional, and its function is perceived by the senses. A tree is no longer an ordinary tree; it now exists with different meaning, as shown in haiku 809:

Why did this spring wood
Grow so silent when I came?
What was happening?

In the following haiku, Wright tries to suppress egotism and attain a state of nothingness:

As my anger ebbs,
The spring stars grow bright again
And the wind returns. (721)

As he relieves himself of anger, he begins to see the stars "grow bright again" and "the wind" return. Only when he reaches a state of nothingness is he able to perceive nature with his enlightened senses.

In some of his haiku, as the following examples show, Wright offers simple scenes in which human beings and nature exist in harmony in contrast to complex, intriguing scenes in society where people are at strife.

Seen from a hilltop,
Shadowy in winter rain,
A man and his mule. (42)

In the winter dusk,
A thin girl leads a black cow
By a dragging rope. (377)

After the sermon,
The preacher's voice is still heard
In the caws of crows. (541)

"Seen from a Hilltop" (42) finds unity in humankind and nature: a man, a mule, a rain, a meadow, and a hill. "In the Winter Dusk" (377), like "Seen from a Hilltop" (42), is a direct description of the scene where a girl lives in harmony with an animal. It is not clear whether a girl leads a cow or a cow her. Since the rope is dragging, neither the girl nor the cow is forcing the other to move. Creating such an ambiguous image intensifies the unity and harmony between the living. In "After the Sermon" (541), the seasonal reference is ambiguous, but Wright finds a continuity between humanity and nature, "the preacher's voice" and "the caws of crows."[30]

Whether perceiving nature for its own sake or in its relation to humankind, Wright's haiku thrive on the subtle interactions among the senses captured in seventeen syllables. For instance, in haiku 47, the poet seems to detach himself from a natural scene:

The spring lingers on
In the scent of a damp log
Rotting in the sun.

The feeling of the warm sun, the scent of a damp log, the sight and silence of an outdoor scene, all coalesce into an image of spring. In the process the overall image has evolved from the separate images of the sun, of the log, and of the atmosphere. The images of sight, moreover, are intertwined with the images of warmth from the sun and the rotting log as well as with the image of smell from the log, all these images interacting with one another.

In trying his hand at haiku, Wright initially modeled his on those of the classic Japanese poets such as Moritake (1472–1549), Bashō (1644–1694), Kikaku (1661–1707), Buson (1715–1783), and Issa (1762–1826). Two of the haiku in *This Other World* have a thematic resemblance to a famous haiku by Moritake:

Off the cherry tree,
One twig and its red blossom
Flies into the sun. (626)

A leaf chases wind
Across an autumn river
And shakes a pine tree. (669)

Here is Moritake's poem, quoted in Blyth's book of haiku:[31]

Rakka eda ni	Fallen petals
Kaeru to mireba	Seemed to return to the branch,—
Kocho kana[32]	A butterfly!

Both of Wright's haiku "Off the Cherry Tree" (626) and "A Leaf Chases Wind" (669) create an illusion similar to that in Moritake's haiku. In "Off the Cherry Tree" a twig with its red blossom flies into the sun as if a bird flew off the cherry tree. Likewise "A Leaf Chases Wind" captures a scene as though a leaf were chasing wind and shaking a pine tree rather than the other way around.

It is this haiku by Moritake that influenced Ezra Pound's famous two-line poem, "In a Station of the Metro." Pound acknowledged for the first time in his career his indebtedness to the spirit of Japanese poetry in general and the art of haiku in particular. In the "Vorticism" essay, he quoted Moritake's haiku "The fallen blossom flies back to its branch: A butterfly," just before discussing his "In a Station of the Metro," often regarded as the first haiku imitation written in English.[33] What impressed Gwendolyn Brooks in calling Wright's haiku "a clutch of strong flowers," as noted earlier, suggests that the images in Wright's haiku are charged with energy. To demonstrate his poetic theory, Pound thought of an image not as a decorative emblem or symbol but as a seed capable of germinating and developing into another organism. As an illustration he presented what he called "a *hokku*-like sentence" he had written:

The apparition of these faces in the crowd;
Petals on a wet, black bough.

"In a poem of this sort," he explained, "one is trying to record the precise instant when a thing outward and objective transforms itself, or darts into a thing inward and subjective."[34] The image of the faces in the crowd is based in immediate experience at a metro station in Paris; it was "a thing outward and objective." In Wright's haiku, as in Pound's imagistic poems, the description of nature is an imagistic one that directly derives from the perception of a natural object or event itself without thought, emotion, or point of view.

A year after his Metro poem appeared, Pound stated that a poetic image "may be a sketch, a vignette, a criticism, an epigram or anything else you like. It may be impressionism, it may even be very good prose." The image, he argued, does not constitute simply a picture of something. As a vortex, the image must be "endowed with energy."[35] Imagism, in turn, is likened to the painter's use of pigment. "The painter," Pound remarked, "should use his colour because he sees it or feels it. I don't much care whether he is representative or nonrepresentative. . . . It is the same in writing poems, the author must use his *image* . . . *not* because he thinks he can use it to back up some creed or some system of ethics or economics."[36]

According to Margaret Walker, Wright was fascinated by American modernist poets, including Pound. "In the last years of his life," she notes, "Wright discovered the Japanese form of poetry known as Haiku and became more than a little interested in what was not just a strange and foreign stanza but an exercise in conciseness—getting so much meaning or philosophy in so few words."[37] Pound's theory that the poet's use of an image is not to support "some system of ethics or economics" coincides with a theory that haiku express the poet's intuitive worldview. Wright, then, found the haiku poet's intuitive worldview akin to that of the African. Because both views have little directly to do with politics or economics, Wright's haiku remain a radical departure from his earlier work in prose.

Whether Wright was influenced by Pound's imagism is difficult to determine, but many of Wright's haiku bear a close resemblance to classic Japanese haiku. In both style and content, a pair of his haiku in *This Other World* are reminiscent of two of Bashō's most celebrated haiku. Wright's "In the Silent Forest" echoes Bashō's "It's Deadly Quiet":

In the silent forest
A woodpecker hammers at
The sound of silence. (316)

It's deadly quiet
Piercing into the rocks
Shrills of cicada.[38]

As Bashō expresses awe at quiet, Wright juxtaposes silence in the forest to the sound of a woodpecker. Similarly, Wright's "A Thin Waterfall" is akin to Bashō's "A Crow":

A thin waterfall
Dribbles the whole autumn night,—
How lonely it is. (569)

A crow
Perched on a withered tree
In the autumn evening.[39]

Bashō focuses upon a single crow perching on a branch of an old tree, as does Wright upon a thin waterfall. In both haiku, the scene is drawn with little detail and the mood is provided by a simple, reserved description of fact, a phenomenon in nature. In both haiku, parts of the scene are painted in dark colors, as is the background. Both haiku create the kind of beauty associated with the aesthetic sensibility of *sabi* that suggests loneliness and quietude, the salient characteristics of nature, as opposed to overexcitement and loudness, those of society.[40] As Bashō expresses *sabi* with the image of autumn evening, so does Wright with the line "How lonely it is," a subjective perception. The two haiku, however, are different: while Bashō describes nature for its own sake, Wright interjects his own feelings in his description. Whether Wright and Bashō actually felt lonely when writing the haiku is moot.

Legend has it that Bashō inspired more disciples than did any other haiku poet; Kikaku is regarded as Bashō's most innovative disciple. Two of Wright's haiku bear some resemblance to Kikaku's "The Bright Harvest Moon" since both poets emphasize an interaction between humanity and nature in the creation of beauty:

Beads of quicksilver
On a black umbrella:
Moonlit April rain. (106)

A pale winter moon,
Pitying a lonely doll,
Lent it a shadow. (671)

The bright harvest moon
Upon the tatami mats
Shadows of the pines. (Kikaku)[41]

In Kikaku's haiku, the beauty of the moonlight is not only humanized by the light shining on the man-made objects but also intensified by the shadows of pine trees that fall upon the mats. The intricate pattern of the shadow of the trees intensifies the beauty of the moonlight. Not only does such a scene unify an image of humanity and an image of nature, but it also shows that humanity and nature can interact positively. In Wright's first poem, an element of nature, "beads of quicksilver," is reinforced by a man-made object, "a black umbrella." In "A Pale Winter Moon," while the second line projects loneliness onto a doll, the beauty of the winter moon is intensified by the presence of a man-made object. In contrast to the four haiku quoted above (Wright's "In the Silent Forest" and "A Thin Waterfall," Bashō's "It's Deadly Quiet" and "A Crow"), these three haiku by Wright and Kikaku do lightly include human subjectivity in appreciating natural beauty although the focus of their visions is nature.

Wright's "I Would Like a Bell" is comparable to Buson's well-known "On the Hanging Bell" in depicting a spring scene, but Wright's poem focuses on a human subjectivity, a desiring self:

I would like a bell
Tolling in this soft twilight
Over willow trees. (13)

On the hanging bell
Has perched and is fast asleep,
It's a butterfly.[42]

Buson was well known in his time as an accomplished painter, and many of his haiku reflect his singular attention to color and its intensification. Wright's "A Butterfly Makes," for example, is reminiscent of Buson's "Also Stepping On"; both imply a subjective perception:

A butterfly makes
The sunshine even brighter
With fluttering wings. (82)

Also stepping on
The mountain pheasant's tail is
The spring setting sun.[43]

In another fine haiku, Wright portrays humanity's relationship with nature in terms of art:

From across the lake,
Past the black winter trees,
Faint sounds of a flute. (571)

Unlike "The Spring Lingers On" (47), discussed earlier, this haiku admits a human involvement in the scene: someone is playing the flute as the poet is listening from the other side of the lake. Through transference of the senses between the faint sounds of a flute and the black winter trees, a positive interaction of humanity and nature takes place. "From Across the Lake" has an affinity with Kikaku's "The Harvest Moon," noted earlier, for both haiku are expressions of beauty perceived by subjects in an interaction of natural and human objects.

Wright's haiku in their portrayal of humankind's association with nature often convey a kind of enlightenment, a new way of looking at human beings and nature, as in the following examples:

A wilting jonquil
Journeys to its destiny
In a shut bedroom. (720)

Lines of winter rain
Gleam only as they flash past
My lighted window. (722)

"A Wilting Jonquil" (720) teaches the poet a lesson that natural things out of context cannot exhibit their beauty. In "Lines of Winter Rain" (722), the poet learns that sometimes only when an interaction between human beings and nature occurs can natural beauty be savored.

While haiku poets often tried to suppress subjectivity in depicting nature, some of Wright's haiku bring the poet to the fore. While haiku 720, "A Wilting Jonquil," focuses on an object, haiku 722, "Lines of Winter Rain," insists on the importance of "my lighted window." None of the classic haiku Wright emulates express the poet's thoughts or feelings. The first haiku in Wright's *Haiku: This Other World* ("I am nobody: / A red sinking autumn sun / Took my name away"), as noted earlier, suppresses subjectivity by depicting the red sun that erases his name. And yet the poet is strongly present, even by negation. The same is true of some of his other haiku discussed earlier, such as haiku 809, "Why did this spring wood / Grow so silent when I came? / What was happening?" and haiku 721, "As my anger ebbs, / The spring stars grow bright again / And the wind returns."

Writing a haiku to depict a spring scene, quoted earlier, Wright and Buson take different approaches in terms of subjectivity: "I would like a bell / Tolling in this soft twilight / Over willow trees" (Wright); "On the hanging bell / Has perched and is fast asleep, / It's a butterfly" (Buson). Wright's focus is on imagining a bell ringing softly over willow trees while Buson's is on a butterfly actually fast asleep on a hanging bell. The two haiku are quite different: subjectivity is present in Wright's haiku while it is absent in Buson's. Another pair of haiku by Wright and Bashō portray autumn scenes: "A thin waterfall / Dribbles the whole autumn night,— / How lonely it is" (Wright); "A crow / Perched on a withered tree / In the autumn evening" (Bashō). Subjectivity is absent in Bashō's haiku while it is directly expressed by Wright's third line, "How lonely it is." In depicting the moon, for example, Wright and Kikaku write remarkably different haiku: "A pale winter moon, / Pitying a lonely doll, / Lent it a shadow" (Wright); "The bright harvest moon / Upon the tatami mats / Shadows of the pines" (Kikaku). Subjectivity is entirely absent in Kikaku's haiku while it is strongly expressed in Wright's with the middle line, "Pitying a lonely doll."

Absent subjectivity in composing haiku is akin to Lacan's concept of the subject. Lacan, as a postmodern psychoanalyst, challenges the traditional concept of subjectivity. On the basis of his analytic experience, he sees subjectivity as a concept that concerns neither the autonomy of the self nor the subject's ability to influence the other. Subjectivity is deficient because of the deficiencies inherent in language: "The effects of language are always mixed with the fact, which is the basis of the analytic experience, that the subject is subject only from being subjected to the field of the Other, the subject proceeds from his synchronic subjection in the field of the Other. That is why he must get out, get himself out, and in the *getting-himself-out*, in the end, he will know that the real Other has, just as much as himself, to get himself out, to pull himself free."[44] Because the subject, an infinitesimal fraction in time and space, is isolated from the world, the subject is only capable of imagining the other: society, nature, and life. Only when the subject is conscious of the deficiencies of language, as Lacan theorizes, does the subject of the unconscious emerge. Only then is the subject able to approach and encounter the truth of life—what Lacan calls "the real" and "the unsymbolizable." To Lacan, the motive for subjectivity aims at the symbolic—what constitutes tradition, religion, law, and so on—whereas the motive for absence of subjectivity aims at the unconscious, a state largely derived from the other and partly derived from the imaginary on the part of the subject. The unconscious, then, is closer to the real than it is to the symbolic; the imaginary is closer to the real than it is to the symbolic. Lacan posits, however, that "there exists a world of truth entirely deprived of subjectivity," universal truth, "and that . . . there has been a historical development of subjectivity manifestly directed towards the rediscovery of truth," historically subjective truth, "which lies in the order of symbols."[45] Lacan sees the door as language; the door is open either to the real or to the imaginary. He says that "we don't know quite which, but it is either one or the other. There is an asymmetry between the opening and the closing—if the opening of the door controls access, when closed, it closes the circuit."[46] He considers language either objective or subjective; the real is objective whereas the imaginary is subjective. Applied to traditional haiku composition, language aims at the real through the imaginary rather than at the symbolic through the historically subjective.

The Lacanian distinction of the imaginary and the symbolic has an affinity with one of the disagreements between Pound and Yeats in reading Japanese poetry and drama. Pound regarded symbolism as "a sort of allusion, almost of allegory." The symbolists, Pound thought, "degraded the symbol to the status of a word. . . . Moreover, one does not want to be called a symbolist, because symbolism has usually been associated with mushy technique."[47] For Pound, symbolism is inferior to imagism, the imaginary in Lacan's theory, because in symbolism one image is used to suggest another or to represent another whereby both images would be weakened. Pound's theory of imagism was derived from haiku, as noted earlier, which shuns metaphor and symbolism, rather than from the Noh play, which Yeats considered "indirect and symbolic." If Yeats's ideal language has the suggestiveness and allusiveness of symbolism as opposed to the directness and clearness of imagism, then his sources certainly did not include Pound. Even though Yeats dedicated *At the Hawk's Well* (1917) to Pound, Yeats was not enthusiastic about Pound's theory. "My own theory of poetical or legendary drama," Yeats wrote to Fiona Macleod, "is that it should have no realistic, or elaborate, but only a symbolic and decorative setting. A forest, for instance, should be represented by a forest pattern and not by a forest painting."[48] Yeats, a symbolist and spiritualist poet, was fascinated by the Noh play, while Pound, an imagist, was influenced by Japanese poetry and by haiku in particular.

In any event, Lacan moreover envisions a domain of the real beyond "the navel of the dream, this abyssal relation to that which is most unknown, which is the hallmark of an exceptional, privileged experience, in which the real is apprehended beyond all mediation, be it imaginary or symbolic." Lacan equates this domain with "an absolute other . . . an other beyond all intersubjectivity."[49] In Lacanian terms, the haiku poet is motivated to depict the real directly without using symbols. In this process the poet relies on the imaginary, a domain that is closer to nature, where subjectivity is suppressed as much as possible, or minimized. The poets avoided symbols in writing haiku in an attempt to be objective and yet creative. "If the symbolic function functions," Lacan laments, "we are inside it. And I would even say—we are so far into it that we can't get out of it."[50]

That symbolism is an obstacle in writing haiku can be explained in terms of Lacan's definition of the symbolic order. Lacan observes that language symbolizes things that do not exist, nonbeing: "The fundamental relation of man to this symbolic order is very precisely what founds the symbolic order itself—the relation of non-being to being. . . . What insists on being satisfied can only be satisfied in recognition. The end of the symbolic process is that non-being come to be, because it has spoken."[51] To Lacan, then, language makes nonbeing become being. Because haiku aim to represent being rather than non-being, what Lacan calls "language" or what is "spoken" does not apply to the language of haiku.

Not only is Lacan's theory of language applicable to the unsymbolic characteristic of haiku, it clearly accounts for the absence of subjectivity in traditional haiku. Those haiku by Wright that express subjectivity directly or indirectly might be considered modern rather than traditional. The first line in Wright's haiku 13 ("I would like a bell / Tolling in this soft twilight / Over willow trees"), quoted earlier, constitutes an expression of subjectivity, but the second line, "Tolling in this soft twilight," is an image created by the imaginary. Pound's haiku-like poem "In a Station of the Metro," noted earlier, has been regarded as imagistic and modernistic: "The apparition of these faces in the crowd: / Petals on a wet, black bough." Since the image of the apparition, as well as that of petals, as Pound explains in his "Vorticism" essay, are derived from the subject's experience at the metro station, this poem indirectly expresses subjectivity. Pound also expresses subjectivity directly in another haiku-like poem, entitled "Alba":

> As cool as the pale wet leaves
>   of lily-of-the-valley
> She lay beside me in the dawn.[52]

As the image of "the pale wet leaves," a creation by the imaginary in Lacanian terms, indirectly expresses the subject's desire, the last line explicitly brings in the desiring subject. One of the disciplines in classic haiku composition calls for restraining the expression of desire. "Desire" as Lacan observes, "always becomes manifest at the joint of speech, where it makes its appearance, its sudden emergence, its surge forwards. Desire emerges just as it becomes embodied in speech, it emerges with symbolism."[53]

As Wright's and Pound's modernist haiku demonstrate, subjectivity in such haiku is expressed through the use of a personal pronoun, and the subject's desire is evoked in an image that reflects subjectivity. Subjectivity and desire, its dominant construct, are both expressed through pronominal language rather than through an image in nature that embodies the real or the unconscious. Because Wright wrote haiku under the influences of classic Japanese haiku poets in the seventeenth and eighteenth centuries, a great majority of his haiku, perhaps eight out of ten, can be categorized as traditional haiku, in which an image of nature is the focus of the poem and subjectivity is absent.

Wright saw the images of nature he created in his haiku as expressing the "primal outlook upon life" he acquired in Africa. As he traveled to Ghana in 1953 to write *Black Power*, a postmodern and postcolonial nonfiction, he was deeply impressed with the African worldview that human beings are not at the center of the universe, a worldview that corresponds with that of Zen. Ashanti culture and belief, in particular, convinced Wright that the world of nature is preeminent over the subjective vision of that world. In writing traditionalist haiku, Wright adopted a poetic form in which subjectivity, egotism, and desire stand in the way of seeking truth. Not only do most of his haiku thrive on poignant images of nature, they admonish the reader that only by paying nature the utmost attention can human beings truly see themselves.

Notes

1. Michel Fabre, *The Unfinished Quest of Richard Wright* (New York: Morrow, 1973), 447.
2. Richard Wright, *Black Power: A Record of Reactions in a Land of Pathos* (New York: Harper, 1954), 266.
3. Fabre, *Unfinished Quest*, 505.

4. Ibid., 505–6.

5. Constance Webb, *Richard Wright* (New York: Putnam, 1968), 393.

6. According to Toru Kiuchi, this South African poet, identified as Sinclair Beiles in Michel Fabre's *Richard Wright: Books and Writers* (Jackson: University Press of Mississippi, 1990), 14, was "one of the Beat poets and . . . his and their interest in Zen led Wright to the knowledge of haiku." Kiuchi further notes that "because the Beat Hotel was in the Latin Quarter and Wright lived very close to the hotel, he must have haunted the hotel bar. I assume that Wright took an interest in Zen, which some of the Beat poets brought up as one of the important topics, and that Wright then must have known haiku through his conversations with Beiles" (Kiuchi's letter to Hakutani, August 7, 2005).

7. Webb, *Richard Wright*, 387.

8. Ibid., 393.

9. Ibid., 394.

10. This manuscript consists of a title page and eighty-two pages, page 1 containing the first seven haiku and each of the other pages ten, altogether 817 haiku. The manuscript, dated 1960, is deposited among the Wright collection in the Beinecke Rare Book and Manuscript Library, Yale University, New Haven, CT. The manuscript was published as *Haiku: This Other World*, ed. Yoshinobu Hakutani and Robert L. Tener (New York: Arcade, 1998; repr., New York: Random House, 2000). References to Wright's haiku, including numbers, are to this edition.

11. See the cover of the Random House edition of *Haiku: This Other World*.

12. Julia Wright, introduction to *Haiku: This Other World*, xi.

13. Michel Fabre, "The Poetry of Richard Wright," in *Critical Essays on Richard Wright*, ed. Yoshinobu Hakutani (Boston: G. K. Hall, 1982), 271.

14. Richard Wright, "Blueprint for Negro Writing," in *Richard Wright Reader*, ed. Ellen Wright and Michel Fabre (New York: Harper, 1978), 45.

15. See J. B. Danquah, *The Akan Doctrine of God: A Fragment of Gold Coast Ethics and Religion* (London: Frank Cass, 1944).

16. Wright, *Black Power*, 214.

17. Ibid., 215–17.

18. Wright, "Blueprint," 45.

19. Wright, *Black Power*, 266.

20. Ibid.

21. Ibid., 267.

22. See R. H. Blyth, *Haiku: Eastern Culture* (Tokyo: Hokuseido, 1981). This is a paperback edition of vol. 1 of R. H. Blyth, *Haiku*, 4 vols. (Tokyo: Hokuseido, 1949). Page references to this book are to the 1981 paperback edition.

23. R. H. Blyth, *A History of Haiku*, 2 vols. (Tokyo: Hokuseido, 1963), 1:1.

24. Wright, *Black Power*, 159.

25. Ibid., 261–62.

26. Blyth, *Haiku*, 1:9.

27. Ibid., 176.

28. Ibid., 162.

29. Yone Noguchi, *Selected English Writings of Yone Noguchi: An East-West Literary Assimilation*, ed. Yoshinobu Hakutani, 2 vols. (London: Associated University Presses, 1992), 2:73–74.

30. "After the Sermon" can be read as a *senryu*, a subgenre of haiku that expresses humor. Wright might have likened "the preacher's voice" to "the caws of crows," which sound least mellifluous. Senryu originated from Karai Senryu, an eighteenth-century Japanese haiku poet.

31. The original and the translation are quoted from Blyth, *History of Haiku*, 2:56.

32. Moritake. A literal translation of the first two lines, "Rakka eda ni / Kaeru to mireba," reads "A fallen flower appears to come back to its branch."

33. See Ezra Pound, "Vorticism," *Fortnightly Review* 96, no. 573 (September 1, 1914): 461–71. For the influence of haiku on Pound's imagism, see Yoshinobu Hakutani, "Ezra Pound, Yone Noguchi, and Imagism," *Modern Philology* 90, no. 1 (1992): 46–69.

34. Pound, "Vorticism," 467. *Hokku* is an older term for haiku. Bashō and other haiku poets in the seventeenth and eighteenth centuries called haiku *hokku*.

35. Ezra Pound, "As for Imagisme," *The New Age: A Weekly Review of Politics, Literature, and Art* 16, no. 13 (1915): 349.

36. Pound, "Vorticism," 464.

37. Margaret Walker, *Richard Wright: Daemonic Genius* (New York: Amistad, 1988), 313–14.

38. The original of the haiku is in Harold G. Henderson, *An Introduction to Haiku: An Anthology of Poems and Poets from Bashō to Shiki* (New York: Doubleday, 1958), 40. The translation is by Hakutani.

39. The original of the haiku is in ibid., 18. The translation is from Blyth, *History of Haiku*, 2: xxix.

40. The word *sabi*, a noun, derives from the verb *sabiru*, to rust, implying that what is described is aged. *Sabi* is traditionally associated with loneliness. Aesthetically, however, this mode of sensibility intimates grace rather than splendor; it suggests quiet beauty as opposed to robust beauty. Many of Wright's haiku thrive on the use of the word "lonely." For further discussion of *sabi* and of other aesthetic principles, see Yoshinobu Hakutani, *Richard Wright and Racial Discourse* (Columbia: University of Missouri Press, 1996), 275–82.

41. The original of Kikaku's haiku is in Henderson, *Introduction to Haiku*, 58. The translation is by Hakutani.

42. The original of Buson's haiku is in ibid., 104. The translation is by Hakutani.

43. The original of Buson's haiku is in ibid., 102. The translation is by Hakutani.

44. Jacques Lacan, *The Four Fundamental Concepts of Psychoanalysis*, ed. Jacques-Alain Miller, trans. Alan Sheridan (New York: Norton, 1881), 188.

45. Jacques Lacan, *The Seminar of Jacques Lacan*, bk. 2, *The Ego in Freud's Theory and in the Techniques of Psychoanalysis, 1954–1955*, ed. Jacques-Alain Miller, trans. Sylvana Tomaselli (New York: Norton, 1988), 285.

46. Ibid., 302.

47. Pound, "Vorticism," 463.

48. William Butler Yeats, letter to Macleod, quoted in E. A. Sharpe, *William Sharp: A Memoir* (London: Heinemann, 1910), 280–81.

49. Lacan, *Seminar*, 176–77.

50. Ibid., 31.

51. Ibid., 308.

52. Ezra Pound, *Ezra Pound: Selected Poems* (New York: New Directions, 1957), 36.

53. Lacan, *Seminar*, 234.

Zen Buddhism in Richard Wright's Haiku

— TORU KIUCHI —

Wright had little understanding of haiku as well as Zen in 1937 when he wrote the articles "Harlem Party to Protest Japan's Action," "Picket Lines Win Withdrawal of All Goods Made in Japan," and "Pickets Force Stores to Ban Japan Goods" in the July 27, November 1, and November 30 issues of the *Daily Worker*, the official organ of the Communist Party in the United States. These articles were written to protest against the Japanese invasion of China. At that time, however, his knowledge of Japan was based on hearsay only, not on personal experience.

Japan seemed quite different to Wright four years later when he wrote a letter to the Department of State on May 13, 1941, requesting a passport to visit Russia, Japan, and China as an African American foreign correspondent: We intend to depart on July 21, 1941 on the S. S. *President Hayes* from the port of San Francisco, bound for Vladivostok via Kobe, and the duration of our stay will range from three months to one year.[1] For him, Japan was no longer a country to criticize and condemn but an important place to visit. His request for the above-mentioned document was, however, turned down by the Department of State.

"The Man Who Lived Underground," a novella that was first published in *Accent* 2 (spring 1942) and then in *Cross-Section: A Collection of New*

Previously published in *Valley Voices* 8, no. 2 (2008). Reprinted with permission of the author.

American Writing in 1945, is indicative of Wright's change regarding his view of Japan because it was written with a Zen state of mind according to Yoshinobu Hakutani in his work *Richard Wright and Racial Discourse*. Before he wrote his novella Wright had sent a letter to the governor of California on October 27, 1941, asking for permission to access Herbert C. Wright's criminal record. Indeed, Herbert C. Wright had been arrested for burglary from his underground hideout as reported in the August 1941 issue of the *True Detective* magazine.[2] The November 5, 1941, letter by Arna Bontemps to Langston Hughes stating that the novella was being "written at white heat, as [Wright and his wife, Ellen] say"[3] shows evidence of Wright's feverish writing of the novella as early as November 1941 just after he decided to visit Japan as a foreign correspondent. It is difficult to prove that Wright already had a rather precise knowledge of Zen Buddhism when he started to write the novella, but Hakutani argues in his study concerning the protagonist Fred Daniels:

> Among Wright's characters, Daniels is the closest to an individual unconcerned about the matter of life and death . . . . A significant aspect of Daniels's kinship with Zen is his self-reliance. . . . Like Emerson, Wright in this parable is emphasizing man's independence from God's power and influence. For Wright, an individual must achieve enlightenment by himself or herself even at the risk of losing sight of God, and this is somewhat akin to the doctrine of Zen . . . . Not only is Zen's self-enlightenment analogous to Daniels's, but the outlook of life Wright's protagonist achieves at the end of the story is not as negative and annihilative as that of a nihilist.[4]

Amy Tory, a second-generation Japanese American who was twenty-two years old at the time, provides us with an interesting testimony regarding Wright's keen interest in Japanese culture. She arrived at Wright's home at 2:00 P.M. on January 14, 1945, and all afternoon he probed her "for some idea, some notion, some attitude toward life that escapes the stock-in-trade answers" (Wright, "Journal"). Wright later tried to learn how to write two Chinese characters, one representing a tree 木 and another representing life 生 on the back of the January 9, 1948, letter from the Syndicate of Czeck Authors.[5]

By the time he took an interest in African culture in the late 1950s, as Hakutani argues that "Wright's interpretation of African philosophy recalls a teaching in Zen Buddhism" and that "Wright's discussion of the African concept of life is also suggestive of Zen's emphasis on transcending the dualism of life and death,"[6] it is clear that Wright was familiar with Japanese culture as well as Chinese culture, and he was aware of the similarity between the Akan religion in Africa and Zen Buddhism. On reaching Kumasi, Gold Coast (now the Republic of Ghana) during a field trip that preceded his writing of *Black Power*, Wright wrote as follows concerning the Japanese attitude toward death in comparison with the African concept of death: "DEATH IS GOOD. . . . Is that the key here? It makes more sense than any other idea that has occurred to me. If that is it, then these are the freest people I've ever encountered. It means that I must talk to George [Padmore] more, much more seriously than I've ever talked to him before. . . . The Japanese feel that. The Chinese feel that. Deep dose in all of us the urge to sleep tell us that . . ."[7]

In August 1959, Wright met a young South African, Sinclair Beiles.[8] It is important to note that Beiles was one of a group of intellectuals known as the Beat poets. According to the Web site "Sinclair Beiles and the Beat Hotel," Beiles was born in Uganda in 1930 and educated in Johannesburg, South Africa, and went to London and then to Paris in the early 1950s. It was here that he became acquainted with Albert Camus, Jean-Paul Sartre, Tristan Tzara, André Breton, William Burroughs, Gregory Corso, Allen Ginsberg, and Jack Kerouac.[9]

When Beiles was in Paris, he lived in a hotel—the Beat Hotel at 9 Rue Git-le-Coeur in the Latin Quarter—where he helped William Burroughs complete his manuscript, *Naked Lunch*, for Maurice Girodias. The Beat poets were quite interested in Zen; likewise, the Beat Generation writers were attracted to Zen, as testified by Jack Kerouac's book titles such as *The Dharma Bums* (1958) and *Satori in Paris* (1966), for instance. As I previously mentioned, because Wright was already familiar with Japanese culture and because he was aware of the similarity between the Akan religion and Zen Buddhism, he probably met Beiles through the interest in Africa and Zen by way of the introduction of Camus or Sartre and other Beat poets at the Beat Hotel close to the rue Monsieur le Prince where he used to live. There, he enjoyed talking with Beiles about Africa, Zen, and Japanese culture before Beiles happened to mention haiku.

Fascinated by it at once, Wright set about composing his haiku. On Wright's request, Beiles lent him the four volumes of *Haiku* by R. H. Blyth on the art of haiku,[10] and later on in September, Wright even asked Ellen to buy a copy of Blyth's book in London.[11] After reading sections I and II in the first volume of Blyth's *Haiku,* Wright noticed that the book emphasized Zen as one of the spiritual origins of haiku and, therefore, should represent the state of a haiku poet's mind. Consequently Wright started doing some research on Zen Buddhism before composing haiku. By the end of 1959, Wright bought seven volumes of *The Complete Works of D. T. Suzuki*, Daisetz Suzuki's second series of *Essays in Zen Buddhism,*[12] and Christmas Humphreys's *Zen Buddhism.*[13] Because the second series of *Essays in Zen Buddhism* was the only one available, Wright even wrote to Celia Hornung, a good friend of his, on January 19, 1960, asking her to send the first and third series of *Essays in Zen Buddhism* by Suzuki as well as *Zen in English Literature* by R. H. Blyth.[14] After reading these books on Zen, Wright gradually began concentrating on haiku in summer, fall, and winter in 1959.

Around January 11, 1960, the number of haiku that Wright had composed amounted to 3,050,[15] and around January 18, it was 3,300.[16] In early February, the number went up to 3,700,[17] and to 4,000 by mid-March. On March 19, he wrote to Margrit de Sablonière, his Dutch translator and friend, and declared that: "I wrote some 4000 of them and am now sifting them out to see if they are any good."[18] Then he stopped writing haiku and selected 1,066 out of those he had composed up to then.[19] Until April, he reduced the number to approximately 800 so that they only weighed a pound or two and he could carry them in his hands.[20]

Wright wrote Sablonière on April 8, 1960, in reference to the weight of haiku:

> These haikus, as you know, were written out of my illness. I was, and am, so damnably sensitive. Never was I so sensitive as when my intestines were raw. So along came that Japanese poetry and harnessed this nervous energy. Maybe I'm all wrong about them. Maybe they have no value, but I'll see.

> The problem of selecting them is agonizing. I'm trying to figure out a scheme. But at last I can carry them around in my hands. Before, they were strung on steel bars and weighed kilos. . . . Now, only a pound or two. What crazy things I think of. Yet the physical weight of those haikus is an important thing to me.[21]

Christmas Humphreys quotes from Alan Watts that "essentially Satori is a sudden experience, and it is often described as a 'turning over' of the mind, just as a pair of scales will suddenly turn over when a sufficient amount of material has been poured into one pan to overbalance the weight in the other."[22] When he read the passage in *Zen Buddhism*, Wright must have thought that the lightened weight of his haiku was connected with the turning over of the scale.

By mid-April 1960 Wright definitely brought down the total of haiku to 817 and had a girl type up the manuscript.[23] On April 22, Wright left Paris for Leiden, Holland,[24] and he brought the manuscript of 817 haiku with his baggage[25] so that, while in Leiden, Sablonière could introduce Wright to the Japanese professor Shibika (this cannot be a Japanese name: probably Shibaki) to have his haiku checked.[26] By the middle of May, Wright had changed the order of 817 haiku within the sequence of seasons.[27] At that time, Wright received a booklet on Zen as well as Daisetz Suzuki's *An Introduction to Zen Buddhism*[28] from Sablonière, and in his May 22 letter to thank her, he said that he was proofreading the typed manuscript of the haiku. Besides, he added: "It's a funny feeling when you finish a work; you are lost when you no longer have it to bother you. But as soon as it is over, you start looking around for something else to do, even though you are glad that you are free of the last job."[29]

In June, Wright finally sent the eighty-page manuscript of haiku to William Targ, editor for World Publishing, first to ask for his advice as a friend and second to find out his editorial reactions. Although he did not expect his haiku to be a commercial success, and although he was not certain as to their spiritual value, Wright felt a need for them to be read by those for whom he wrote them.[30] However, on July 6, Targ wrote to Wright to inform him as to his decision to turn down the manuscript: "You do have the poetic gift. . . . But after reading a few hundred, a quiet monotony sets in. . . . I should say that a fine little book could be produced from a careful selection; but frankly, I don't have the courage to undertake such a publication, publishable though it be. Commercially speaking it simply would not get off the ground."[31] Thus Wright gave up the idea of publishing them. Hence, Hakutani's and Tener's edition of *Haiku: This Other World* was published posthumously, thirty-eight years after the writer's death.

Zen Buddhism was the first to enter Wright's mind when he set about composing haiku during the months in summer 1959 with the help of Blyth's *Haiku*. Thanks to Beiles, he was aware of the impact of Zen as well as Japanese culture in the composition of haiku before he noticed how many pages Blyth had spared for the basic explanation of haiku in the first volume of *Haiku*. One hundred and two pages out of 344 pages constitute an impressive percentage with 6 pages for Buddhism, 11 pages for Taoism, and 16 pages for Confucianism.

Wright tried to have a full understanding of the practice of Zen, in light of Daisetz Suzuki's theoretical explanation of Zen: "It is not a religion in the sense that the term is popularly understood; for Zen has no God to worship, no ceremonial rites to observe, no future abode to which the dead are destined, and, at last of all, Zen has no soul whose welfare is to be looked after by somebody else and whose immortality is a matter of intense concern with some people."[32] Wright also tried to extract the essence of Zen out of haiku and maxims that Blyth had quoted in *Haiku*, in order to add a flavor of Zen to his haiku.

Zenrinkushu, which Blyth often quotes in *Haiku*, is a collection of sagacious maxims and famous sayings selected from old Chinese collections of poems and records of Zen monks' quotations. This book is still in use today by monks who study Zen in monasteries and "who select the passage which seems to them to solve the problem they are given by the master."[33] In section I of the first volume of *Haiku*, Blyth cites many maxims from the collection to give his readers a general idea of the relationship between Zen Buddhism and haiku. He says that "Zen is the putting into practice, the realizing (making real) of Mahayana Buddhism in daily life."[34] Mahayana Buddhism was a reformed Buddhism that developed in India shortly before Christ's lifetime as a reaction to the original Hinayana Buddhism, that appeared five hundred years earlier and was narrowly restricted to believers. Zen is the transcription of dhyana in Sanskrit, that means "thinking quietly." In ancient India, mental concentration was integrated into Buddhism from a meditation method called yoga. Above all, this method was extremely sophisticated all over China and Japan and was developed as a unique religion.

Here is one of the examples that Blyth quotes from *Zenrinkushu* to show how close the Zen Buddhist view of the world is to haiku:

> Meeting, the two friends laugh aloud;
> In the grove, fallen leaves are many.[35]

Two friends meet, but all they can do is laugh, watching leaves falling outside since they know that there is nothing to talk about. Similarly, two Zen thinkers, R. H. Blyth and Daisetz Suzuki, met for the first time in Kamakura, Japan, in 1946 soon after World War II,[36] but they did not talk eloquently about Zen. A simple glance at the following verses in Wright's *Haiku: This Other World* is sufficient to convince us of the deep influence of Zen:

> With shy yellow smiles,
> Baby pumpkins are hiding
> Under yellow leaves. (111)

The difference between the quoted sample maxim in *Zenrinkushu* and Wright's haiku is that in the former, we are dealing with friends and in the latter, with baby pumpkins. Such a change or variation on a theme testifies to Wright's sense of humor. Both friends and pumpkins know that Zen cannot be explained and that the "Ah!" of things is Zen without adding anything to the beauty and quietness of nature. Using different material, Wright is successful in creating a Zen flavor in his haiku.

Another example can be found in *Zenrinkushu*:

> The cock announces the dawn in the evening;
> The sun is bright at midnight.[37]

The Zen way of thinking is more or less associated with *satori*, or Enlightenment, which, according to Suzuki, "is the *raison d'être* of Zen without which Zen is no Zen."[38] It connotes a Japanese proverb, "Clear your mind of all mundane thoughts, and you will find even fire cool." Once one reaches *satori*, one can see the bright sun at midnight and find fire cool. Likewise, the following haiku also reflects the influence of Zen:

A cock's shrill crow
Is driving the spring dawn stars
From out of the sky. (202)

By contrast, in this haiku that uses *satori*, Wright describes an ordinary morning in the countryside, recollecting his country life at the Moulin d'Andé, an old flour mill about seventy-five miles northwest of Paris.[39] If the cock crows, then the dawn stars are necessarily bright in the dark. Here *satori* works humorously, as it leads the cock's crow to force the dawn stars out of the sky.

To Wright, the next excerpt from *Zenrinkushu* is very different from Western poetry:

Just one pistil of the plum flower,—
And the three thousand worlds are fragrant.[40]

In Zen thought, one flower makes three thousand worlds fragrant. This is what Humphreys calls "the jump of Zen": "We in the West are growing used to Kierkegaard and his 'existential leap,' and it is but the jump of Zen. You may, if you wish, be dramatic about it. Drag yourself with the last ounce of your intellect to the jaws of the abyss."[41] Wright makes use of "the jump of Zen" in his haiku as follows:

Lifting the lantern,
The scent of plums on the tree
Became more fragrant. (270)

If you lift up the lantern, the scent of plums, in reality, may become more visible but does not become fragrant. But if you can see more plums on the tree, they can at least seem more fragrant than in the dark. This is an example of Wright's jump of Zen. He just described what he actually saw and felt.

In section II of the first volume of *Haiku*, "Zen, the State of Mind for Haiku," Blyth asserts that there are thirteen characteristics of the Zen state of mind that the creation and appreciation of haiku demand: selflessness, loneliness, grateful acceptance, wordlessness, nonintellectuality, contradictoriness, humor, freedom, nonmorality, simplicity, materiality, love, and courage.

In the working draft of haiku, sorted by seasonal headings such as spring, summer, autumn, and winter, Wright provided a variety of additional subcategories: absence, agreement, contrast, delicate, humor, illusion, pathos, personification, projection, religion, sensation, tension, time, timelessness, and cryptic mystery.[42] Even though Eugene Miller in *Voice of a Native Son* declares: "The proposed title for Wright's planned book of haiku indicates his intention that the poems be analyzed from the point of a schema that differed from Japanese Zen,"[43] categories such as "absence," "contrast," "humor," "timelessness," and "religion" must be related to Zen because Wright's categorization is quite similar to Blyth's thirteen headings under which Zen is related to the mind of the haiku poet. Wright classified haiku in the working draft after the manner of Blyth.

Selflessness is listed as one of the most important characteristics of Zen. The following tanka—another Japanese short type of poem—was written by Ikkyu (1394–1481), who was said to be one of the Emperor's sons but became a Zen Buddhist monk, a man who preached all over Japan against the corruption of Zen monasteries at that time:

Myself of long ago,
In nature
Non-existent:
No final destination,
Nothing of any value.[44]

Regarding Ikkyu's tanka, Blyth says: "The realization of the selflessness of things comes through a realization of non-ego."[45] In the poem Ikkyu asserted that he was the only one in the legitimate line of orthodox Zen Buddhism, criticizing Zen practiced by the Gozan School which, in those days, was controlled by the government, and he made the artistic tanka rich with the essence of Zen Buddhism to show that only selflessness conveys the truth of Zen in opposition to corruption. Ikkyu's tanka is a good example of selflessness or non-ego. Wright put Ikkyu's theory in practice in haiku 1:

I am nobody:
A red sinking autumn sun
Took my name away.

"I" in the haiku becomes selfless and nameless having the Zen state of mind just as Ikkyu did in his *tanka*. In *Zen Buddhism*, which Wright read very carefully, Christmas Humphreys theorizes that, on one hand, haiku is "a means, not an end, a hint of the unspeakable. The western poets attempt to describe what they see, or feel, or think" and that haiku, on the other hand, "helps you to grasp the sensation directly, as a means or device for 'seeing into the soul of man.'"[46] From the theory, a hint came to the mind of the African American writer in exile, leading him to see into his own soul and grasp the selfless sensation. Twelve years of exile had elapsed since his departure from the United States in 1947. He was neither an American nor a French man but a cosmopolitan without a nationality. That's what Robert Tener means when he declares that Wright "turns the red autumn sun into a symbol, perhaps of a Western world, America, that has deprived the speaker of his name and identity, perhaps that of a black African?"[47] It is true that Wright suffered from namelessness and loss of nationality just as much as Cross Damon does in *The Outsider*, for instance. Damon loses his name and identity and becomes a different person, Lionel Lane; Wright himself employed a new principle of Zen to voice his namelessness and selflessness in his haiku.

Wordlessness, another characteristic of Zen, lies deeply in haiku 1 because of "the recognition that the individual can no longer define his being when the star of light and meaning disappears with his name."[48] Blyth also writes in *Haiku*, "It is essentially a wordless state, in which words are used, not to express anything, but rather to clear away something that seems to stand between us and the real things which (in being not in fact separate from ourselves) are then perceived by self-knowledge."[49]

As loneliness is another Zen characteristic of a haiku poet's mind, Blyth says that "*Sabishisa*, loneliness, is the haiku equivalent of *Mu* in Zen, a state of absolute spiritual poverty in which, having nothing, we possess all."[50] Quoting Bashō's famous haiku, Blyth proves that loneliness is nothingness:

Along this road
Goes no one,
This autumn eve.[51]

The similarity between two haiku by Bashō and by Wright is striking:

Autumn moonlight is
Deepening the emptiness
Of a country road. (501)

Wright categorized the haiku under the heading "religion" in the working draft.[52] This shows that the haiku has something to do with religion and is characterized by a mixture of loneliness and nothingness possessing all in "a state of absolute spiritual poverty." In *Zen Buddhism,* which Wright read, Humphreys explains the presence of Zen in haiku: "A *haiku* has no point; nor does it strive to be beautiful. It is in Zen the expression of the Zen state of mind, and merely points at the moon; it does not attempt to describe it. In itself it has no value; it is not to be parsed, or 'analysed,' as the beauty of English poems is torn in shreds by an age that knows not the meaning of poetry."[53] Wright did not attempt to give a beautiful description of the moon; he did not try to emphasize the emptiness of the road either. He just depicted the deepening loneliness and nothingness, possessing all, of the country road.

In the following, Wright gave another proof of the similarity between loneliness and nothingness possessing all:

That road is empty,
The one leading into hills
In autumn twilight. (136)

Nobody goes along the road and there is but one road whose end is disappearing into dusk. The season is fall when everything withers. The absolute loneliness contrarily produces poetical richness. This is *sabishisa,* or *Mu* in

Zen, nothingness possessing all in haiku. Wright is successful in extracting the essence of Zen flavor out of Bashō's haiku and in seasoning his own haiku with a Zen feature.

Blyth tells us that "Zen is often conveyed by some intellectual contradiction, explicit or implicit, expressed in the form of paradox or dilemma, that is somehow resolved by a living experience,"[54] and he gives the following example by Issa:

A Time of Congratulation;
About average for me,—
This is my spring.[55]

Wright interprets contradiction in Zen as:

From these warm spring days,
I can still see her sad face
In its last autumn. (186)

Even warm spring days cannot relieve the sadness of a woman's face. In Wright's haiku, even on a warm spring day, a girl's face looks sad and unhappy just as spring is not fully but averagely congratulated in Issa's haiku. Nature usually turns loneliness in autumn to happiness in spring but the woman's intellectual contradiction sets the clock back against the round of seasons.

Humor is an indispensable element not only for Zen but also for haiku. Teishitsu's haiku is a good example:

A handle
On the moon,—
And what a splendid fan![56]

On the other hand, Wright's version of Zen humor is as such:

A spring moon so round
That my fingers are itching
To touch its sharp edge. (289)

This short statement may be classified as hyperbole if we are to follow Blyth's analysis and enumeration of the different kinds of humor to be found: "the laughter of disillusionment, the laughter of studied idiocy, spontaneous idiocy, hyperbole, dilemma, scatological humor, dry humor, breaking with conventionality, and dropping from the sublime to the ridiculous."[57] Teishitsu's and Wright's haiku have what Humphreys calls "the jump of Zen" as well as humor of exaggeration. It is possible for the Zen state of mind to put a handle on the moon and touch the sharp edge of the moon at the psychological level where the unspeakable can be spoken. The roundness of the beautiful spring moon is so exaggerated that you can touch the sharp edge.

Among other types of Zen humor, a good example of scatological humor—quoted by Blyth—can be found in *Mumonkan*, a book of forty-eight official ancient Zen rules which were chosen by Keikai Mumon (1183–1260), a Chinese monk who lived during the Sung dynasty:

> A monk asked Mumon, "What is the Buddha?"
> "A dry shit-stick," replied Mumon.[58]

Wright's application of scatological humor to haiku is:

> While urinating,
> I feel slightly self-conscious
> Before the spring moon. (754)

Aside from scatological humor, according to the third series of Suzuki's *Essays in Zen Buddhism*, there are two important elements of the expression of Zen intuition: the realization of the Unconscious and facing the moon.[59] When the realization of the Unconsciousness is done, "all their karma-hindrances vanish and the chain of birth and death is cut asunder."[60] On the top of the picture of a Zen monk facing the moon reads: "Read on, read on, and when there is nothing more to read, there shines out the meaning of the whole scripture, and the moon too is forgotten."[61] "I" in the haiku is on the way to *satori*, self-conscious with his mind not yet clear enough and far from forgetting the moon.

Zen is nonmoral, according to Blyth, as in the next haiku by Taigi:

Not a single stone
To throw at the dog,—
The wintry moon.[62]

This is poetry, however inhumane it is. The point lies in the fact that the beauty and clearness of the moon in winter is not hindered by morality from doing the nonmoral activity of throwing a stone at the dog. Wright applied nonmorality to his haiku in the following:

Little boys tossing
Stones at a guilty scarecrow
In a snowy field. (191)

The scarecrow in Wright's haiku is guilty. The characteristic of nonmorality in Zen is the guileless nature of little boys. Unlike an innocent dog in Taigi's haiku, the scarecrow is guilty enough to be thrown a stone at. But, what is the guilt of the scarecrow? This is the image of crucified Christ. By contrast, the little boys should feel guilty. Thus Zen and haiku do not declare who is guilty or innocent but just describe what happens in front of the poet. Zen is beyond morality, in other words, it is amoral. Zen exists between nonmorality and simplicity in the sense that Blyth quotes Bashō's words that "Get a three-foot child to write haiku."[63] An innocent young child would be at once a good haiku poet and a practical observer of Zen Buddhism. Bashō shows us an appropriate illustration for nonmorality and unconsciousness:

The Rose of Sharon
By the roadside,
Was eaten by the horse.[64]

What Bashō tries to say is that we must not try to write an excellent poem, which Blyth interprets in the following way: "but do it as naturally, as freely, as unselfconsciously as a child does everything."[65] In the following haiku, Wright presents a barking dog at night. He concentrates on the simplicity of a barking dog as "unselfconsciously as a child does":

No star and no moon:
A dog is barking whitely
In the winter night. (268)

Courage is the last manifestation of Zen. Citing from a passage written by Bashō, Blyth writes: "Abide by the rules, then throw them overboard, and for the first time you will achieve freedom."[66] Courage provides us with the power to accept gratefully whatever happens around us, as Bashō also says, "There is nothing you see that is not a flower; there is nothing you can think of which is not the moon."[67] Thus, even his very particular situation, as he was living alone in a shabby and dirty apartment on rue Régis in Paris, while his family was living away in London, Wright made into poetry:

I am paying rent
For the lice in my cold room
And the moonlight too. (459)

Even in such a situation, Wright did not forget the beauty of moonlight. He also categorized this haiku under the heading of religion in the working draft of *Haiku: This Other World*. Haiku and Zen provided him with the power to accept a Zen monk-like life. According to Suzuki, Zen monks' meals simply consist of rice, gruel, and pickled vegetables. The bedding for each monk never exceeds one large five-square-foot quilt whether in winter or summer. Poverty and simplicity are the basic rule. Suzuki says, "The central idea, however, of the monk's life is not to waste but to make the best possible use of things as they are given us, which is also the spirit of Buddhism everywhere."[68] Wright answers to Roy Wilder's interview in the August 17, 1941, issue of the *New York Herald Tribune* that "I live simply and I can't write unless it's quiet and simple. There are no fireworks in my life. Just work day in and day out."[69] Wright never changed this quiet and simple lifestyle until his death in 1960. His love of nature since his Mississippi days, his unchanging quiet and simple lifestyle, and his preference of farm life to urban life were somewhat deeply rooted in his experiences long before he met the unique aspect of Zen. He was partly of Native American descent, as on his father's side; his grandmother, Laura Calvin, was partly Choctaw Indian.[70] Native Americans are believed to have originally come from the Eurasian Continent after crossing the Bering Strait tens of thousands of years ago. It would be interesting to think that Wright's ancestor's Asian blood was what aroused his enthusiasm for Asian and Japanese culture and what eventually led him to haiku and Zen.

Notes

1. Hazel Rowley, *Richard Wright: The Life and Times* (New York: Henry Holt, 2001), 251.

2. Michel Fabre, *The World of Richard Wright* (Jackson: University Press of Mississippi, 1985), 93–94.

3. Charles H. Nichols, ed., *Arna Bontemps—Langston Hughes Letters, 1925–1967* (New York: Paragon, 1990), 94.

4. Yoshinobu Hakutani, *Richard Wright and Racial Discourse* (Columbia: University of Missouri Press, 1996), 231–33.

5. Letter to Richard Wright, January 9, 1949, in Box 106, Folder 1630, JWJ Collection, Beinecke Library, Yale University.

6. Hakutani, *Richard Wright and Racial Discourse*, 266–67.

7. Richard Wright, "Travel Journal," August 8, 1953, in Box 22, Folder 344, JWJ Collection, Beinecke Library, Yale University.

8. Michel Fabre, *Richard Wright: Books and Writers* (Jackson: University Press of Mississippi, 1990), 14.

9. "Sinclair Beiles and the Beat Hotel," January 24, 1997. http://www.111.co.za/beathotel.

10. Michel Fabre, *The Unfinished Quest of Richard Wright* (Urbana: University of Illinois Press, 1993), 505.

11. Fabre, *Wright*, 14.

12. Fabre, *Wright*, 156.

13. Ibid., 75.

14. Richard Wright, letter to Hornung, January 19, 1960. Michel Fabre Private Collection.

15. Ibid., January 12, 1960.

16. Ibid., January 19, 1960.

17. Ibid., February 5, 1960.

18. Fabre, *Quest*, 505.

19. Wright, Letter to Hornung, March 16, 1960.

20. Wright, Letter to Sablonière, April 8, 1960. Michel Fabre Private Collection.

21. Fabre, *Quest*, 508.
22. Christmas Humphreys, *Zen Buddhism* (London: Allen & Unwin, 1957), 162.
23. Fabre, *Quest*, 508.
24. Ibid., 510.
25. Wright, Letter to Sablonière, April 20, 1960.
26. Fabre, *Quest*, 510.
27. Ibid., 508.
28. Fabre, *Wright*, 156.
29. Wright, Letter to Sablonière.
30. Fabre, *Quest*, 509, 620 n. 24.
31. Rowley, *Richard Wright: The Life and Times*, 515.
32. Daisetz T. Suzuki, *An Introduction to Zen Buddhism*, ed. Christmas Humphreys (London: Arrow, 1959), 39.
33. R. H. Blyth, *Haiku* (Tokyo: Hokuseido, 1949–52), 1:24.
34. Ibid.
35. Ibid., 1:26.
36. Kansho Ueda and Mihoko Okamura, eds., *Suzuki Daisetz towa Dareka* [*Who Is Daisetz Suzuki?*] (Tokyo: Iwanami Shoten, 2002), 300.
37. Blyth, *Haiku*, 1:26.
38. Suzuki, *An Introduction to Zen Buddhism*, 95.
39. Fabre, *Quest*, 497.
40. Blyth, *Haiku*, 1:30.
41. Humphreys, *Zen Buddhism*, 150.
42. Richard Wright, "This Other World: Projections in the Haiku Manner," in Box 70, Folders 832 and 833, JWJ Collection, Beinecke Library, Yale University.
43. Eugene Miller, *Voice of a Native Son: The Poetics of Richard Wright* (Jackson: University Press of Mississippi, 1990), 248.
44. Blyth, *Haiku*, 1:159.
45. Ibid., 1:158.
46. Humphreys, *Zen Buddhism*, 190.
47. Robert L. Tener, "The Where, the When, the What: A Study of Richard Wright's Haiku," in *Critical Essays on Richard Wright*, ed. Yoshinobu Hakutani (Boston: G. K. Hall, 1982), 283.
48. Michel Fabre, "The Poetry of Richard Wright," in *Critical Essays on Richard Wright*, ed. Yoshinobu Hakutani (Boston: G. K. Hall, 1982), 269.
49. Blyth, *Haiku*, 1:176.
50. Ibid., 1:162.
51. Ibid., 1:169.
52. Wright, "This Other World."
53. Humphreys, *Zen Buddhism*, 189–90.
54. Blyth, *Haiku*, 1:189.
55. Ibid., 1:93.

56. Ibid., 1:196.

57. Ibid., 1:200.

58. Ibid., 1:202.

59. Daisetz T. Suzuki, *Essays in Zen Buddhism*, no. 3 (London/New York: Rider, 1960), 256–57.

60. Ibid., 26.

61. Ibid., 256.

62. Blyth, *Haiku*, 1:212.

63. Ibid., 1:217.

64. Ibid.

65. Ibid.

66. Ibid., 1:236.

67. Ibid., 1:237.

68. Suzuki, *An Introduction to Zen Buddhism*, 121.

69. Keneth Kinnamon and Michel Fabre, eds., *Conversations with Richard Wright* (Jackson: University Press of Mississippi, 1993), 37.

70. Rowley, *Richard Wright: The Life and Times*, 4.

Healing and Loss

Richard Wright's Haiku and the Southern Landscape

— META L. SCHETTLER —

In her study *Richard Wright: A Biography,* Constance Webb describes how Richard Wright immersed himself in writing haiku, and she emphasizes the sheer quantity Wright produced: "Lying back on his pillows and scribbling with pen or pencil, whichever his fingers touched first, he began to write the small poems. They poured out like a flood and formed in his brain asleep and awake. Everything he observed or had experienced began to shape itself in a natural flow into a poem. Within a few months he had written 4,000."[1] In her introduction to *Haiku: This Other World,* which collects 817 of the total 4,000, Wright's daughter Julia also reflects on her father's process of writing and his desire to remember the South: "His vow not to break the fast of self-imposed exile could never entirely suppress his mother-hunger and the yearning for the world of childhood she had given him. A form of poetry which links seasons of the soul with nature's cycle of moods enabled him to reach out to the black boy part of himself still stranded in a South that continued to live in his dreams."[2] Here, Julia Wright asserts the importance of Wright's Southern identity and consciousness, even at the end of his life, and speaks of the haiku as attempts to reclaim this essential part of his life. Although Wright famously wrote, "Tradition is no longer a guide. The world has grown huge and cold,"[3] many of his haiku do affirm a distinctly African American tradition of remembrance. In the landscapes of his haiku, the world is no longer "huge and cold," but deeply personal and intimate.

In *The Location of Culture,* Homi Bhabha describes the strategy of postcolonial and black critique as a fundamentally transformative process. He writes, "The intervention of postcolonial or black critique is aimed at transforming the condition of enunciation at the level of the sign—where the intersubjective realm is constituted—not simply setting up new symbols of identity, new 'positive images' that fuel an unreflective 'identity politics.'"[4] Likewise, Wright's haiku do not promote flatly positive alternatives to negative stereotypes. Rather, they attempt to complicate the space and process of representation itself. By drawing on African American history and alluding to negative experience, such as lynching, Wright brings a social realist approach to his haiku. He does not attempt to transcend race but instead analyzes its influence from many different angles within the haiku form. Furthermore, his combination of African American history with a traditional Japanese form creates a hybrid, transcultural space in the haiku, confounding any essentialist or simplistic notions of what "black" writing should be and innovating new themes for the modern haiku.

I would argue also that Wright's haiku, written as they were in exile and written at a time when decolonization and independence swept the globe, might easily be considered part of an emerging body of "postcolonial" literature. As an expatriate, Wright stood outside the boundaries of the United States and continued to develop antiracist and anticolonialist critiques of American hegemony and influence. In *The Location of Culture,* Bhabha also writes that "the struggle against colonial oppression not only changes the direction of Western history, but challenges its historicist idea of time as a progressive, ordered whole"[5] and that "the challenge to modernity comes in redefining the signifying relation to a disjunctive 'present': staging the past as *symbol,* myth, memory, history, the ancestral—but a past whose iterative *value as sign* reinscribes the 'lessons of the past' into the very textuality of the present."[6] Wright's haiku, which explore African American and Southern history, culture, and tradition, certainly accomplish this redefinition, redirection, and interruption of the linear Western construct of time, weaving the past into the present space of the haiku. In this retelling, Wright revives and recreates African American history, keeping alive a sense of community and continuity. This painful history requires, as Toni Morrison suggests in *Beloved,* some "fixing ceremony,"[7] to overcome the abuses of racism and exploitation. And as bell hooks writes in her essay, "Whiteness in the Black Imagination," this exploration must be intentional, "to bear the burden of memory one must willingly journey to places long uninhabited, searching the debris of history for traces of the unforgettable."[8] Like Toni Morrison, bell hooks calls for "ritual reenactment" to "conquer terror"[9] for "it is the telling of our history that enables self-recovery."[10] For Wright the haiku begin this process of ritual reenactment, healing, reconciliation, and self-recovery. As Paul Gilroy puts it in *The Black Atlantic*, "Even when exploring the depths of that spontaneous 'nihilism' which he felt to be modern American racism's most significant contribution to black culture, his focus remained on the scope for agency which blacks enjoyed even in the most restricted conditions."[11] In the haiku, Wright voluntarily accepts restricted conditions, but he also expresses a limitless sense of agency.[12]

Overall, very little critical attention has been given to the published haiku in *Haiku: This Other World*, and because of this scant criticism, many more lessons can still be gathered from this last phase of Wright's life. This essay will examine images of the Southern landscape and images of color and race as shifting constructs within the haiku. While undergoing many personal changes and personal struggles during the last years of his life, as a writer, Wright continued to connect to larger contexts politically, socially, and culturally. In exploring images of African American history he affirmed his connections to the African American community and American society at one and the same time.

In *Black Boy*, Wright frequently examines the harshness of race relations and the damaging psychological effects of Jim Crow racism. To describe the overall atmosphere of threat, he writes: "Tension would set in at the mere mention of whites and a vast complex of emotions, involving the whole of my personality, would be aroused. It was as though I was continuously reacting to the threat of some natural force whose hostile behavior could not be predicted. I had never in my life been abused by whites, but I had already become as conditioned to their existence as though I had been the victim of a thousand lynchings."[13]

Interestingly, Wright describes racism as a dangerous "natural force," hostile, unpredictable, and capable of being all pervasive. The biographer Michel Fabre claimed that for Wright nature was the "touchstone of his poetic sensitivity: it was the Mississippi country that restored his strength during a childhood of struggle and deprivation."[14] Wright demonstrates this love of nature from early childhood in these lines from *Black Boy*: "There was the vague sense of the infinite as I looked down upon the yellow, dreaming waters of the Mississippi River from the verdant bluffs of Natchez. . . . And there was the quiet terror that suffused my senses when vast hazes of gold washed earthward from star-heavy skies on silent nights."[15] Here Wright sows the seeds for his later haiku, with his sharp attention to detail and immersion in nature.[16] Notably, the sky in the South creates a "quiet terror." Rather than granting freedom, these images of nature spring traps and restrict. Like the ambivalence expressed in his haiku, Wright reveals beauty and threat wrapped together in the Southern landscape.

In *Haiku: This Other World*, Wright seems to rehabilitate images of nature from the South, projecting more positive images, while also at times he still expresses a deep ambivalence. For example, he writes a number of haiku with the Southern magnolia as a central image, as in haiku 304 and 725:

> Lonelier than dew
> On shriveled magnolias
> Burnt black by the sun.

> From a cotton field
> To magnolia trees,
> A bridge of swallows.

First Wright shows the wet dew contrasting with burnt flowers, a close-up view of nature infused with negative emotion while in the second poem the swallows connect elements of the landscape, cotton and magnolias with a more expansive view conveying interconnectedness as well as detachment from emotion. Wright's interest in landscape here reclaims Southern earth as his earth. He claims iconic symbols of the South as his own. However, Southern trees inevitably point to the tragic history of lynching, even in the haiku.

In earlier works, such as "Between the World and Me," Wright describes lynching in excruciating detail, putting himself in the center of a lynch fire:

And in a blaze of red I leaped to the sky as pain rose like water,
boiling my limbs.
Panting, begging I clutched childlike, clutched to the hot sides
of death.
Now I am dry bones and my face a stony skull staring in yellow
surprise at the sun . . .[17]

In the haiku Wright approaches the subject more obliquely as in the following two poems:

Burning autumn leaves,
I yearn to make the bonfire
Bigger and bigger. (49)

A dog's blood-red bark
Lights up the summer forest
And blanches the moon. (258)

In the first haiku Wright claims his autonomy by stoking the bonfire, an image of fire that recalls the fires of lynching and the violence of white mobs. Wright's yearning to make the bonfire "Bigger and bigger" suggests the enormity of loss caused by racial violence and simultaneously reveals his desire to combat it. In the second poem the dog's "blood-red bark" carries an automatic threat which frightens the moon itself. Here Wright proposes that the violence of racism creates a break within nature itself, destroying our assumption of the autonomy and innocence of the natural world. The dog appears as an intimidating hunter, and the forest setting recalls many other African American narratives of escape and hiding in the face of white violence. Without knowledge of the history of slavery and lynching, these two poems might seem innocuous or apolitical, but the stories they tell create a commentary as powerful as Billie Holiday's rendition of "Strange Fruit." In *Black Boy*, Wright describes the lynching of Uncle Hoskins as one of the most traumatizing events of his childhood, "Uncle Hoskins had simply been plucked from our midst and we, figuratively, had fallen on our faces to avoid looking into that white-hot face of terror that we knew loomed somewhere above us. This was as close as white terror had ever come to me and my mind reeled."[18] In addition, many of Wright's first published short stories, such as "Big Boy Leaves Home" and "Bright and Morning Star," confront the danger and damage caused by lynching. Continuing this theme within the haiku shows the crucible of Wright's discomfort with and ambivalence toward nature.

In other haiku Wright seems to take a step away from narratives of lynching, and he explores the beauty of trees alone without the inclusion of any people or reminders of human society. For example, he writes:

> Enough of dawn light
> To show pearly pear blossom
> Burning from within. (219)

And also,

> Fiery apples
> Are searing the tree leaves
> And singeing the grass. (252)

In both poems the fire of the trees does not automatically invoke the tragic legacy of lynching, but instead the burning apples and pear blossoms seem to glow from within in a mystical way. Wright composes many haiku similar to these two combining trees and fire, and in Wright's characteristic style, his description of fiery images appeals to our sense of touch as much as sight. Like the lynch fire in "Between the World and Me," he makes us feel the heat of the fire itself. By reworking images of trees in the haiku, Wright pulls them away from narratives of lynching into another world where racial violence does not prevail. In so doing he achieves reconciliation with nature perhaps not possible on Southern ground. The whole body of Wright's haiku can perhaps be seen in this light, as part of a long journey in writing to overcome, resist, and combat the damage inflicted by racism and racial violence and also part of a new journey to reclaim his connection to the earth and the Southern landscape, even while living in exile.

Yoshinobu Hakutani and Robert L. Tener claim that "Wright never tired of trying to fuse his two dreams—of black union with white and of his personal symbolical union with nature."[19] In many haiku Wright's attention to black and white becomes aesthetic and painterly, only sometimes evoking the South. For example, the two following haiku continue his preoccupation with magnolias:

The sudden thunder
Startles the magnolias
To a deeper white. (228)

White as it is young
And as black as it is dead,—
One magnolia! (330)

Here the darkness of thunder sets off the paleness of magnolias, and death becomes the equalizer between black and white. These haiku provide a new space for Wright to explore the meaning of color, and he does not always seem heavily burdened with the grim realities of white supremacy. In other words, the haiku allow Wright the freedom to explore nonracial definitions and relationships between black and white without the burden of politics. At the same time this exploration transforms our assumptions about black and white, creating new connections. In the broad range of his prolific production of haiku, Wright records the play of light and dark in minute detail with a large backdrop of seasons and landscape. Effectively, it is the neutrality and largeness of the natural world within the haiku that absorbs division:

Beads of quicksilver
On a black umbrella:
Moonlit April rain. (106)

Heaps of black cherries
Glittering with drops of rain
In the evening sun. (58)

In both haiku the light moves while reflected in raindrops, and Wright's attention to black and white reveals an intimate interconnectedness within nature. The cherries need both rain and sun, and the umbrella becomes an organic shape within the spring setting. In describing this mutable space of light and dark, Wright shows a richness of color joined with the life-giving element of water while the seasonal references of "April" and "cherries" heighten our sense of immediacy and temporality. A strong sense of presence and awareness of the present moment becomes intensified by the sharp contrast between light and dark and the sensory appeal of the rain. The intransigence of racial categories is replaced by transience and transformation in nature.

In *Haiku: This Other World* Wright still occasionally refers to race, but his depictions of race are less graphic than his representations in earlier writings:

In the falling snow
A laughing boy holds out his palms
Until they are white. (31)

The first day of spring:
The servant wears her blonde hair
In a new manner. (375)

Race is implied in both poems, but no overt critiques or judgments are made connected to race. Instead, the seasonal setting of the haiku eclipses the social meanings of race, and the natural world contradicts our narrow perceptions of race. Race is implicitly present, but racism is not. As other critics have pointed out, though the boy's race remains ambiguous, the symbolic weight of the color white resonates with Wright's readers.[20] This reserved approach to race differs greatly from Wright's treatment of race in most of his other writings, and he opens up multiple interpretations of the poem with this subtlety. In the second poem, the newness of spring creates a sense of new possibilities, and Wright's empathetic portrait emphasizes connection.

With some of his haiku, Wright also bridges the gap between African and African American culture, and between France and the United States, with images of black culture and black labor. By depicting images of ironwork, music, and black workers in the timeless setting of the haiku, Wright, like many other African American writers, explores the struggle for survival and the need for continuity and remembrance. At times criticized for being alienated from the African American community while he was in exile, Wright shows the maintenance of connection here. He writes:

> The summer moonlight
> Gleams upon a blacksmith's forge,
> And cools red embers. (179)
>
> Sun is glinting on
> A washerwoman's black arms
> In cold creek water. (60)
>
> A black woman sings:
> Filling the sunlight with steam,
> Bubbling molasses. (452)

The blacksmith, whose race is not identified, works at night with a traditional African craft while the washerwoman uses her natural surroundings productively and creatively. They both seem strongly connected to the elements that surround them, and the singer seems to be a force of nature herself. Here Wright portrays endurance and innovation, and he erases the lines between the social and natural worlds. He creates timeless images without any specific geographical reference. These subjects could be African immigrants in France or memories of African Americans in the South. The poems contain elements possible in both landscapes and both periods of his life, Southern and French, past and present, literal and imaginary. As a writer in exile, Wright faced the dilemmas of separation, loss, and even isolation, but the vividness of his memories of the South shines through in these haiku healing the rift.

Wright also combines rural and urban images within the haiku expanding our notion of "landscape" and preserving core images of African American community and culture. As Camille Dungy suggests in the introduction to her recent anthology *Black Nature: Four Centuries of African American*

Nature Poetry, pastoral poems from African American poets describe "elements of an environment steeped in a legacy of violence, forced labor, torture, and death. Are these not meditations on nature? We find poems set in urban streets. Can these not be landscape poems?"[21] Wright's haiku mirror this tradition exactly. Like the ambivalence inherent to rural Southern landscapes, urban landscapes also hold possible betrayal. For example, as Wright tells us in *Black Boy*, his father was "a black peasant who had gone to the city seeking life, but who had failed in the city; a black peasant whose life had been hopelessly snarled in the city . . . that same city which had lifted me in its burning arms and borne me toward alien and undreamed-of shores of knowing."[22] The city can lift people up or tear them down. In the haiku, he writes:

> From a tenement,
> The blue jazz of a trumpet
> Weaving autumn mists. (253)

And also,

> Black men with big brooms
> Sweeping streets in falling snow,
> Are absorbed by flakes. (609)

A sense of anonymity emerges from both poems with the musician remaining invisible in the first poem and the black men disappearing in the snow in the second. Similar to his father's loss, the urban landscape swallows up individual identity, and again the natural world obscures the significance of race through the power of the elements. Although anonymous, the music of the trumpet, like the black woman singing, becomes a force of nature itself, creating autumn mists with the power of its sound. Wright imagines a natural process emerging from the music that softens the urban landscape. Similarly, the softness of the snow covers the streets in the second poem creating a natural blanket that softens the scene.

Wright also explores the traditional bridge between rural and urban landscapes, the bridge between North and South, with numerous poems on trains. As in the poems above, Wright could be observing trains cutting through the French countryside, or he could be recording memories of trains from the South:

Empty railroad tracks:
A train sounds in the spring hills
And the rails leap with life. (155)

The low of a cow
Answers a train's long whistle
In the summer dusk. (387)

The train awakens life in the first poem, which is further emphasized by the springtime setting, and the cow's reply to the train whistle suggests an organic relationship between natural and man-made or urban and rural elements. Rather than division between rural and urban life, Wright sees wholeness. These two haiku both serve as good examples of Wright's creation of a transcultural space as he combines elements of Western and Eastern principles and cultures. The train acts as a modern and industrial Western anchor while the hills, the cow, the seasonal settings, and Wright's holistic approach to the subject matter all emphasize the Zen principle of unity with nature. Wright treats the train as a natural object, an object as essential to the Southern landscape as trees.

In *Voice of a Native Son: The Poetics of Richard Wright*, Eugene E. Miller stresses that Wright's primary interest "was the integration of the individual with society, not nature,"[23] but he also writes that "haiku is the expression of the individual's infinity within the limitation of finite things."[24] Similarly, in their afterword to *This Other World*, Hakutani and Tener write, "In haiku, two entirely different things are joined in sameness: spirit and matter, present and future, doer and deed, word and thing, meaning and sensation."[25] For Richard Wright, this list could be extended to include differences in color, race, place, culture, memory, and even urban and rural settings. In the expansive body of his haiku, he fuses together past and present, the American South and rural France, and African and African American culture, seeking new transitions and new bridges.

In *The Location of Culture* Homi Bhabha writes: "If we are seeking a 'worlding' of literature, then perhaps it lies in a critical act that attempts to grasp the sleight of hand with which literature conjures with historical specificity, using the medium of psychic uncertainty, aesthetic distancing, or the obscure signs of the spirit-world, the sublime and the subliminal."[26] The subtleties of Wright's haiku create this "worlding" of literature, this global view including both the sublime and the subliminal as they transport us from the surface of existence to the heart of living, beyond thin-skinned judgments to multilayered spaces of memory, history, and culture.

Finally, Wright's haiku bring to mind lines from Amiri Baraka's poem "Ka 'Ba":

> We have been captured,
> brothers. And we labor
> to make our getaway, into
> the ancient image, into a new
>
> correspondence with ourselves
> and our black family. We need magic
> now we need the spells, to raise up
> return, destroy, and create. What will be
>
> the sacred words?[27]

It seems that with his haiku Wright began this search for sacred words, conjuring new images and initiating a new correspondence in exile. The violence inherent to African Americans' particular history, the extremities of racism, challenged Wright to examine his own relationship to the natural world and to create a space of healing within this new genre reviving and reclaiming core images of African American and Southern history. This process of reconciliation remained for him disappointingly incomplete when the manuscript of *Haiku: This Other World* was rejected, but the haiku themselves allow the process of dialogue and reconnection to continue. In his introduction to *Black Boy,* Jerry W. Ward writes that part of Wright's success "is demonstrated by his ability to subvert the discourse of the dominant culture and bring it under the terms of his own control."[28] Like his mastery of the autobiographical form, with this new form, Wright powerfully infiltrates the dominant culture, combats the losses of exile, and reconnects to the American South. Wright's fierce sense of individualism illumines all of his writing, and especially *Black Boy,* but in the haiku, he starts to move in another direction, losing self to find a resting place, peace, connection, and a broader communal ground.

Notes

1. Constance Webb, *Richard Wright: A Biography* (New York: Putnam, 1968), 393.

2. Richard Wright, *Haiku: This Other World,* ed. Yoshinobu Hakutani and Robert L. Tener (New York: Arcade, 1998), xi.

3. David Levering Lewis, ed., *The Portable Harlem Renaissance Reader* (New York: Viking Press, 1994), 204.

4. Homi Bhabha, *The Location of Culture* (New York: Routledge, 1994), 247.

5. Ibid., 41.

6. Ibid., 247.

7. Toni Morrison, *Beloved* (New York: Vintage International, 2004), 101.

8. bell hooks, *Killing Rage: Ending Racism* (New York: Henry Holt and Company, 1995), 41.

9. Ibid.

10. Ibid., 47.

11. Paul Gilroy, *The Black Atlantic: Modernity and Double Consciousness* (Cambridge, MA: Harvard University Press, 1993), 154.

12. Hakutani and Tener emphasize this combination of freedom and restriction as a characteristic of the traditional haiku form in their afterword to *This Other World,* 249. However, Gilroy's focus on "agency" rather than "freedom" narrows this idea and contradicts the traditional Zen ideal of losing self.

13. Richard Wright, *Black Boy (American Hunger)* (New York: HarperCollins Publishers, 1998), 74.

14. Hakutani and Tener, afterword to *This Other World* by Wright, 274.

15. Wright, *Black Boy (American Hunger),* 8–9.

16. Floyd Ogburn also stresses this connection in his essay, "Richard Wright's Unpublished Haiku: A World Elsewhere," *MELUS* 23, no. 3 (1998). Ogburn also links this passage to Wright's descriptions of nature and the Southern landscape in *12 Million Black Voices.*

17. Ellen Wright and Michel Fabre, eds., *Richard Wright Reader* (New York: Harper & Row, 1978), 247.

18. Wright, *Black Boy (American Hunger),* 54–55.

19. Hakutani and Tener, afterword to *This Other World* by Wright, 282.

20. Hakutani and Tener discuss the symbolic quality of the color white in this poem in their afterword to *This Other World*, 278.

21. Camille T. Dungy, ed., *Black Nature: Four Centuries of African American Nature Poetry* (Athens: University of Georgia Press, 2009), xxi–xxii.

22. Wright, *Black Boy*, 35.

23. Eugene E. Miller, *Voice of a Native Son: The Poetics of Richard Wright* (Jackson: University Press of Mississippi, 1990), 246.

24. Ibid., 241.

25. Hakutani and Tener, afterword to *This Other World* by Wright, 253.

26. Bhabha, *Location of Culture*, 12.

27. Maria Mazziotti Gillan and Jennifer Gillan, eds., *Unsettling America: An Anthology of Contemporary Multicultural Poetry* (New York: Penguin Books, 1994), 156.

28. Jerry W. Ward Jr., introduction to *Black Boy* by Wright, xviii.

Female Imagery, Exploitation, and Richard Wright's Journey to His Other World

Haiku

— SHAWNRECE D. CAMPBELL —

After Jim Crow Mississippi causes Richard Wright to lose his sense of cosmos, he tries to find his way to an ordering of life. However, Wright soon finds that although his fiction and nonfictional works allow him to restore some order to the chaos in his soul, after enduring years of physical and psychological hardships in his life, this achievement does not fully satisfy his soul's thirst for humanistic fellowship with society. Even though in his prose works Wright shows mastery for distinguishing the shades of gray between good and evil, he is unable to balance the opposite truths he has experienced in his lifetime with the artistry of his works. Neither do his personal, social, and political aims overtake the artistry, nor does his focus upon the artistry leave room to effectively espouse his personal, social, and political aims. As a result, Wright's interest turns more toward humanism. Unfortunately, Wright's political, radical, and ideological commitments to promote humanism in the Third World nations often clash with his career as a novelist. Michel Fabre states that for Wright "to reach the widest possible public, by the most direct route, he now returned to journalism and lecturing as the mediums best suited to expressing his opinions."[1] Lamentably, Wright's nonfiction works were not as well received as he had hoped,

A small portion of this essay was previously published under a different title in *Modern Haiku* 32, no. 3 (2001): 54–57. Reprinted with permission of the author.

a fact that eventually led him to start questioning his talent as a writer and his ability to make a living as a writer.

By the time Wright begins writing haiku, according to Fabre, he has come to realize that the major theme—individual freedom and fulfillment in relation to organized society—of all his works as well as his lifelong concern is an issue he cannot answer.[2] It is only in his haiku that Wright the poet is able to achieve a wholeness of vision after an organic view of existence that Wright the intellectual thinker could not. As Julia Wright puts it, for Wright, haiku is "a form of poetry which links seasons of the soul with nature's cycle of moods [which] enabled him to reach out to the black boy part of himself still stranded in a South that continued to live in his dreams. With the haiku, a self-nurturing could begin, albeit so close to his own death."[3] This self-nurturing allows Wright to depict distilled truths in his haiku. These portraits are less likely to be misinterpreted because there is no social, political, or intellectual baggage surrounding them. For Wright, haiku is an imprint of life in its purest form.

Although many of Wright's haiku represent some of his best poetry, according to the editors—Yoshinobu Hakutani and Robert L. Tener—of *Haiku: This Other World,* "he never totally learned to eliminate his political and personal attitudes in them. Clearly he was experimenting with his own African-American approach to the haiku form."[4] The editors also agree with Constance Webb's observation that Wright is trying "to bring the life and consciousness of a black American" to this form of Japanese poetry.[5]

Unable to demonstrate the unity and harmony of all things in his prose without colonialism as well as the moral, intellectual, social, and political problems of racism, Wright finds in haiku the peace and harmony in society he so insatiably desired. Wright's fiction and nonfiction works exhibit an intertextuality centered on religiosity (primarily how it is used as an instrument of oppression), female characters (Wright's presentation of them), and humanism (Wright's personal search for an interconnectedness between all human beings). In *Haiku: This Other World,* humanism emerges once again as a theme of not only a fraternal bonding of all peoples but as a portrayal of life at its most profound level. As Hakutani declares, Wright longed to be a part of two cultures:

> American and African, as *Black Power* demonstrates, he was at times torn between the two worlds and remained an exile in Europe. His haiku, on the other hand, poignantly express a desire to transcend social and racial differences and a need to find union and harmony with nature. While his prose exhibits a predilection for a rational world created by human beings out of their narcissistic image of themselves, the humanism expressed in his haiku goes beyond a fellowship of human beings. It means an awareness of what human beings share with all living things. The human images in his haiku represent life at its deepest level.[6]

Haiku is a world where Wright's sense of cosmos is restored. Unable to make that connection with his African American community in his works of fiction, Wright finds himself an accepted member of every community in the world of haiku, and his haiku represent an achievement that allows him to finally quiet areas of turmoil within his soul.

Because of Wright's tendency to include his political and personal attitudes in his haiku, many of them can be read as senryu—a satirical form of haiku developed by Karai Senryu during the eighteenth century. In their afterword to *Haiku: This Other World*, Hakutani and Tener further define senryu "as a kind of 'mock haiku' with humor, moralizing nuances, and a philosophical tone, expressing 'the incongruity of things' more than their oneness, dealing more often with distortions and failures, not just with the harmonious beauty of nature."[7] This type of haiku appeals more to one's reason than to one's intuitiveness. Consequently, it is a great vehicle for Wright to create a synergistic relationship among images of black, white, and nature. It is also a form that defends Wright's haiku style against the following assessment by Tener: "But the ability to reject metaphor and symbol did not come easily to Wright. Much more at hand was his own preoccupation with the black and white symbolism in his life, a concern that became intrusive in his haiku and at times prevented them from communicating that special moment."[8] While Wright's haiku do not often conform to the "pure" content of the Japanese haiku, they definitely satisfy the moment of epiphany in the senryu.

In traditional haiku, nature is not a representation of goodness, truth, or beauty but often uncovers truths. These truths are often revealed in a relationship between the human subject and nature. Traditional haiku often include a clear reference to the season in which they were written, often showing how nature transforms sensations to the human psyche—where nature's tangible presence stimulates a cathartic experience. Wright's haiku reveal that there can be a conflict between nature and culture. Nature on its own is neither good nor bad; the interiority of the seer defines what is seen. When there is a conflict between nature and culture it sometimes suggests that certain members of this culture are exploited and made unnatural by their culture and its demands of the subject, such as women exploited for labor and sex.

Like writers of traditional haiku, Wright uses nature in his poems; however, his use of nature often does not show the wonders or mysteries of the natural world and how these wonders or mysteries correlate to the wonders of the internal (the human heart, psyche, etc.). It is Wright's use of human nature—its ability to exploit, abuse, and injure—that exposes suffering. His natural world discloses women and young girls suffering exposure to natural elements like rain and snow rather than learning from them, pondering them, or enjoying them, something they are unable to do because of cultural exploitation and/or economic deprivation. Thus, nature itself is not necessarily a wellspring of either transcendent sensationalism or horrific pain in and of itself; rather, it is the subject's social/cultural position in the world that causes suffering and that enables him or her to see what he or she sees in nature. If one is treated unjustly, exploited, and/or hurt, nature can be an agent of pain and suffering.

Wright reveals in his use of nature that the social position of the speaker and his object in the haiku are relevant to the haiku's meaning—to meaning-making in general. This seems to be very much in line with Wright's views of nature and culture in *Native Son*. What one sees is made possible because the culture provides the means, or lack thereof, for one to see it (or not). Instead of nature revealing epiphany-like, transcendent moments, in Wright's haiku nature reveals the truths of his subjects—women and young girls who suffer and who are separated from the natural world because they are physically and economically exploited by their culture.

The female imagery in Wright's haiku reveals his concern for the exploitation and suffering of women. Wright's female subjects' perceptions of the natural world rely on their experiences in their unnatural "natural" worlds. Unlike the Japanese noblemen, priests, writers, singers, and artists who had the time to find beauty and pleasure in natural phenomena, Wright's female subjects have to contend with the negative aspects of nature.

Nature often has a dual role in Wright's haiku, occupying not only the position of mother nature but playing the role of human nature as well. It is overwhelmingly human nature that impedes Wright's female subjects' abilities to enjoy mother nature. As a result, many of the female subjects in Wright's haiku experience the type of cultural determinism Wright emphasizes as controlling the fate of the male protagonists in his prose. The following haiku (number 60) is an example of Wright's harking back to the theme of cultural determinism present in his fictional works:

Sun is glinting on
A washerwoman's black arms
In cold creek water.

A washerwoman's black arms which should "naturally" be warmed by the sun are actually cold. Why? Historically, this seems a critique of the unnatural labor practices (slavery and colonialism) that prevent the black woman's, as well as all black people's, ability to be a natural person in the world. She cannot feel the warmth of the sun (nature) because culture, the "unnatural" economy that has required African Americans to become its laborers—women especially as domestics, "washerwomen"—will not allow her to experience nature as it is or feel warmth, life, and beauty. The fact that it is a creek suggests the passing of time, which indicates it has been this way a long time.

Similarly, in haiku 415,

In a drizzling rain,
In a flower shop's doorway,
A girl sells herself.

The theme of human nature causing women to suffer natural elements because of cultural demands is clearly presented in this haiku. Rain sets the tone—something death-like, melancholy, gray, unhappy. The speaker does not reverse the reader's expectations. The "girl" (youth—connection to growth, spring, promise of "flower" shop flowers) "sells herself"—prostitutes herself as the flower (nature) is prostituted/appropriated/exploited in order to fulfill man's (culture's) desires. Note that it is a drizzling rain and not a torrential downpour. This suggests that the girl's prostitution and suffering are not particularly cataclysmic to the culture that demands them. The drizzling rain suggests a slow, steady experience of suffering rather than a quick or sudden injury or death. That she stands in the flower shop's doorway is significant also because the doorway is a bridge, a transition between two worlds—the outside world as human nature and the inside world as mother nature.

However, culture exploits nature both inside and outside the flower shop. Inside the flower shop, the natural world of flowers is exploited and sold because of culture's demands. Outside the flower shop, the girl representing the natural is also exploited and sold because of culture's demands. The girl and the flowers are exploited by culture's desires to own and to use whatever it desires. Instead of being in nature and permitted their own natural experiences of life, the flowers are cut and sold in order to fulfill human (cultural) desires. Likewise, instead of being in nature as a young girl who can experience sex for its pleasures, the girl is a commodity that is cut off from her youth and its pleasures as she is bought and sold in an economy of exploitation that denies its member's humanity.

Exploitation of women's bodies echoes again in haiku 378:

Upon crunching snow,
Childless mothers are searching
For cash customers.

Here a woman's nature—her sexuality—is exploited for culture's (the cash customers') desires. Being a mother is not, for these women, a part of this sexual economy of exploitation. Because prostitution relies on the use, abuse, and exploitation of women's sexuality but not its natural result (children), the natural world and result of women's sexuality (her own and her offspring's) are annihilated by economic and cultural demands on her flesh which the culture sees as a commodity for its own use. Unfortunately, Wright is aware of far too many women who are represented by the plights of the women in the haiku above. He can only watch as they lose the innocence he expresses in haiku 363:

A little girl stares,
Dewy eyes round with wonder,
At morning glories.

During their youth, young girls wait patiently for some unknown good to touch their lives. As this promise of hope turns into a dream deferred, the girls become victims of cultural demands who are made to suffer while they are waiting. The word "stares" suggests something unnatural about this young girl's gaze. It eliminates the romance one might expect from such an idyllic scene which is an indication that the myriad opportunities available in life, represented by the morning glories, also will be eliminated in this young girl's life.

Haiku 186 represents Wright's memory of a woman toward the end of her life of suffering:

From these warm spring days,
I can still see her sad face
In its last autumn.

The focus here is on the juxtaposition of seasons. The speaker is calling to mind an old memory during warm spring days. Because spring represents growth, renewal, and rebirth and autumn represents decay, death, and the onset of old age, this haiku suggests that the speaker may not be in tune with nature because he recalls her sad face during these warm spring days. It also suggests that the female subject is out of tune with nature since the speaker remembers her sad face in its last autumn, "last autumn" suggesting that she has experienced deaths before as a metaphor for loss.

The conflict in many of Wright's haiku containing female imagery is between the natural human subject and her experiences in a corrupt culture. Wright's haiku seem to emphasize that it is a cultural determinant that is to blame for his subjects' being out of tune with nature: sun, rain, spring, autumn, flowers, and snow. Wright's female subjects suffer because cultural elements—men's (sexual) desires, cultural demands, forced labor, loss, pain, suffering, and injustice—will not allow them freedom to fully be or to be at one with nature.

Margaret Walker believes that "despite his constant fight against dehumanizing forces of racism, anti-Semitism, imperialism, including colonialism and neocolonialism, [Wright] never found that common ground of humanity."[9] I disagree. Wright finds the common ground of humanity through his haiku, particularly in the way he connects the experiences of his subjects to one another. For instance, Wright connects the experiences of the girl in haiku 52 with those of the washerwoman in haiku 60. Haiku 52 reads:

> Gazing at her face
> Reflected in the spring pond,
> The girl grimaces.

The face of the girl does not reflect the season of life (spring) that she is in. In the place of a youthful face reflecting the blossoming of life is a reflection of a face that has lost its blossom. The pain of life—represented by her grimace—has weathered the girl's face and caused it to look as though she is approaching the autumn of her life rather than approaching the summer years of her life. Her gaze implies she is looking beyond her face, contemplating all that has happened in her life up to this moment and that is now reflected in her face. The girl's face tells those who look upon it that life has been hard for her. Cultural exploitation and/or economic deprivation have not allowed her to experience the energizing renewal or the peaceful tranquility reflected in a "spring pond." Her young life has been full of pain.

In discussing Wright's ability to depict pain and suffering, Jianqing Zheng remarks: "In most of his fiction, Wright used his pen as a loudspeaker to cry out the pain and suffering of African American people in a segregated country and as a weapon to accuse the social injustice he had witnessed and experienced. But, in his haiku, he used his pen as a brush to paint his tender feelings of nature and human nature. In fact, his haiku collection shows a change in his writing."[10] I agree with Zheng's observation of Wright using his pen in his fiction as a loudspeaker for pain and suffering. However, I believe Wright continued to use his pen in his haiku to inform the world about the pain and suffering he had witnessed throughout his life. I also concur with Zheng's observation that the pen had turned into a brush as the tone employed in Wright's haiku was softer than the tone of his fiction. Nonetheless, as that brush painted the picture of nature and human nature it did not stop portraying the theme of human nature inflicting suffering upon human beings in order to satisfy its insatiable desires. These nuances are best exemplified in Zheng's discussion of the South in Wright's haiku:

> One prominent part of Wright's haiku is the use of the image of the sun or the moon to present the south. Haiku 38 is a good example:
>
> That abandoned house,
> With its yard of fallen leaves,
> In the setting sun.
>
> This haiku presents a desolate picture of the South. Instead of telling us directly, Wright conveys the meaning through the combination of images that make a reader feel intuitively. Further, the montage of the close-up of the abandoned house and fallen leaves followed by the long shot of the setting sun creates a perspective that Wright is not unfamiliar with when he was a black boy living in the villages and small towns in Mississippi and Arkansas. Although the sun functions as an intensifier of desolation in this haiku, in other haiku of his, it functions as a soothing power that brings warmth to a person's poor life, as in haiku 60:
>
> Sun is glinting on
> A washerwoman's black arms
> In cold creek water.[11]

Although the sun does attempt to bring some comfort to the washerwoman, as I discussed above, her arms still remain cold. The sun is unable to penetrate the coldness (exploitive inhumanity) that surrounds the washerwoman's life just as the spring pond is unable to bring peace to the young girl so that she grimaces when gazing at her face. This is Wright's tender way of saying that both of these females continue to live in the hardness and discomfort of life despite nature's (the naturalness of humanity) efforts to mitigate the unnaturalness of their lives. Zheng has it right when he states, "In a word, the South in Wright's haiku is a place full of dreams, memories, hardships, and loneliness."[12] Yet, I would go even further and say this is not just true of the South in Wright's haiku but of his entire published collection.

Clearly, it is true of the female imagery in Wright's haiku. Hardships, loneliness, dreams, and memories connect these haiku that bring out the oneness of these females' lives. This is represented in the implied connection between haiku 52 (discussed above) and haiku 123:

And now this thing too:
A drunken girl vomiting
In the autumn rain.

The first line of haiku 123, "And now this thing too," indicates a continuation of events, as though the girl the reader was introduced to in haiku 52 is the girl that is now drunk in haiku 123. Given the harshness of life that causes the girl in haiku 52 to grimace when looking at her face in the "spring pond," it would be understandable that she attempts to cope with that pain by numbing it with alcohol. However, even this desperate comfort eludes her as her body violently rejects the intoxicating liquid. This leaves the girl in a death-like, melancholy, gray, unhappy, steady experience of suffering, a tone set by the "autumn rain." Again, there is juxtaposition between the age of the female and the season. She is a drunken youth in an autumn rain. The cultural exploitation and/or economic deprivation she has experienced have separated her from the natural order of the world. It has robbed her of experiencing the benefits of what should be an energizing season in her life. At the very time in her life when she should be experiencing continuous renewal, there is only the steady drone of death (autumn rain).

As one continues to follow the strain of female imagery in Wright's haiku, the next time the reader encounters the girl she is dead.

A spring pond as calm
As the lips of the dead girl
Under its water. (140)

The first line of this haiku highlights the unnaturalness of the girl's death, which harkens back to the unnaturalness of her life. A calm spring pond would be one full of death as a "spring pond" should be full of the chaotic noises of life beginning again after a season of death. Although a spring pond could have a calming, comforting effect on individuals enjoying its natural pleasures, a calm spring pond is a symbol of death. The second line confirms this when the speaker compares the calmness of the spring pond to the lips of a dead girl.

Could this be the same subject that was in haiku 52, 123, and 140? The third line indicates that it could be. The girl's dead body is under the water instead of floating on top of it. This also highlights the unnaturalness of the girl's death as dead bodies float on top of the water. Yet in reading the female imagery in Wright's haiku as a strain, it would make sense that the girl's body is under the water because it would represent the cultural exploitation and/or economic deprivation that rained upon the female subject in the previous haiku. However, this time the water did not stop until it completely beat her down as signified by the unnatural state of the water reigning over her dead body instead of her dead body reigning (floating) over the water.

The water covering the female subject's dead body would also imply that in death, the girl still does not find the release from the oppressive forces of her life or else her dead body would float on top of the water. Unfortunately, the unnatural position of her body in death also indicates that the portrayal of cultural and economic oppression will continue in other female imagery encountered in Wright's haiku as the oppressive cultural and economic forces which killed the girl were not defeated. Again, this is indicated by the image of the girl's body being submerged beneath the water instead of floating on top of it. Ultimately, I believe Wright is saying that until all women are free of cultural and economic exploitation, no woman is free—dead or alive—from these exploitive forces.

By illustrating the suffering of female subjects in his haiku, Wright is able to find the common ground among humanity. The female subjects in his haiku, as well as in his fiction, do not possess agency. They are not free to create or adopt a philosophy that could bind them together with women from other cultures to work as a united group defending women and the rights of women. They are the victims of institutionalized worldviews.

Wright demonstrates this by portraying how and why the female subjects in his haiku are relegated to a script dictated by the conjunction of institutional capitalism, racism, sexism, and Judeo-Christian ethics. Within this worldview no one is free to create oneself but is required to submit to the roles already available to one. "According to popular notions of masculinity and femininity," as explained by Nafueyalti Warren, "the truly feminine person is supposed to adapt naturally to roles requiring submissive behavior"[13] as a part of this institutionalized worldview. Wright paints this perspective as he depicts the suppression and exploitation of female subjects in his haiku; however, he also fights against the continuation of these practices. In portraying the commonality of women in all cultures, Wright seeks to expose and defeat materialism and greed that result in the cultural exploitation of women of all cultures. He achieves this in his haiku by creating a connective strain among the subjects in his female imagery. After writing 4,000 haiku, Wright seems to be more vehement than ever in his belief that two of human beings' vices, materialism and greed, are the twin culprits of racial discord and poverty. While his fiction and nonfiction works explicitly advocate his position, he is able to express this only indirectly in his haiku.

In his journey as a writer, commentator, journalist, and finally poet, Wright finds that the only entity that can defeat materialism and greed is humanism. In "Blueprint for Negro Writing," he implores the African American writer to seek out the commonality among all cultures. Wright argues, "Every iota of gain in human thought and sensibility should be ready grist for his mill, no matter how far-fetched they may seem in their immediate implications."[14] Wright believes that finding what is common among all cultures and defending it increases those cultures' faith in themselves. This conviction is something he observes in the Ashanti Kingdom in West Africa, as he writes, "The truth is that the question of how much of Africa has survived in the New World is misnamed when termed 'African survivals.' The African attitude toward life springs from a natural and poetic grasp of existence and all the emotional implications that such an attitude carries; it is clear, then, that what the anthropologists have been trying to explain are not 'African survivals' at all—they are but the retention of basic and primal attitudes toward life."[15]

Wright also observes the tenacity to retain their culture in the Asian mind at the Bandung Conference. He affirms, "The more I examined the relationship between Communism and Christianity at Bandung, the more complicated I found that relationship to be. In the West one is inclined to feel that the two doctrines of life, Christianity and Communism, are opposed, but, at bottom, they are not as opposed as one would think. There are deep underground, emotional connections."[16] Instead of allowing Western philosophies to consume their own cultural philosophies, Asians combine the two philosophies since they see them as sharing much of the same assumption of hope. In this way, their own cultural philosophies do not die out. Yet they still show that they are willing to cooperate for the good of their country.

The primal outlook on life to which Wright is a witness coincides with his belief that there is a preeminence of intuition over knowledge in the search for truth. This is what leads Wright to call into question the basic assumptions of existence; that is, questioning the life one is socially and politically taught to live. In his haiku, as in all of his works, Wright admonishes us that for us to see ourselves truly as human beings, we must give our utmost attention to comprehending the relationship between humanity and nature.

Notes

1. Michel Fabre, *The Unfinished Quest of Richard Wright* (New York: William Morrow, 1973), 408.

2. Ellen Wright and Michel Fabre, eds., introduction to *Richard Wright Reader* (New York: Harper & Row, 1978), xx.

3. Julia Wright, introduction to *Haiku: This Other World* by Richard Wright (New York: Arcade, 1998), xi.

4. Yoshinobu Hakutani and Robert L. Tener, afterword to *Haiku: This Other World*, 282.

5. Ibid.

6. Yoshinobu Hakutani, *Richard Wright and Racial Discourse* (Columbia: University of Missouri Press, 1996), 262.

7. Hakutani and Tener, afterword to *Haiku: This Other World*, 255.

8. Robert L. Tener, "The Where, the When, the What: A Study of Richard Wright's Haiku," in *Critical Essays on Richard Wright*, ed. Yoshinobu Hakutani (Boston: G. K. Hall, 1982), 283.

9. Margaret Walker, *Richard Wright: Daemonic Genius* (New York: Amistad Press, 1988), 212.

10. Jianqing Zheng, "Richard Wright's Haiku," *Southern Quarterly* 46, no. 2 (2009): 61.

11. Jianqing Zheng, "The South in Richard Wright's Haiku," *Notes on Contemporary Literature* 37, no. 2 (2007): 8.

12. Ibid., 9.

13. Nagueyalti Warren, "Black Girls and Native Son: Female Images in Selected Works by Richard Wright," in *Richard Wright Myths and Realities*, ed. C. James Trotman (New York: Garland Publishing, 1988), 61.

14. Ellen Wright and Michel Fabre, eds., *Richard Wright Reader*, 45.

15. Richard Wright, *Black Power: A Record of Reactions in the Land of Pathos* (New York: Harper & Brothers, 1954), 266.

16. Richard Wright, *The Color Curtain: A Report on the Bandung Conference* (Cleveland: World Publishing Company, 1956), 168.

"I Am Nobody"

The Haiku of Richard Wright

— RICHARD A. IADONISI —

When Richard Wright's typescript *Haiku: This Other World* was first published in 1998,[1] it seemed logical to expect a fair amount of critical attention to be focused on the volume. After all, the dramatic shift that Wright makes from writer of realistic and naturalistic fiction to haikuist is so unusual that it seems to beg for explication. Moreover, Wright is the first noteworthy American minority writer to produce the highly popular poetic form. Such, however, has not been the case. To this point, Wright's collection has received even less notice than did the twenty-three haiku that were published during the author's lifetime and collected in *Richard Wright Reader*.[2] This neglect is unfortunate because examining the whole collection allows us to see how Wright radically reinvents the haiku form, making of it a revolutionary poetry that offers and then savagely undercuts the possibility of Zen oneness; in the process, the haiku serve as a vehicle that articulates the author's anticolonial position.

Because a number of biographers have chronicled Wright's relationship with the haiku, only a brief summary is required here. While suffering from a relapse of amoebic dysentery in 1959, Wright picked up a volume of Japanese haiku, which he read repeatedly and with fascination. Finding the form irresistible, Wright began composing in August 1959 and, within a few months, he had written 4,000 haiku. By March of 1960, Wright had typed the poems; by the middle of April, he had selected 817 that he hoped

Previously published in *MELUS* 30, no. 3 (2005). Reprinted with permission of the author.

to publish. After devoting the next month to rearranging the sequence of these haiku, Wright submitted them in June to editor William Targ of World Publishing. The eighty-page typescript was rejected and, following the author's death and the disbursal of his estate, the typescript remained in the Rare Book Collection of Yale's Beinecke Library until its publication under the auspices of editors Yoshinobu Hakutani and Robert L. Tener.[3]

Because haiku in the United States grew in popularity following World War II, Wright had at his disposal a number of major critical treatises on the verse form. However, little question exists as to the work that most influenced him. That work is R. H. Blyth's four-volume *Haiku*.[4] From Blyth, Wright learned the history of the haiku form from its beginnings as the opening stanza in thirteenth-century Heian court poetry contests to its inception as a single, three-line, seventeen-syllable poem with Buddhistic, impressionistic, and/or realistic overtones. Attempting to capture the exact form of haiku, Wright reproduced the three unrhymed lines of five, seven, and five syllables and sought to include a seasonal reference, sometimes implicit, other times explicit. He also learned that Japanese haiku are classified by seasons and subjects. From Blyth, Wright also learned that haiku are loosely "syllogistic" because they present "step by step in each line, an independent but related image"[5] although these relationships may not be overtly signaled.

In addition to the external characteristics of haiku, Wright learned from his encounter with Blyth that concepts taken from Zen Buddhism often underlie the poems. Specifically, Wright became familiar with such Zen concepts as *mu*, "a state of nothingness that is absolutely free of any human-centered thought or emotion"; *sabi*, a quiet beauty or lonely grace; *wabi*, an aesthetic appreciation of beauty stemming from poverty; and *yugen*, the "mystery and inexplicability, which surround the order of the universe,"[6] as well as the proper state of mind required to write haiku: a state of selflessness, a condition of rest and ease.[7]

Relying on this Zen foundation to contextualize Wright's haiku, a number of important Wright scholars seek to connect the haiku with flight, escape, and transcendence. An overview of the commentary will demonstrate what I feel has been an erroneous or at least misleading approach. In an article appearing in *Tamkang Review* (and reprinted in his book *American Poetry and Japanese Culture*), Kodama asserts that Wright's very "Japanese" haiku possess "a sense of contentment" that brings to the reader "a fresh sense of calmness," and they show Wright attaining a state of selflessness and condition of rest and ease.[8] Kodama's key point is that Wright, exhausted by his lifelong battle against racism, sought a genre that he could construct as race-free. Finding that genre to be haiku, Wright was able to dispense with his "strong and uneasy consciousness at being a black American" and succeed at "accepting and transcending his fate," something he was unable to accomplish in his novels, which were "the outlet for his violent, black consciousness."[9]

Robert L. Tener makes a similarly limited move in "The Where, the When, the What: A Study of Richard Wright's Haiku," arguing that haiku appealed to Wright because the short poems contain what the critic Joan Giroux terms a "haiku moment," an intuitive flash in which the object and the poet are united.[10] Feeling a keen desire to escape the sickness and loneliness of his final years, Wright sought poetic escape in "the 'ah-ness' or moment of nature, intuitively becoming one with the object of his vision."[11] For Tener, the evaluative standard for Wright's haiku is how well they capture the "haiku moment." Thus, Tener feels that Wright is at his best when he identifies with nature without humanizing or sentimentalizing it. Conversely, all haiku that contain a speaker who intrudes on the natural scene are unsuccessful, and, by implication, any haiku that presents racial tension (symbolically or otherwise) causes a speaker to intrude on the natural scene. Tener ultimately criticizes Wright's haiku because Wright did not succeed in either mastering the form of haiku or separating his political ideas from "the sensitive lyricism of this intimate poetry."[12]

Michel Fabre goes so far as to evacuate Wright's haiku of political intent altogether, commenting in *The Unfinished Quest of Richard Wright* on how the haiku consoled Wright "in the face of illness, isolation, financial hardship, and personal and critical attacks"; these poems enabled Wright to counter his anger and frustration with sensitivity and delicacy rather than vituperation.[13] In "The Poetry of Richard Wright," Fabre explores the evolution of Wright's poetry from the early leftist poems to the haiku, arguing that the lyricism which Wright had used to praise Communism in the 1930s came to praise "a universal transformation" because it is "in harmony with Nature that [people] will most fully realize [their] humanity," and people's overriding need is to establish "a meaningful relationship with the objective world."[14] For Fabre, the evolution from the harshness and brutality of the revolutionary poems to the sensitivity and intimacy of the haiku is indicative of Wright's increasing desire for detachment. Wright on his deathbed was still interested in racial inequality, but he "had gradually reserved the poetic form, initially the sole vehicle of his social and political message, for the expression of feeling. Poetry served to paint scenes at once more personal and more universal, while his prose works reflected his ideological stands."[15] A final "transcendent" reading occurs in Jean-Francois Gounard's *The Racial Problem in the Works of Richard Wright and James Baldwin,* which connects the twenty-three published haiku to the issue of race, arguing that the haiku served Wright as "the literary means of freeing himself from his anguish," his struggle against exhaustion and illness.[16] These haiku reveal Wright's "unconscious desire to recapture the innocence and purity of his childhood."[17]

I would agree that both Wright's life and a number of his writings lend themselves to the theme of escape. Wright's decision to relocate to France, to journey to Argentina, Ghana, Indonesia, and various other countries, and to seek residence in England indicates a man fleeing his own culture. The "I" of both *Black Boy* and its companion piece *American Hunger,* Fred Daniels, Big Boy, Fishbelly (the main character of *The Long Dream*), and Bigger Thomas all choose flight as the at-best marginally workable solution to the problem of racial oppression. It is tempting, then, to see the haiku that Wright composed in his last years as a further attempt at flight, to see an older man, sick with dysentery, bedridden, seeking to escape the complexities of being a black man in a white world for transcendent moments of poetic union with nature. However, whether we consider Wright's haiku as a seamless union of poet and nature, a way of achieving a state of nothingness, or a race-free genre that allows the poet to dispense with his angry black consciousness, on a theoretical level the haiku are detached from Wright's sense of identity (except, perhaps, insofar as the writing of lyric poetry expands the poet's soul). Yet such a theoretical foundation crumbles when it is juxtaposed with Wright's own aesthetic expounded in *Black Boy* (*American Hunger*) and other works.[18]

At the heart of this aesthetic, as I see it, is what Wright's Richard terms in *Black Boy* "the secret, the thing, the reality I felt somewhere beneath all the words and silences."[19] (47). Since this "secret" that Richard is denied concerns his grandmother's whiteness, it is clear that the secret is race, the "white threat." For Richard, oral report is limiting: at best it is untrustworthy, and at worst dangerous. Questioning his family, Richard is reminded to stay in his place with verbal rebukes and often blows to the face. Failing to say "sir" to a white man, Richard is hit with a whiskey bottle and threatened with death.

Although these examples relate to social privilege and expectation, they also clearly relate to spoken language, which denies Richard dignity and humanity. As a consequence, he turns to written language. Reading H. L. Mencken, Theodore Dreiser, Sinclair Lewis, and other writers, Richard thinks about life and people, and he learns "what being a Negro meant."[20] Richard recognizes that he has learned experientially what he could not learn through utterance: the "white threat" is no longer a secret that is denied him. The one missing essence has been replaced with another; however, as Richard realizes, "There were feelings denied [him], that the very breath of life itself was beyond [his] reach."[21] He cannot fully embrace this "sense of life itself" through reading alone; he must capture the essence in writing. As Wright implicitly acknowledges in "Richard Wright Describes the Birth of Black Boy," "writing of one's life was vastly different from speaking of it" because he finds it easier to render "a close and emotionally connected account" of his experience orally than in writing. "[T]o tell the truth [in writing] is the hardest thing on earth."[22]

This aesthetic develops, of course, out of Wright's awareness that as an artist he must use the language of the dominant culture as a transformative tool. Wright's writing constantly deterritorializes the major language, subverting that language. Wright continues "fighting with words," using words as a weapon[23] in his later works, including *Black Power*, a record of a visit to the Gold Coast (1954); *The Color Curtain* (1956), based on his observations of the 1955 Bandung Conference, a gathering of leaders of the developing nations; and *White Man, Listen!* (1957), a collection of previously unpublished essays and lectures on the subject of race. These works, especially the latter two, focus on the debilitating effects of colonialism on the psychology of oppressed peoples.

If Wright's own aesthetic and his concerns with the developing nations raise questions about the essentializing meta-language that codes haiku as a "pure" literary form and arena, so too does an examination of the haiku themselves as in a number of them Wright poses complex ontological questions through their presentation of an overt and menacing disjunction between the narrative "I" and contingent reality. Haiku 1 foregrounds the affective powers of nature:

> I am nobody:
> A red sinking autumn sun
> Took my name away.

In this, the first haiku appearing in the volume, it is possible to read the speaker's awareness of self as nobody as his attainment of the state of *mu*. Or it could be what Blyth sees in many haiku as a transcendent moment in which the poet moves to "a nameless realm where the human and the non-human . . . meet and are one."[24] Yet, implicit in the involuntary loss of identity and disembodiment is a sense of violence. The autumn sun, after all, has taken the speaker's name away. Another haiku—

> It is September,
> The month in which I was born;
> And I have no thoughts. (508)

—at first glance seems to demonstrate the seamless union of poet and nature. In fact, were the poem to consist merely of lines one and three, it might then be making a move to close the gap between human and non-human, with the speaker stepping into the world of nature and outside of all-too-human cognition. The second line is included, however, and it grounds the poem not in the natural but in the human. The significance that the speaker attaches to September is based not on the fact that it is autumn. Indeed, the speaker focuses on the calendar and not the season—but on the fact that September is the month of his birth. The absence of thought is connected with the anniversary of the speaker's birth: How? We are not certain. Is there a causal relationship between the month and the lack of thought? Or is there some other unspecified relationship at play?

A number of haiku on the first several pages, which set the tone for the volume, are equally illustrative of a disjunction between self and nature. For instance, the second haiku of the volume—

For you, O gulls,
I order slaty waters
And this leaden sky!

—hardly presents a seamless union of poet and object or an attainment of *mu*, that state of nothingness free of human-centered thought or emotion. On the contrary, this poem is decidedly "human-centered," as the poem contains a sense of hostility toward the gulls as well as humor, the speaker's mock audacity to project his will onto what is beyond human control. In that sense, the choice of the adjectives "slaty" and "leaden" serve to yoke solid (metal) with liquid (water) and air; such a yoking foregrounds not a union with nature but the poet whose art(ifice) connects the disparate elements.

An alternate reading of this haiku treats the speaker's lack of connection with the natural scene around him as a serious desire to control the sea and sky and offer a service to the gulls. Such service is, however, illusory. After all, if the speaker were as fully in control of nature as his words suggest, why would he order "slaty waters" and a "leaden sky" rather than clear or bright blue ones? The lack of parallelism in the last two lines also calls into question the speaker's control. A parallel construction would consist of either "[these] slaty waters / And this leaden sky" or "slaty waters / And [a] leaden sky"; its absence imposes limitations on the speaker's degree of control. Finally, if the haiku suggests the poet's ability to control nature, it also implies a request, an order, of something to be supplied. This would place the speaker not in the position of absolute power but somewhere above the gulls and below the something of which he makes the request.

Other human-centered haiku are prevalent in the early pages of Wright's collection. Observe these two separate haiku:

I give permission
For this slow spring rain to soak
The violet beds. (5)

I grant to sparrows
The telegraph wires that brought
Me such glad tidings! (14)

The verbs "order," "give," and "grant" in each of the three haiku could be read as expressions of acceptance, thereby endowing each poem with a Zen quality. However, in each, the speaker seems more at odds than at peace with his surroundings as he is "giving" something that he does not really own to begin with. In the haiku about sparrows, what the speaker possesses are "glad tidings" that have prompted his "generosity" toward the sparrows, again giving what the poet himself does not possess but what the speaker does in his fictive world. It would, of course, be possible to read this poem as a successful union of poet and nature. The speaker could desire to share his happiness with the sparrows, saying, in effect, "I'm happy, so you can be happy on the wires." But clearly the happiness of the sparrows is not contingent on the happiness of the speaker; consequently, the worth of the "grant" is called into question. Also, the idea of the speaker's "granting" could be a concession, indicating that the speaker is giving up the wires rather than offering them to the sparrows, an act that would, figuratively speaking, put an end to further good tidings. Moreover, even if the speaker desires to share his happiness with the sparrows, the fact that what he gives to creatures of nature are emblems of the very technology that threatens to destroy their habitat undercuts the union of the two worlds.

Similarly, the following haiku undercuts the union of human and natural world through the presentation of an ambivalent consciousness.

O finicky cat,
Forgive me for this spring rain
That disgusts you so! (8)

In attributing to the cat society's expectations that humans are above animals and that humans should have control over the environment, the speaker's consciousness emerges as dialogic. Obviously, the act of seeking forgiveness of the cat reluctant to go out in the rain is an ironic one on the speaker's part since he knows fully well that he is not responsible for the rain or for the cat's fastidiousness or disgust. At the same time, the speaker ironically assumes a position of power over nature, situating himself as the rain's agent when, in fact, he has no more control over the rain than does the cat. Thus, he asks the cat's forgiveness for failing to live up to expectations that he controls nature.

The three haiku by Wright I have cited (and there are others that could also have been included) are examples of what J. L. Austin terms performative utterances, aimed at getting something done.[25] Haiku 5 and 14 are illocutionary utterances, doing something in the saying; haiku 8 is a perlocutionary utterance, attempting to bring about an effect by the saying. Whether illocutionary or perlocutionary, however, the haiku present self-conscious performances and mock gestures: the desire to order, grant, and beg forgiveness. Most likely aimed at a predominantly white audience, these haiku enable Wright to challenge society's expectations of what it means to be human: for an African American, he suggests simply yet elegantly, control is illusory.

Thus, we see in the haiku attempts on the part of Wright to constitute himself by constituting nature. We also see a disjunction between the speaker and the natural world that runs the gamut from contingent reality as mildly, amusingly intrusive to the fear that a too-close communion with nature causes Wright to lose name and hence identity, a concept that runs throughout Wright's works. It almost goes without saying that such a relationship between speaker, self, and nature is very un-Japanese.

I should note at this point that Wright does generate a number of haiku that successfully replicate their classic Japanese forebears. The two haiku below, though very different, share characteristics of traditional haiku:

> The spring lingers on
> In the scent of a damp log
> Rotting in the sun. (47)
>
> The crow flew so fast
> That he left his lonely caw
> Behind in the fields. (117)

Both make use of *kigo* (season words), the first by mentioning the season and the second by depicting a crow, usually associated with autumn in classical Japanese haiku, as Wright would well know from reading R. H.

Blyth. The first poem also suggests the unity of disparate elements; probably written in early summer, this poem juxtaposes an image of nascence (the lingering scent of spring) with an image of decay (the rotting log). The second haiku, presenting a picture of a crow that has flown away immediately after cawing, connects nature and human nature. Observing the scene, the poet is left in the fields as lonely as the "lonely caw."

Nevertheless, even those haiku that seem quite close to Japanese sensibility adhere more closely to the aesthetic set forth by Wright in the 1940s. Read haiku 7:

Make up your mind, Snail!
You are half inside your house
And halfway out!

This poem is similar to a haiku by the famed haikuist Kobayashi Issa that is included in Blyth's book: "O snail, / Climb Mt. Fuji, / But slowly, slowly!" Issa gently laughs at the snail's ponderous progress up the mountainside, yet his humor is tinged with a sense of fellowship for the struggling creature. The haiku thus demonstrates that the fusion of humor and Zen that Blyth mentions is expressed in the delight we feel reading the poem. This delight is evidence that "we are momentarily enlightened, Buddhas, raised above mortality and religion, beyond life and death."[26] In the same way, in Wright's poem, the reader can laugh at and identify with the snail's indecision. However, it is possible to see the speaker's sympathy with the snail as a conscious identification with a creature both in and out of its shell, denizen of two "worlds" belonging wholly to neither.

Here is another haiku that seems to be "Japanese" in its sensibility:

The dog's violent sneeze
Fails to rouse a single fly
On his mangy back. (20)

Yet the poem contains an image that is rooted in a moment of degradation. Compare it with Issa's most famous haiku: "One man / and one fly / waiting in this huge room," in which the poet identifies with the fly, sharing its sense of aloneness. Wright's poem contains a different sort of pathos.

Instead, the reader is confronted with a diseased dog, its back without fur. And whether the failure "to rouse a single fly" means the solitary fly on the dog's back refused to move, or whether it means that not a single one of numerous flies moved, the harshness of the image still strikes the reader.

Other haiku, too numerous to analyze, ground themselves in material poverty, as do many classical Japanese haiku. However, the classical Japanese haiku, as Wright knew from his studies, relied on *sabi* and *wabi*. The first is a quiet beauty or lonely grace, and the second is "the uniquely human perception of beauty stemmed from poverty."[27] The perception of poverty in Wright's haiku is not overlain with quiet beauty. Instead, the poverty speaks of pain and misery. A few examples will suffice.

> This tenement room
> In which I sweat this August
> Has one buzzing fly. (421)

Again, we can juxtapose Wright's piece with Issa's famous fly haiku. Supposedly envisioned while Issa waited in an anteroom to meet an important person, this haiku is generally seen as the speaker's awareness that he and the fly are both isolated and even insignificant. Issa is able to connect with the fly, as the parallel construction of the first two lines (at least in this translation) makes clear, thus easing that sense of loneliness and insignificance. In Wright's haiku, the anteroom is reduced to a too-hot tenement room. Even the fellowship of speaker and fly is gone. The speaker's only connection to the room is the fact that he sweats in it; the room itself "has" the single fly.

The following haiku seems closer to attaining a sense of *wabi*, an aesthetic appreciation stemming from poverty:

> I am paying rent
> For the lice in my cold room
> And the moonlight too. (459)

It is possible to see the speaker as the beneficiary of his poor living quarters. The room may contain lice, but it also affords a "priceless" view of the moonlight. Still, the speaker makes it clear in the first two lines that he is an exploited consumer whose money allows him to purchase a lack of heat and parasites (lice that, in a manner of speaking, "consume" the consumer). The moonlight is akin to a retail offer in which a less valuable item is included with the purchase of a more valuable one. Any appreciation for the moonlight, it seems, is offset by the room's material conditions. The moonlight may also be read as an unexpected beauty that no degree of poverty or injustice can deny one, whatever rent one pays.

Wright further diverges from the concepts of *sabi* and *wabi* in his two haiku about tuberculosis:

The consumptive man,
Who lives in the room next door,
Did not cough today. (121)

and

An old consumptive
Coughs so spasmodically
He disturbs the birds. (590)

The first one implies that the next-door neighbor has ceased coughing because he has died; the second one suggests that the old man's medical condition is unnatural both because it disturbs the birds and because it is undoubtedly exacerbated by lack of medical care. These haiku, when taken with Wright's pieces on prostitutes, suggest the utter desperation of the poor, a desperation that can be contrasted with the poverty in haiku 459 above in that the renter's condition is at least relieved by the moon's beauty.

Other haiku take on the subject of rats; in so doing, they force us to make an intertextual leap to *Native Son*. These two in particular—

The sound of a rat
Scampering over cold tin
Is heard in the bowels. (294)

and

The sound of a rat
Gnawing in the winter wall
Of a rented room. (453)

—remind us of the scene in which the Thomas family discovers the rat in their apartment:

> A huge black rat squealed and leaped at Bigger's trouser-leg and snagged it in his teeth, hanging on.
> "Goddamn!" Bigger whispered fiercely, whirling and kicking out his leg with all the strength of his body . . .
> Bigger aimed and let the skillet fly with a heavy grunt . . .
> "I got 'im," he muttered, his clenched teeth bared in a smile. "By God, I got 'im."
> He kicked the splintered box out of the way and the flat black body of the rat lay exposed, its two long yellow tusks showing distinctly. Bigger took a shoe and pounded the rat's head, crushing it, cursing hysterically:
> "You sonofa*bitch*!"[28]

However much we may seek to extrapolate the rat from its unnatural surroundings and view it as a "natural" creature with which the speaker in the haiku is somehow attuned, we cannot escape the image of the savage rat, trapped, wheeling, and attacking Bigger. Even if such an intertextual elision were possible, the two haiku contain a sense of menace: the first results from the disconcerting noise of claws on tin, and the second from the rat attempting to chew its way through the wall and into the speaker's apartment. The point of view of the haiku is also interesting. Rather than using a subjective "I" to personalize the experiences, Wright suggests that they are universal; anyone who is impoverished could have the same experience. The fact that the listener in the first haiku is located in "the bowels" of the building makes a further connection between that haiku and the Thomas family. "Bowels" suggests not only a stomach-turning feeling of fear but also a person who has been "chewed up" and "digested" by the building, an apt description of the Thomases in their tiny one-room "garbage dump" of an apartment with its "thinly plastered walls."[29]

The haiku that I have examined, particularly those that foreground materiality and the subjectivity of the impoverished and oppressed, form an important and largely unexplored strain in Wright's collection. They are connected with colonialism's greatly negative influence on minority subjects. Abdul R. JanMohamed, in discussing the construction of Wright as subject, argues that "the hegemonic formation of minorities is itself based on an attempt to negate them—to prevent them from realizing their full potential as human beings and to exclude them from full and equal participation in civil and political society,"[30] and that minority subjects must negate this hegemonic negation before they can participate in the dominant culture.

Wright, of course, is quite conscious of hegemonic negation, especially its base in language, as he demonstrates in works that precede the haiku. In *The Color Curtain,* he recalls coming across a booklet designed to teach Bahasa, the language of Indonesia, to Dutch officials, tourists, and anyone else who might be spending time in Indonesia. This booklet includes no words or sentences of polite conversation; instead, it is comprised of orders and accusations. Wright includes some of the most egregious examples:

> Gardener, sweep the garden!
> Babu, wash the clothes!
> You are stupid.
> I think you are lying.

Wright notes the racial shame that these sentences convey, and he concludes ironically that "the sentences I have quoted above were designed to maintain 'law, order, peace, and tranquility.'"[31] In *White Man, Listen!* Wright quotes an African scholar who notes "that 'savages' are the products of a Western, a morally imperialistic, influence upon us, a wrong kind of an attempt to 'change' us."[32] The imperialistic influence is, in large part, discursive as the linguistic designation "savage" conveys.

This hegemonic negation attempts to make of minority subjects subhuman creatures devoid of initiative and entirely compliant to the will of white imperialist designs. In *Black Boy,* however, Wright produces a text that "demonstrates his ability to overcome that drastically limiting societal formation."[33] By establishing through writing "a specular relation with society's attempt to negate him," Wright makes of the narrator "Richard" and himself "a mirror that reflect[s] the negation back at the hegemony."[34]

Wright's haiku perform a related function, altered slightly by the author's adoption of a "foreign" literary form. Such a move reflects Wright's advice to African American writers in *White Man, Listen!* to "stand on [their] own two feet and express [themselves] not in purely racial, but human terms."[35] By expressing themselves in human terms, African American writers will provide evidence of "the oneness of man, of the basic unity of human life on this earth."[36] Haiku, grounded as it is in Eastern spirituality and philosophy, is a logical form with which to express the "oneness" of people. Wright's move away from the United States as a source of literary inspiration and subject matter seems to be his way of moving beyond the specular relation which JanMohamed suggests and a way of negating the negators through the formation of his own subjectivity by establishing a link between his subjective self and the cosmos.

However, this link is not as unproblematic as it may appear. Arguing along lines that parallel my positioning of Wright's aesthetic, Eugene E. Miller bases his discussion of Wright's poetics on the "progenic myth" advanced by Dexter Fisher and Robert Stepto: "The antecedent quest for literacy and freedom which lies behind the generation of all African-American literary forms" and on the attempts of African American art to "deal as directly as possible with black American life . . . to put on paper the very consciousness of black Americans."[37] In the midst of both this quest and this need to put his black consciousness on paper, Wright searches for a "'something' which exists at the core of African-American folk expression."[38] Earlier in his life, Wright sensed this "something" in his grandmother and her religious beliefs; he then became aware of it in all African American folk utterances, particularly in blues lyrics. Later, Wright searched for and found the "something" in various places, including Ghana with its newly freed population and Spain with its religious peasants. Ultimately, he looked to a radically different verse form, the haiku.[39]

By applying both the idea of the "progenic myth" and the need to "negate the negators," we can see that Wright succeeds in many of the haiku in triangulating the master-slave dialectic in relation to the mainstream and turning this dialectic into a different kind of language game. Wright's haiku are on one hand deliberately open-ended, as my various alternative readings throughout this article have suggested. On the other hand, Wright is able to build on classic Japanese haiku by poets such as Issa and Bashō without riding rough shod over them. This is a striking contrast to dominant Anglo-American appropriations of the haiku (such as those of John Gould Fletcher, Jack Kerouac, and Gary Snyder, who frequently ignore the syllable counts and sometimes even the three-line format) and a way for Wright to defamiliarize these imperialist appropriations.

When I position Wright's haiku as anticolonialist and anti-imperialist, I am not alone. Two recent critics, Eugene E. Miller and Yoshinobu Hakutani, argue that the haiku function to combat racism. Miller feels that Wright's haiku capture what R. H. Blyth calls a union of all entities "in the ceaseless activity of their Buddhist nature."[40] Through the haiku, Miller claims, Wright came to believe that knowing and becoming one with nature (reality) "was to become one with oneself,"[41] and Wright found in this becoming a way to integrate himself into society. Similarly, Hakutani sees the haiku as Wright's attempt to achieve an independent vision, a double vision that "enables the nonwhite people of the world to acquire the basic ideas of democracy and freedom from the West," but to reject greed and materialism, the inhuman elements of capitalism.[42] Where I differ with both Miller and Hakutani, however, is in their emphasis on the aesthetic value of the haiku. Miller sees Wright taking an art-for-art's sake stand, with the idea that artistic expression is a vessel containing the values which bourgeois life lacks.[43] Hakutani feels that Wright's haiku "describe his poverty and isolation" only so they can demonstrate "the transcendence of materialism and the creation of beauty."[44] With such readings, we have seemingly come full circle: Wright's haiku are again configured along racial lines, but only as "pure" poetic forms that are able to transcend race and materiality.

What I have shown in this article is that Wright's haiku do not transcend race and materiality; instead, they bring to the poems a dialogic consciousness that plays with the transcendence generally associated with Japanese haiku. R. H. Blyth observes, "The strange thing is that this world, which we wish to be free from, is yet the one that we really desire to live in, somehow or other,"[45] and his observation on the ambivalence that Zen practitioners feel can be applied ironically to Wright and his haiku. Any desire for escape or transcendence is tempered by the world we live in, and that world forces upon African Americans what W. E. B. Du Bois terms "double-consciousness."

The following haiku, one of several that specifically allude to blackness, contains Wright's double vision.

The green cockleburs
Caught in the thick wooly hair
Of the black boy's head. (455)

One could argue that the poem provides a detached, objective—we might say "Japanese"—view of a natural scene. The color contrast of the green burrs and the youth's black hair is mildly interesting. Still, the poem has a level of consciousness that goes beneath the pictorial level. In *The Color Curtain*, Wright mentions an encounter he had with a white woman. This woman came to Wright to discern if her roommate, an African American woman, was practicing voodoo. The reason for the white woman's suspicions was that her roommate was combing her hair with a can of sterno when she thought the white woman was asleep. Wright explains that the woman was straightening her hair and further explains that "It's her way of saying: 'Forgive me. I'm sorry that I'm black; I'm ashamed that my hair is not like yours. . . .'"[46] The haiku, with its burrs sticking to the boy's hair, draws attention to the "thick wooly hair" as a mark of shame, a racial stigma. An alternate reading of this haiku suggests that the burrs are drawn to the hair, "forgiving" it in a way the roommate cannot.

Two other haiku express this sense of double-consciousness. In haiku 355:

An Indian summer
Heaps itself in tons of gold
Over Nigger Town.

The beauty of the late summer sunshine is compared to gold, and the richness of that gold is contrasted with the undoubtedly impoverished town on which it shines. This haiku arranges lines to emphasize liminality. The first and last lines allude to "Indians" and "Niggers," so historically dispossessed groups are placed on the poem's margins; conversely, the "heaps" of "gold," symbolic of wealth, are accorded both the poem's center and its longest line. In contrast to the preceding, haiku 609 demonstrates an awareness of double-consciousness through its color images:

Black men with big brooms
Sweeping streets in falling snow,
Are absorbed by flakes. (609)

What might first strike us on reading the poem is the pictorial elegance of street sweepers lost in contemplation of the snow. Yet, we are also forced to see the stereotypical African American laborers working at menial tasks. More important, the image of these black men being covered by the snow reminds us of a dominant "snow-white" society. This society may claim to welcome African Americans as equals but in fact "absorbs" them, often accepting them only insofar as they can act "white."

As a way of concluding my discussion of Wright's haiku, I would like to take another look at *Native Son*. In one of the first scenes in the novel, Bigger and his friend Gus see an airplane fly overhead. Bigger's initial impulse is a desire to fly away himself: "I *could* fly a plane if I had a chance." His friend Gus responds, "If you wasn't black and if you had some money and if they'd let you go to that aviation school, you *could* fly a plane." Bigger answers Gus's reminder of the material conditions that "ground" Bigger: "Maybe they right in not wanting us to fly. 'Cause if I took a plane up I'd take a couple of bombs along and drop 'em as sure as hell."[47] The desire to escape collapses into feelings of anger and a desire to lash out.

As I have demonstrated, a number of critics have interpreted Wright's haiku as a vehicle that enabled Wright to fly away from his economic, physical, and racial concerns. In a sense, the classic Japanese haiku do serve as a vehicle to Wright. However, while Wright adopts the traditional seventeen-syllable form and description of nature so successfully that many critics praise the authenticity of his haiku, he does so not merely to escape concerns. On the contrary, like Bigger's dreamed-of airplane, Wright loads his haiku with linguistic "bombs" that he drops to remind his readers of social inequities. While the haiku themselves serve as a suitable vehicle for Wright, the fact that he looks to Japan for literary inspiration is also significant. Wright argues that colonizers historically require "an Arcadia, a Land's End, a Shangri-la, a world peopled by shadow men, a world that would permit free play for [their] repressed instincts."[48] Because Japan has served historically as this "Shangri-la,"[49] Wright finds it to be an ideal "airport" from which to launch his "sorties" against the dominant culture. Resisting colonial impulses, Wright peoples his haiku not with "shadow men" but with an African American subjectivity that strongly resists the kind of "free play" of repressed instincts that many Westerners would seek in the poems.

Notes

1. Yoshinobu Hakutani and Robert L. Tener, eds. (New York: Arcade).

2. Ellen Wright and Michel Fabre, eds. (New York: Harper & Row, 1978).

3. See Constance Webb, *Richard Wright: A Biography* (New York: Putnam's, 1968), 386–87, 393–94; and Michel Fabre, *The Unfinished Quest of Richard Wright*, trans. Isabel Barzun (New York: William Morrow, 1973), 505, for more on the history behind the haiku. Note also that Fabre incorrectly lists the number of haiku as 811, suggesting a typographical error on the part of Fabre's publishers.

4. 4 vols. (Tokyo: Hokusiedo, 1949–52). Among other sources from which Wright may have gleaned his knowledge of haiku are *The Four Seasons*, ed. and trans. Peter Bielenson (Mt. Vernon, NY: Peter Pauper Press, 1958); *Japanese Haiku*, ed. and trans. Peter Bielenson (Mt. Vernon, NY: Peter Pauper Press, 1955); Donald Keene, *Japanese Literature: An Introduction for Western Readers* (New York: Grove Press, 1955); Kenneth Yasuda, *The Japanese Haiku* (Rutland, VT: Charles E. Tuttle, 1957); Earl Miner, *The Japanese Tradition in British and American Literature* (Princeton, NJ: Princeton University Press, 1958); *Zen and Japanese Culture*, Daisetz T. Suzuki Bollingen Ser. 64 (Princeton, NJ: Princeton University Press, 1959); *An Introduction to Haiku*, ed. Harold G. Henderson (New York: Doubleday, 1958); and *Haikai and Haiku*, the Japanese Classics Translation Committee (Tokyo: Nippon Gakujutsu Shinkokai, 1958).

5. Sanehide Kodama, "Japanese Influence on Richard Wright in His Last Years: English Haiku as a New Genre," *Tamkang Review* 15, no. 1–4 (1984–1985): 66–67.

6. Yoshinobu Hakutani, *Richard Wright and Racial Discourse* (Columbia: University of Missouri Press, 1996), 276–77, 280, 290.

7. Kodama, "Japanese Influence," 67.

8. Ibid., 65.

9. Ibid., 67–68.

10. In *Critical Essays on Richard Wright*, ed. Yoshinobu Hakutani (Boston: G. K.

Hall, 1982), 273–96. This essay was revised and published as "Union with Nature: Richard Wright and the Art of Haiku," *Chiba Review* 10 (1988): 19–34. It was also revised and published as "Richard Wright's Haiku: This Other World," in *Modernity in East-West Literary Criticism*, ed. Yoshinobu Hakutani (Madison, NJ: Fairleigh Dickinson University Press, 2001), 137–57.

11. Ibid., 273.

12. Ibid., 288.

13. Fabre, *The Unfinished Quest of Richard Wright*, 488, 508–9.

14. Michel Fabre, "The Poetry of Richard Wright," in *Critical Essays on Richard Wright*, ed. Yoshinobu Hakutani, 265.

15. Ibid., 271.

16. Jean-Franfois Gounard, *The Racial Problem in the Works of Richard Wright and James Baldwin*, trans. Joseph J. Rodgers Jr. (Westport, CT: Greenwood, 1992), 132–33.

17. Ibid., 134.

18. For a different take on the connection of Wright's haiku to his personal aesthetics, see Floyd Ogburn Jr., "Richard Wright's Unpublished Haiku: A World Elsewhere," *MELUS* 23, no. 3 (1998): 63–64. Ogburn uses Wright's "A Blueprint for Negro Writing" to show that Wright felt that the creative process has as its goal a "search for the meaning of some common human experience of nature and man."

19. Richard Wright, *Black Boy*, in *Richard Wright: Later Works*, ed. Arnold Rampersad (New York: Library of America, 1991), 47.

20. Ibid., 239.

21. Ibid.

22. Richard Wright, "Richard Wright Describes the Birth of Black Boy: An Autobiography Destined to Disturb White Egotism," *New York Post*, November 30, 1944, B6.

23. Wright, *Black Boy*, 237.

24. R. H. Blyth, *A History of Haiku*, 2 vols. (Tokyo: Hokuseido, 1963), I:177.

25. J. L. Austin, *How to Do Things with Words* (Cambridge, MA: Harvard University Press, 1962).

26. Blyth, *A History of Haiku*, 219.

27. Hakutani, *Richard Wright and Racial Discourse*, 277, 280.

28. Richard Wright, *Native Son* (New York: HarperPerennial, 1998), 5–6.

29. Ibid., 4, 8.

30. Abdul R. JanMohamed, "Negating the Negation as a Form of Affirmation in Minority Discourse: The Construction of Richard Wright as Subject," in *The Nature and Context of Minority Discourse*, ed. Abdul R. JanMohamed and David Lloyd (New York: Oxford University Press, 1990), 103–4.

31. Richard Wright, *The Color Curtain* (Cleveland: World, 1956), 179–82.

32. Richard Wright, *White Man, Listen!* (Garden City, NY: Doubleday, 1957), 34.

33. Wright, *Black Boy*, 103.

34. JanMohamed, "Negating the Negation," 104.

35. Wright, *White Man, Listen!* 149.

36. Ibid., 150.

37. Dexter Fisher and Robert Stepto, *Afro-American Literature: The Reconstruction of Instruction* (New York: Modern Language Association, 1979), xi–xii.

38. Ibid., 7.

39. Eugene E. Miller, *Voice of a Native Son: The Poetics of Richard Wright* (Jackson: University Press of Mississippi, 1990), 95. Miller believes that, in order to capture this "something," Wright fuses together disparate elements, a technique he gleaned from a variety of sources. Kenneth Burke's notion of "perspective by incongruity" helps Wright to understand that the chief characteristic of African American folk expression is "[i]ts penchant for juxtaposing discordant elements" (184–85). Blues lyrics show Wright the benefits of superimposing diverse elements. Also at the heart of Wright's poetics were psychoanalyst Wilhelm Reich's theories of orgone, a "universal energy" that is "practically identical to life and its processes . . . present in the atmosphere and soil," and absorbed and released by all animate things (228). One receptive to orgone energy, Reich felt, would be able to see connections in all things, as well as the reality of these connections.

40. Ibid., 242.

41. Ibid., 246.

42. Hakutani, *Richard Wright and Racial Discourse*, x.

43. Miller, *Voice of a Native Son*, xv–xvi.

44. Hakutani, *Richard Wright and Racial Discourse*, 287.

45. Blyth, *A History of Haiku*, 219.

46. Wright, *The Color Curtain*, 182–87.

47. Wright, *Native Son*, 17.

48. Wright, *White Man, Listen!* 43.

49. Kenneth Rexroth, "The Influence of Classical Japanese Poetry," in *The Elastic Retort* (New York: Seabury Press, 1973). Rexroth describes Japan in terms that Wright would understand but not condone. Japan, Rexroth argues, provides "those nutriments for which the West was starved, or at least Western intellectuals persuaded themselves it did" (150–51). He goes on to say that "[t]he myth of Japan provides a dream world in which the suppressed half of Western civilization can find imaginary fulfillment" (151).

Inverting the Haiku Moment

Alienation, Objectification, and Mobility in Richard Wright's Haiku: This Other World

— THOMAS L. MORGAN —

Richard Wright's haiku—both the 4,000 he wrote at the end of his life and the 817 he selected for inclusion in *Haiku: This Other World* (1998)—remain something of an enigma in his larger oeuvre; critics variously position them as a continuation of his earlier thematic concerns in a different literary form, an aesthetic departure from the racialized limitations imposed upon his earlier work, or one of several positions in between. Such arguments debate the formal construction as well as the strategic reinvention of Wright's haiku. The present essay engages both sides of this conversation, arguing that Wright's inversion of the logic of the "haiku moment" offers him a new generic form with which to explore the themes of alienation, dehumanization, and inequality appearing in his earlier works. Wright's reformulation of the haiku moment allows him to reengage the same cultural and social mores seen in his earlier works in a different generic context, one stripped of the pre-inscribed notions of identity that influence the critical reception of his prior works. Mapping out the revisions Wright strategically employs to manipulate the formal construction of his haiku reveals the way those manipulations allowed Wright to refine and extend his artistic vision.

In the afterword to Richard Wright's *Haiku: This Other World,* Yoshinobu Hakutani and Robert L. Tener discuss the "haiku moment." Quoting Joan Giroux's definition, they observe that "the haiku moment 'may be defined as an instant in which man becomes united to an object, virtually becomes that object and realizes the eternal, universal truth contained in being.'"[1] This moment of unification between nature and humanity, where the two become inseparable, is mediated by the author's evacuation of subjectivity in the act of representation, and "[a]ll nature is unified with human beings through the poet's perception and expression," making the author's perspective "almost imperceptible."[2] As such, the haiku moment is created by the writer's contemplation of a natural object that, when presented as a visual image in the haiku, allows the writer to merge with nature via that contemplation. In this definition, the relationship between nature and humanity is located as an essential requirement to create the seamless fusion of form and content found in haiku. Applied to Wright's haiku, this definition positions the conceptual logic that his work would ostensibly be expected to fulfill. However, while Wright was undoubtedly aware of the formal configurations of haiku—critical work consistently points to Wright's working knowledge of R. H. Blyth's four-volume collection entitled *Haiku* (1949–52)—Wright's haiku do not always reflect these expectations.

This deviation should not be too surprising. As Eugene E. Miller explains in *Voice of a Native Son* (1990), "It is unlikely that [Wright] would have attempted to reproduce the Japanese haiku precisely. He would have known, from the first lines of Blyth's first volume, if not from some other source, that authentic haiku are intimately connected with a whole cultural tradition of which he was not a part."[3] As Miller implies, an exclusively formalist reading of Wright fails to consider Wright's own awareness of the connection between culture and art as well as the importance of this relationship to identity. Richard A. Iadonisi, in "'I Am Nobody': The Haiku of Richard Wright" (2005), further argues that Wright's deviations are both strategic and intentional and that an exclusive reliance on the formal definition of haiku limits our understanding of Wright's poetic experimentation. For Iadonisi, moving beyond traditional definitions of form "allows us to see how Wright radically reinvents the haiku form, making of it a revolutionary poetry that offers and then savagely undercuts the possibility of Zen oneness; in the process, the haiku serve as a vehicle that articulates the author's anti-colonial position."[4] Drawing Miller's and Iadonisi's claims about Wright's aesthetic project into conversation with the comments in the last paragraph concerning the formal definition of the haiku moment reveals the connections to be made between the two ostensibly opposing perspectives. Wright's revision inverts the basic formulations that locate the haiku moment to suit his own ends, using a logic of disjunction in regard to humanity's relationship with nature rather than of unification to organize a good number of his haiku. While this inversion subverts the rhetorical thrust of the haiku moment as defined by Joan Giroux, it does so through utilizing the same framework to achieve opposite ends: the realization of universal truth comes through the disjunction created with nature, not humanity's unification with nature.

Aesthetic Interests, or Wright and Perspective

To best understand Wright's aesthetic interest in revising the haiku moment, it is necessary to revisit Wright's earlier beliefs about the role and function of art. In "Blueprint for Negro Writing" (1937), Wright argues that authors in general, and black authors in particular, need to have an "angle of vision [that] can show them all the forces of modern society in process."[5] Labeling this "The Problem of Perspective," Wright states that perspective "is that part of a poem, novel, or play which a writer never puts directly upon paper. It is that fixed point in intellectual space where a writer stands to view the struggle, hopes, and sufferings of his people." Wright proceeds to note that the black author hoping to use perspective successfully "must create in his readers' minds a relationship between a Negro woman hoeing cotton in the South and the men who loll in swivel chairs in Wall Street and take the fruits of her toil."[6] This relational perspective, one that creates connections between the different possible poles of experience within the space of the nation (or even a global context), is intended to ameliorate the *perceived* differences that readers incorrectly believe exist between these two subjects. The relationship that Wright advocates here moves beyond the assumed differences of race, gender, class, and even regional affiliation to argue for a common humanity and a common dignity that exist across the spectrum of experience. It is thus no coincidence that Wright also connects the idea of "perspective" to both "awareness" and "consciousness,"[7] further indicating the connection he sees between art, representation, and consciousness-raising.

Wright makes a similar appeal for a shared humanity in a 1955 interview with *L'Express*, asserting "[i]f my writing has any aim, it is to try to reveal that which is human on both sides, to affirm the essential unity of man on earth."[8] In this quote, the relationship between the two "sides" is framed as a commonality or as a unified whole that is not readily understood by either group; Wright's interest in revealing "that which is human" to the other side points to his desire to foreground their shared humanity. As both quotes indicate, Wright embraces art for its transformative possibilities, and numerous examples from his work pursue this aesthetic agenda. For example, in "Long Black Song" from *Uncle Tom's Children* (1938), Sarah thinks to herself that "[s]omehow, men, black men and white men, land and houses, green cornfields and grey skies, gladness and dreams, were all a part of that which made life good. Yes, somehow, they were all linked, like the spokes in a spinning wagon wheel. She felt they were. She knew they were."[9] Coming as this does when Sarah's husband, Silas, is about to be lynched, Wright's observation about the "linked" connections that "made life good" points to the types of collective humanity that the violence and "old river of blood"[10] portrayed in the story attempt to erase.

Obviously, Wright was not alone in pointing out the importance of establishing connections between different groups for readers. As Ralph Ellison points out in "Richard Wright's Blues" (1945), "[t]he welfare of the most humble black Mississippi sharecropper is affected less by the flow of the seasons and the rhythm of natural events than by the fluctuations of the stock market."[11] In highlighting the economic dependence created by this relationship, Ellison not only mirrors the example from Wright's "Blueprint for Negro Writing," he also points out that the social relations created by economic subordination trump the rhythm and flow of the natural world—that economic relationships have a material effect on maintaining perceived notions of established difference in the social realm. Zora Neale Hurston, too, shares with Wright an understanding of the importance of "reveal[ing] that which is human on both sides."[12] As she observes in "What White Publishers Won't Print" (1950), "[b]ut for the national welfare, it is urgent to realize that the minorities do think, and think about something other than the race problem. That they are very human and internally, according to natural endowment, are just like everybody else. So long as this is not conceived, there must remain that feeling of unsurmountable difference, and difference to the average man means something bad. If people were made right, they would be just like him."[13] Here, it is the perception of "unsurmountable difference" between different social groups that precludes the possibility of an "essential unity"[14] for humanity—after all, difference without understanding "means something bad." Hurston's description of this type of transformation as "urgent" for the health of our collective "national welfare" points to the importance of overcoming notions of difference for the larger collective good. The use of "welfare" by both Ellison and Hurston further emphasizes the relational connections between different groups—constructing a collective sense of well-being requires all being treated equitably. For Hurston, as for Wright and Ellison, transforming readers requires art that has the ability to address readers' limitations. As Hurston asserts, until minorities are seen as "just like everybody else"—until they can be imagined as possessing the same hopes, dreams, and aspirations as those who look down upon them—notions of difference will continue to drive social and cultural relationships and prevent the development of a feeling of shared humanity.

Thus, the preoccupation with creating connections between groups and addressing the prejudices minorities face was clearly an important part of Wright's aesthetic agenda. Flashing forward, this is the same artistic sensibility that Wright brought to bear on his experimentation with haiku. And the haiku moment that Wright discovered, as Floyd Ogburn describes, "draws heavily upon the *satori* of Zen. The haiku moment is an aesthetic moment—one in which the words which create the experience and the experience itself are one. Anti-temporal and eternal, the haiku moment culminates 'in a new insight or vision which the poet must render as an organic whole' (Yasuda 24–25)."[15] The unification of words and experience to create an "organic whole" is also dependent upon the fusion of humanity and nature; as Hakutani and Tener observe in the afterword to *Haiku: This Other World,* "Well-wrought haiku thrive upon the fusion of man and nature."[16] They note further that "[i]t is also imperative that a haiku be primarily concerned with nature; if a haiku deals with man's life, that life must be viewed in the context of nature rather than society."[17] However, while Wright's own relationship to nature is well documented,[18] his experimentations with nature in his haiku depart from the traditional relationship between humanity and nature as defined in the haiku moment. This disjunction has helped produce the seeming rift in the criticism surrounding Wright's haiku alluded to at the beginning of the essay. As Miller argues, "Wright's haiku should be analyzed in light of his own poetics, rather than be compared to the Japanese poems he used as models. This approach might not reveal them as any better poems, but it will reveal more about Wright as a creative artist."[19] And, as Meta Schettler observes, Wright's haiku "attempt to complicate the space and process of representation itself [. . .] creat[ing] a hybrid, transcultural space in the haiku."[20] As can be inferred from Miller's comments, Wright's poetics are an integral part of understanding his experimentations with haiku; merely comparing them to their Japanese counterparts does nothing to extend our understanding of Wright. At the same time, Schettler's "hybrid, transcultural space" requires an awareness of haiku aesthetics to understand how hybridity functions in Wright's work as well as the ways in which the cultural fusion Wright creates can challenge representational norms. This fusion of the formal components of the haiku moment with Wright's intentional inversion of haiku aesthetics marks where this essay moves beyond the argument made by Richard A. Iadonisi;[21] connecting Wright's "reinvent[ion of] the haiku form"[22] to the aesthetic conventions that Wright manipulates reveals the correlations between alienation and subject formation that Wright uses to revise his aesthetic project and bring it full circle.

Wright's inversion of the haiku moment follows two main paths: the primary one focuses on humanity's relationship with nature. His initial revision breaks apart or inverts the traditional fusion between humanity and nature seen in traditional haiku. In doing so, Wright foregrounds man's separation from nature and/or nature's isolation of man to highlight the ways in which alienation and estrangement are produced and replicated. In a similar vein, Wright's haiku also personify nature to make nature meet humanity rather than having humanity evacuate subjectivity to meet nature. Iadonisi refers to this type of revision as Wright's "human-centered" haiku, where "the speaker's mock audacity to project his will onto what is beyond human control" highlights a lack of cohesion between the speaker and nature.[23] While the personification of nature ultimately serves as an illusion of humanity's power, it still functions as part of Wright's manipulation of the haiku moment. The process of alienation and imagined power and control that Wright constructs is his inversion of traditional haiku aesthetics; rather than relinquishing subjectivity and perspective to build meaning, Wright uses the disjunction between nature and humanity, as well as a false belief in the ability to control nature, to underline meaning within his haiku.

The second main path of inversion concerns the process of objectification present in Wright's haiku and the Japanese notion of *wabi,* which "refers to the uniquely human perception of beauty stemm[ing] from poverty."[24] Traditionally, the contemplation of a natural object becomes the path through which the writer relinquishes subjectivity and unites with nature. However, in several of Wright's haiku the object of contemplation is itself another human; in conjunction with a focus on the poverty of the subjects depicted, Wright uses the combination to challenge the traditional operation of *wabi.* The shift in contemplation from natural object to fellow subject as object allows Wright to complicate the traditional coming together of writer and object by making this unification dependent upon dehumanizing a fellow subject: readers finding aesthetic pleasure in the contemplation of poverty participate in the processes of dehumanizing and alienating their fellow subjects by turning them into objects of reflection.

The final section of the present essay employs both of these aesthetic inversions to examine the role that intertextuality plays between *Haiku: This Other World* and Wright's other works, specifically in regard to mobility. While mobility and movement are both components of Wright's earlier inversions, they also function in a broader context. For example, there are twenty-two haiku featuring trains in Wright's collection; this intertextual connection work not only points to further connections to be made between Wright's haiku and his other work, it also signals the ways in which Wright saw his haiku as dialogically connected with his earlier work. Linking Wright's conscious inversions of the haiku moment with his larger body of work reveals that Wright's manipulation of the haiku moment examines humanity's isolation from nature as the means to affirm a shared, albeit not acknowledged, set of human experiences. In documenting the alienation and estrangement that all subjects experience, Wright highlights the importance of recognizing "that which is human" as a collective universal process that can create a sense of our shared humanity when built upon mutual dignity and respect. The catalyst of separation becomes the means to examine both the sociological context that produces marginalized subjectivity as well as the resulting effects of that alienation upon the subject. While the means taken to reveal our shared humanity as a universal truth may undercut traditional notions of the haiku moment, it nonetheless allows Wright the textual space to resolve, in his own terms, the themes of alienation and objectification that span his collected works. By locating the existential ennui created by estrangement as a shared human experience, Wright invites his readers to recognize that established notions of difference are illusions most often fostered by self-centered notions of human hubris.

Inverting the Haiku Moment: Alienation and Nature

Wright's inversion of humanity's relationship with nature is at work from the very beginning of *Haiku: This Other World*. The opening haiku observes

> I am nobody:
> A red sinking autumn sun
> Took my name away.

While there is a loss of subjectivity in the opening line, this loss represents not a coming together with nature but rather a break or split from it in that the "red sinking sun" actively removes the writer's "name" to make the speaker into a "nobody." This active alienation, articulated through the verb choice of "took" and created by the natural phenomenon of the sunset, departs from the haiku moment as described by Hakutani and Tener, where the "loss of [the speaker's] individuality within the union [of humanity and nature] involves a generalized melancholy aspect or loneliness as an underlying rhythm."[25] A more traditional reading would argue that the evacuation of subjectivity presented in the opening line and the disappearance of the speaker's name in the third line calls upon the "melancholy" and "loneliness" invoked in Hakutani and Tener; however, the use of "took" to open the final line implies a harsh disjuncture from nature rather than a harmonious cohesion, in that any fusion or union created by the verb "took" can only come via force. The loneliness the speaker experiences is a product of the conscious alienation created by the speaker experiencing nature; as Iadonisi notes, the disjunctive "relationship between speaker, self, and nature [in haiku 1] is very un-Japanese."[26] It is in this way that alienation becomes an active construct in Wright, produced by a confrontation with nature that exerts agency on humanity.

Numerous other haiku in the collection use the same logic of disjunction to build their examination of subjectivity and alienation. Haiku 461 describes the alienation created by a winter snowstorm:

> Entering my town
> In a heavy fall of snow,
> I feel a stranger.

Here, nature creates the isolation the speaker feels through depersonalizing or transforming physical space; the sense of inclusion and possession invoked by the pronoun "my" is transformed into feelings of exclusion and alienation now articulated as being that of a "stranger." While such a feeling is generated in part by the presence of "a heavy fall of snow," it is also reciprocally produced by the speaker's movement, invoked by the departure and subsequent return seen in "entering." Combined with the sense of alienation created through the change in the landscape produced by nature, Wright's use of "feel" further locates the speaker's alienation in terms of an emotional response to nature's explicit estrangement—whether or not nature intends its natural phenomena to create such a response, the speaker's reaction is still an experiential reality connected to the external stimuli of the snow. As with haiku 1, a sense of loneliness is present; the speaker, returning to "my town," does not experience a sense of community or happiness in conjunction with her/his homecoming, but rather the estrangement of feeling out of place. R. H. Blyth observes that "loneliness is the second state of mind necessary for the creation and appreciation of haiku" and that "the loneliness of haiku emanates . . . from the nameless realm where the human and non-human meet and are one."[27] As with haiku 1, there is no union between humanity and nature here; instead, it is the sense of alienation and disjunction created by nature that propels the haiku. While, as Blyth implies, loneliness may be necessary to create and understand haiku, in Wright there is no subsequent coming together of humanity and nature: the creation of loneliness becomes the focal point, not its resolution. In both haiku, the isolation produced through humanity's interaction with nature helps highlight the psychic pain alienation creates in subjects; whether produced by nature or our fellow humans, alienation affects subjectivity by marking it with the psychological burden of exclusion in ways that will continue to manifest itself in later behavior.

Three other examples from Wright's collection are worth noting for their use of snow to develop the sensation of alienation and for their contribution to the use of estrangement from nature as a disruptive inversion of the haiku moment. The first two:

Even my old friends
Seem like newly met strangers
In this first snowfall. (519)

Just enough of snow
To make you look carefully
At familiar streets. (521)

Haiku 519 and 521 build upon the context created by haiku 461. Across the page from each other, these two haiku point to Wright's ability to employ what Blyth refers to as "seasonal words"[28] to build his haiku, while at the same time functioning as a part of his intentional inversion of the union between humanity and nature. In the first haiku, "seem" works much like the use of "feel" in 461, where the focus is more on the speaker's perception than on the outside world. While the qualifier of "first" may position this feeling as the novelty of seasonal change, it still contributes to producing a reaction in the speaker that foregrounds exclusion: "old friends" become "newly met strangers" through the transformation created by seasonal effect. In the juxtaposition of old and new, it is nature that stands between or transforms human relationships, as with the ability of snow to enhance estrangement in haiku 461. As well, the replication of "stranger" in both helps highlight the defamiliarization nature produces in these two haiku.

Haiku 521 points to the importance of visuality and perception. Again, snow disrupts the scene; while the speaker no longer focuses on her/his feelings, as with the first snow haiku, the speaker's response highlights the necessity of assessing one's situation and acting correctly in response to that changed context. This can be seen in the relationship established between "carefully" and "familiar." While the use of "carefully" in connection to "look" implies a need to examine the scene closely to ascertain whether or not the streets are actually "familiar," it also carries with it a note of warning. In this sense, being "careful" implies knowing how to act and behave accordingly; after all one of the products of alienation, and being made to feel like an outsider, is a changed set of behavioral responses to social conditions. The verb choice of "make" further accentuates these connections; the lack of choice and reciprocal implication of force carried by "make" points to nature's ability to dictate human behavior. In this sense, haiku 521 becomes the behavioral response to haiku 461—once becoming a "stranger," the speaker must act "carefully" and in accordance with the expectations accorded to a stranger in an unfamiliar situation. The easy assurances of "familiar streets" normally taken for granted are no longer readily available, having been transformed by nature into something alien and unknown.

The final example, haiku 132, shifts the scene to the contemplation of an actual outsider although, in conjunction with the other haiku, the status of this "stranger" as an actual stranger, as opposed to someone familiar but unrecognized by the speaker, is not readily discernable. Appearing earlier in the collection than the previous three, the poem is nonetheless framed around similar concerns:

What stranger is that
Walking in the winter rain
And looking this way? (132)

In this haiku, the tensions created between the internal and external ascriptions of subjectivity seen in the haiku discussed earlier are intensified—there is no "feel" or "seem" to qualify experience in this haiku; instead, this figure is located as a "stranger." The roles of visuality and identification, which make acknowledgment possible, are not operating, at least not in a sympathetic or compassionate manner. Instead, the speaker sees the "stranger," but there is no indication that the speaker responds to the look of the outsider as a fellow human; the speaker instead positions the subject with the alienating appellation of "stranger." Identification rests on recognition; in this haiku, the speaker's application of learned logic builds barriers between subjects, and the stranger, located as an outsider obscured by the "winter rain," is marked as not worthy of fellow feelings. As with previous examples, nature contributes to and conditions the social ostracism presented in this haiku. And, as the next section of the essay will demonstrate, Wright's manipulation of the speaker's perspective highlights the ways that assumptions of privilege contribute to the process of objectifying and dehumanizing other people.

Projected inward onto the self or outward onto others, assessed in regard to one's own behavior or that of an approaching stranger, Wright's examination of perspective draws connections between the speaker's thoughts and the creation of alienation in others. In doing so, Wright presents the coldness and bleakness of winter as a corollary to the type of human behavior that produces social exclusion and ostracism. Whether merely felt or actually experienced, the end result is the same—subjectivity and behavior are negatively affected. Perception and perspective are conditioned by the natural world in these haiku, separating individuals from both nature and each other and creating the barriers that lead to isolation. The bright sunlight of the first haiku aside (which is an "autumn sun"), many of the haiku that most dramatically focus on alienation are set in fall and winter, foregrounding seasonal images that correspond to the behavior being enacted in the haiku. The relationship between seasonal words and the speaker's perspective indicates that Wright adheres to certain components of haiku aesthetics while intentionally deviating from others. As such, this use of perspective connects back to Wright's comments in "Blueprint for Negro Writing"—Wright's structuring of subjectivity in relation to winter and alienation identifies the awareness needed from readers in relation to identity and their fellow subjects. In learning to identify the effect one's thoughts and actions can have on others, in focusing on the connections between one another rather than the assumptions of difference, Wright gives his readers the tools to treat others with the respect and dignity they deserve.

Another equally important component of Wright's inversion of the haiku moment occurs when he reorders the relationship between humanity and nature rather than having the writer/speaker abandon or evacuate subjectivity to unite with nature, Wright either personifies nature in order to make nature meet humanity, or he restructures the relationship between humanity and nature to privilege humanity's perspective even when such privileging is itself an illusion of humanity's power. These "human-centered"[29] haiku, to use Iadonisi's term, are an important part of Wright's inversion of haiku poetics, specifically as they build upon his initial disjunction between humanity and nature. The lack of awareness embodied in the speaker's thoughts toward nature points to ways in which alienation is produced through the obliviousness of human behavior. This behavior is another instance of the importance of "perspective" for Wright in regard to human action, specifically in relation to the effect it can have on other subjects. Haiku 307 is an example of both personification and the privileging of humanity's perspective; Wright uses humanity's interest in a suitable explanation for an irresolvable condition to anthropomorphize the autumn rain and its attempt to convey mortality to the speaker:

I feel autumn rain
Trying to explain something
I do not want to know.

That the speaker is able to articulate a lack of desire to know about death—after all, the "autumn rain" is "trying" but not succeeding to convey its ominous message—positions human subjectivity as the privileged perspective that nature must attempt to satisfy. The use of "autumn" as a seasonal reference helps to emphasize the looming significance of the information being presented; the waning of the year and the twilight of the speaker's life function in tandem, building the unresolved dilemma of the haiku. However, while the fact of death cannot be explained away, that the autumn rain must stoop to quibble with humanity over nonnegotiable information allows Wright to shift the trajectory for how meaning is created within his haiku. The license claimed by the speaker in this haiku is the privilege to remain ignorant of the way the world operates. This choice, and the assumed agency that comes with it, leaves the speaker unable to recognize her/his connection with the natural world.

Personification also occurs without human participation, as seen in haiku 676:

After a meeting
Held in the corner garden,
The leaves scattered.

Here, the personification of "meeting" functions to explain the reason for the accumulation of leaves in the "corner garden" from both a temporal and spatial perspective. However, the return to natural imagery for the resolution of the haiku—the use of "scattered" rather than departed or left—reinforces the personification required to create the initial image. While the disjunctive nature of Wright's inversion of nature is more pronounced here than in haiku 307, in part because of the omission of human agents within the haiku, Wright makes use of personified nature frequently. Two other commonly quoted examples,

With a twitching nose
A dog reads a telegram
On a wet tree trunk. (22)

and

Whose town did you leave,
O wild and droning spring rain,
And where do you go? (69)

highlight nature's ability to take on human characteristics. To "read," to "leave," or, as with the first example, to "explain" and alleviate humanity's collective concern with a looming and irreversible death, further situates the positive possibilities contained within nature as contributing to the alienation that humanity feels when it seeks solace in the processes of nature or attempts to make nature conform to human guidelines and categories.

The examples of haiku that most specifically privilege humanity's perspective when reordering the relationship between humanity and nature tend to focus on verb choice that empowers human subjectivity:

> For you, O gulls,
> I order slaty waters
> And this leaden sky! (2)

> I give permission
> For this slow spring rain to soak
> The violet beds. (5)

> I grant to sparrows
> The telegraph wires that brought
> Me such good tidings! (14)

These haiku are three occurrences that articulate the speaker's empowered perspective. And in all three, it is the verb choice—"order," "give," and "grant"—that positions the speaker's authority even when such "permission" is merely an empty verbal gesture by the speaker. The speaker's rhetorical assumption of power carries with it a sense of hubris; the control the speaker claims is not only predicated upon an incorrect understanding of the relationship she/he shares with nature but on an attempt to maintain that hierarchical status at the expense of nature. A similar example, although not so straightforward as the previous three, occurs later in the collection:

> As my anger ebbs,
> The spring stars grow bright again
> And the wind returns. (721)

Here, the relationship between the speaker and nature privileges the speaker's perspective; the verb choice of "ebbs" positions the speaker's perspective as the one controlling the cause-and-effect relationship with nature. Thus, when "my anger ebbs," the natural world responds appropriately; "grow bright again" implies that nature has dimmed and then intensified with the "again" signifying repetition while "returns" signifies that wind has left and come back rather than having remained constant all along. Making the speaker's emotional response the perspective through which nature is apprehended—as it "ebbs," nature "returns"—privileges the speaker's perspective even as it simultaneously impedes her/his ability to see, experience, and understand the natural world.

Both of these inversions allow Wright to pursue his interrogation of subject formation in relation to the social and cultural mores that affect the construction of identity. In conjunction with the aesthetic norms connected to the haiku form, Wright's inversion of the haiku moment allows him the aesthetic space to experiment with a generic form that is more racially neutral or ambiguous than his previous prose productions. Coupled with the possibility of manipulating perspective for precise literary effect and for presenting the necessity of carefully examining one's own behavior, Wright is able to expand and continue the development of his earlier themes, including the estrangement experienced by nonwhites, in ways that would not be immediately coded as race-based by his readers. Wright's interest in examining the relationship between privilege and alienation through manipulating the speaker's perspective points to the value Wright sees in using the haiku as a literary tool. Projected forward, this possibility also paves the way for an examination of the way Wright interrogates objectification in his transformation of the haiku moment.

The Politics of Zen: Objectification and the Contemplation of Poverty

As previously noted, one of the central elements of the haiku moment is to create a visual image that allows the writer to merge with nature through the contemplation of the object presented in the haiku. This union requires what Robert L. Tener refers to as a "compassionate irony" or a "compassionate wry humor,"[30] one intended to allow the speaker to understand the equality between humans and things so that she/he may identify and unite with nature. These objects of contemplation, as Ogburn observes when discussing Wright's use of natural imagery in his haiku, "carry the emotional power of the scenes. As the haiku poet should, Wright uses the objects to present experiences simply and succinctly, leaving the reader to intuit or imagine the details necessary to make meaning."[31] As someone interested in the subjectivity of the oppressed, Wright's decision to locate humans as the objects of contemplation within his haiku is significant when examining his revisions of the haiku form, not only for the fact that these subjects must become objects of contemplation—they are objectified for aesthetic enjoyment—but also because this objectification becomes the means through which the speaker unites with nature. Wright's choice to foreground the process of objectification as a component of the alienation and estrangement he revises in regard to the haiku moment is his second main inversion of haiku aesthetics.

In Wright's initial inversion, he employs the disjunctive relationship between humanity and nature to reveal the experiential effects of alienation and/or the illusory components of human control on human perception. Here, Wright engages the relationships between subjects to expose how perspective, when predicated upon assumed notions of power, privilege, and control, functions to impede human relationships and perpetuate inequality. Wright's focus is the concept of *wabi*; as Yoshinobu Hakutani observes in *Richard Wright and Racial Discourse*, *wabi* "refers to the uniquely human perception of beauty stemmed from poverty. *Wabi* is often regarded as religious, as the saying 'Blessed are the poor' suggests, but the spiritual aspect of *wabi* is based upon an aesthetic rather than moral sensibility."[32] The aestheticization of poverty implied in *wabi* is based upon an abstract or idealized logic; as Wright's inversion of *wabi* makes clear, when aesthetics prevail over our shared humanity, we, whether inadvertently or intentionally, participate in the process of objectifying and dehumanizing our fellow humans.

For instance, in one of the most compelling examples in *Haiku: This Other World*, Wright focuses on a black woman washing clothes:

> Sun is glinting on
> A washerwoman's black arms
> In cold creek water. (60)

The vision of the speaker focuses on the interaction between the "glinting" sun, the "cold creek water," and the woman's "black arms," making her arms the object of contemplation within the haiku. While the flashing sunlight playing off the woman's wet skin could be seen as an aesthetic coming together of nature and object, the metonymic use of "arms" to represent the woman's labor—and alienated labor at that, as being a "washerwoman" literally implies doing someone else's dirty work—complicates the normative union between the speaker and object within the haiku. To find aesthetic pleasure in this moment, the speaker (and by proxy the reader) must ignore the unpleasant aspects the woman experiences; in addition to the metonymically reductive use of "arms" to represent the woman's identity, we have the harsh, sharp flashing implied by the "glinting" sun and the frigidity and numbness experienced through repeated immersions in the "cold creek water." Wright's manipulation of perspective—he mediates the speaker's vision in ways that force readers to make aesthetic choices about the scene being represented—allows him to invert the function of *wabi* within the haiku moment. In locating the relationship between the speaker and the subject/object of the haiku as one that finds aesthetic pleasure rather than noting the class- or race-based conditions that should mediate how this moment is viewed, Wright makes readers complicit with the orthodoxy of oppression. After all, while focusing on the dignity of labor may make readers feel good about themselves, doing so elides the connections between this woman and "the men who loll in swivel chairs in Wall Street and take the fruits of her toil."[33]

Wright's focus on the material conditions of the subjects he represents is an important part of his inversion of *wabi*. As Hakutani argues, the hardships experienced by haiku poets are an important part of reaching the "higher state of mind"[34] implied by *wabi*; for Bashō, as Hakutani observes, "an empty stomach was necessary to create poetry."[35] In Wright, however, the focus is not on the speaker's hardship, but that experienced by the subjects the speaker observes, as with the washerwoman, whose labor the speaker represents. Thus, achieving *wabi* through contemplating the washerwoman's labor requires ignoring the material conditions she experiences, transforming her into an object. Iadonisi draws similar conclusions when examining the speaker's contemplation of her/his own poverty as well as Wright's haiku on prostitutes; "[t]he perception of poverty in Wright's haiku is not overlain with quiet beauty. Instead, the poverty speaks of pain and misery."[36] The appropriative pleasure found in the speaker's observation is not mirrored in pleasure of being for the washerwoman, and the privilege enjoyed by the speaker's perspective functions to aestheticize the washerwoman as an object of contemplation. In this sense, Wright's manipulation of the speaker's perspective is intended to create a change in his readers—instead of mirroring the insights discovered by the speaker through contemplating his own poverty, Wright uses the speaker to foreground the disregard created by objectification.

The process of objectifying subjects, specifically those exploited for their lack of power, appears elsewhere in the collection. Haiku 467 focuses on the image of flood survivors in the moonlight:

A radiant moon
Shining on flood refugees
Crowded on a hill.

As with haiku 60, a triad of images constructs the speaker's focus: "radiant" moonlight, "refugees," and the lack of space implied by "crowded." While the use of "radiant" and "shining" carries healthy and even resplendent qualities to the scene, finding aesthetic pleasure in the condition of the "flood refugees / Crowded on a hill" requires the ability to ignore the material condition they face; one need only recall the voyeuristic representation of Katrina victims in New Orleans to get a sense of the scene Wright could be discussing here. The disjunction between the opening and closing lines—between "radiant" and "crowded"—is more difficult to gloss over than the image of the washerwoman presented in haiku 60, however. Continuing the aesthetic effect created by the initial language and description provided by the speaker necessitates a disregard of both the danger that "crowd[s]" these refugees together and the reciprocal economic losses that they have most likely suffered.[37] In addition, the lack of control implied by being "crowded" together carries with it a sense of powerlessness as well as an inability to change such conditions; forced to retreat, these refugees have been herded and trapped by rising floodwaters. Not only has nature turned against those represented in the haiku, the speaker's attempts to render the refugees as a poignant image of human frailty further trades on their suffering, thus locating aesthetic pleasure in the misfortune of others.

The alienating and objectifying gaze of the speaker does at times get turned back on the speaker, as in haiku 615:

Their watching faces,
As I walk the autumn road,
Make me a traveler.

As with haiku 467, the verb choice of "make" calls attention to the connection between the "watching faces" and the estrangement Wright develops in the haiku; "make" indicates the effect that the "watching faces" have on the speaker. In transforming the speaker into a "traveler," the speaker is made aware of her/his exclusion from the community, indication that continued movement and escape appears to be in the speaker's best interests. The speaker is also objectified by these viewers; while being made into a "traveler" may seem to be a bit of stretch here, the speaker is positioned as an outsider, as foreign, as other. The use of "traveler" is also quite similar to Wright's use of "stranger" in the earlier snow haiku, specifically 132, which reads "What stranger is that / Walking in the winter rain / And looking this way?" In 132, the outward gaze of the speaker makes the other subject into an object, while in 615, the speaker experiences the same treatment at the hands of others. Both haiku, however, indicate not only the close connections between Wright's different inversions of the haiku moment, but also the ways in which privilege and power can be used to produce alienation and objectification.

As Wright uses the speaker's perspective to make clear, the making of subjects into objects allows readers to gloss over the inequalities that exist: the privilege to choose consciously to ignore the connections that exist between those laboring and those who enjoy the rewards of that labor. Wright's revision of *wabi* questions the assumptions that privilege often unconsciously carries with it—the ability to objectify and ostracize, to estrange and exclude when refusing to think through any perspective other than your own. In questioning the "higher state of mind"[38] that *wabi* carries, Wright engages the romanticizing gaze that allows the speaker to objectify the labor of others for her/his personal spiritual development while at the same time ignoring their psychological needs and material conditions. After all, there is no higher consciousness to be achieved when the pleasure of watching requires disregarding the humanity of others.

Intertextuality: Trains, Mobility, and Singing the Haiku Blues

Previous critics have noted the connections between Wright's haiku and his earlier work. Richard A. Iadonisi ties two of Wright's haiku that focus on rats with the opening scene of *Native Son* before going on to observe that those haiku, which examine "the subjectivity of the impoverished and oppressed, form an important and largely unexplored strain in Wright's collection."[39] Meta Schettler, in "'The rifle bullet': African American History in Richard Wright's Unpublished Haiku," makes connections between Wright's work and the violence African Americans experienced in the South. Schettler observes that "Wright frequently invokes images of fire or the sun to allude to the South's violent and repressive history" and analyzes his unpublished haiku to argue that "the redness of the cotton makes connections between the exploitation of black labor and the use of racial violence as a form of social control."[40] Applying Schettler's observations to the analysis already provided for haiku 1—"I am nobody: / A red sinking autumn sun / Took my name away"—adds new insights into this work. If the "red sinking autumn sun" is an image connected to the "South's violent and repressive history," then the speaker's alienation and loss of identity, while outwardly stripped away by nature, is also removed by the violence historically done to African Americans in the South. The verb "took" signifies doubly in this sense, both in regard to the literal violence the sunset acts out on the speaker and the metaphoric violence the South performs on black subjects. This reading also connects to the way subjects with privilege and power contribute to objectifying and alienating others—the South's desire to control blacks plays a part in the process of stripping blacks of agency and reinforcing their objectification. As well, there are the connections presented in this essay between the haiku on flood refugees and Wright's short fiction in both *Uncle Tom's Children* and *Eight Men*; not only does this example point out new intertextual connections in Wright's work, it also looks to build and extend an examination of the "impoverished and oppressed" that Iadonisi labels as an "unexplored strain in Wright's collection."[41] However, while initial work has been done to begin connecting Wright's haiku to his larger body of work, much work remains to be done to enrich and expand this line of critical inquiry. In this light, examining Wright's use of trains is one place to begin such an investigation.

That trains are a significant part of the Wright canon should be self-evident; Wright's observation about his "first lesson in how to live as a Negro" in "The Ethics of Living Jim Crow" positions his childhood home as "behind the railroad tracks."[42] Also significant in *Uncle Tom's Children* is the role that trains play in "Big Boy Leaves Home," including the idea of freedom in the North that trains invoke for the boys, the mournful tones of the train whistles, and the tangible danger Big Boy experiences after killing a white man: "In the distance he heard the approach of a train. It jarred him back to a sharp sense of danger . . . As he turned from the road across a plowed field he heard the train roaring at his heels. He ran faster, gripped in terror."[43] *Native Son* opens with Bigger Thomas's mother singing a blues-themed train song: "Life is like a mountain railroad / With an engineer that's brave / We must make the run successful / From the cradle to the grave . . ."[44] while *Black Boy*, to quote Ralph Ellison, is "filled with blues-tempered echoes of railroad trains."[45] Finally, there is also Dave's choice in "The Man Who Was Almost a Man" in *Eight Men* to run away on a train at the end of the story.[46] Collectively, these moments involving trains connect to Wright's larger literary themes: trains as images of freedom, terror, and enforced racial codes, trains as a metaphor for life, carrying with them, to quote Ellison again, the "jagged grain"[47] of blues, and trains as a means of escape. Thus, the inclusion of twenty-two haiku featuring trains in *Haiku: This Other World* indicates that Wright did not turn to haiku with the intention of abandoning his previous artistic endeavors; rather, he was making use of the opportunities provided by the formal structure of haiku to further develop his larger aesthetic interests.

As mentioned previously, the haiku is a more racially neutral generic form than Wright's other prose projects; in making use of the form, Wright's predominantly white readership would be less likely to code the thoughts and actions of the speaker in the haiku along the same white-black dichotomy as his fiction. In other words, they would be less likely to use their own potential biases about difference to read Wright's work.

Wright's previous experiences with the entrenched racism and privilege of white America had undoubtedly exposed him to both blatant racism as well as naive liberalism. Thus, Wright's interest in haiku allowed for the possibility of naming the dread and fear created by alienation and objectification without it being exclusively connected to black experience, precisely because it stripped away the outward configurations of race. While the problem of a shared humanity is particularized by race, in that racial categories help determine and construct the perceived differences that exist between subjects, Wright's aesthetic interest in revealing "that which is human on both sides"[48] necessitates removing the normative framework his readers unconsciously use to perceive the world. And, as this essay has demonstrated, Wright's use of a racially neutral speaker allows Wright the space to foreground the processes of estrangement, isolation, and dehumanization, specifically as they impede our ability to recognize the similarities that exist across the spectrum of human experience.

Wright's interest in trains performs a similar function; trains carry less preestablished meaning than the characters inhabiting Wright's work, but are still marked with poignancy as a symbol. In the haiku, they are further stripped of the specific needs of the speaker, and at times signify and represent on their own. In "Richard Wright's Blues," Ellison observes that "[t]he function, the psychology, of artistic selectivity is to eliminate from art form all those elements of experience that contain no compelling significance."[49] While Ellison is referring to Wright's writing process in regard to *Native Son*, this passage is also prescient in regard to Wright's interest in haiku. For Wright, a lack of awareness of power and privilege is no more a specifically white problem than living with objectification is a black problem; rather, both are human problems. Yet both social norms and the reception accorded to a transgressive African American author interested in challenging accepted hierarchies of power are shot through with just such contradictions and preconceived notions. In choosing the haiku form and then inverting its organizational structure to suit his needs, Wright can "eliminate" precisely "those elements of experience" that impede the construction of his aesthetic vision; the speaker in the haiku carries less baggage that will influence Wright's readership than the characters in his fiction. Trains, too, can serve in this capacity to call upon and remember the "jagged grain" of a blues-tempered past without literally invoking the subjects that experience such treatment. Trains are also able to embody the type of mobility that brings people together as well as pulling them apart. In this sense, Wright's use of trains not only serves as an intertextual moment between his earlier and later works, it also connects mobility to the ideas concerning alienation and objectification examined earlier in this essay and to the way subjects see and experience the world.

Wright uses trains in a variety of ways in his haiku: at times they are personified, as Wright did with nature; in others they are given the agency and power to affect the speaker as well as other subjects; and finally they foreground movement and motion, whether in regard to the speaker, relationships between subjects, or sometimes just the possibility of mobility itself. For example, haiku 526 implies a connection between towns created by the appearance of a train:

> The arriving train
> All decorated with snow
> From another town.

While the snow in this haiku invokes the previously discussed haiku concerning alienation, in this one, snow does not impede or limit perception. Instead, as the use of "decorated" implies, the snow provides the train with a sense of adornment and festivity—the train looks different, but is recognized for what it is as carrying good tidings in the passage from town to town. Compared to haiku 132 and 615, where the latent threat implied by the "stranger" and the "traveler" that pass between towns configures mobility as dangerous, the train in haiku 526 presents mobility in a more positive light—it is welcomed rather than ostracized. The juxtaposition between the benefits of mobility versus the dangers carried by strangers presents movement in a different light when subjectivity is removed from the equation.

Other haiku, however, are not so sanguine in the presentation of movement represented by the train. In haiku 632, the train is personified as more of a malevolent force:

In the rainy dark
A train screams at each village,
Then rolls on to the next.

The verb choice of "screams" personifies the noise that the train makes into a form of address the train uses to speak to the village. While loud and vocal, however, this type of speaking does not effectively communicate the train's point. Instead, "screams" implies a harsh and abrasive sound that signals the breakdown of communication. At the same time, the train's continuing motion, described as "rolls on," seems to indicate that the train behaves similarly at each village—it proceeds through the "rainy dark," screaming at each village it encounters. In this sense, the train is marked as exterior to and apart from the village; unlike the inhabitants the "stranger" and the "traveler" encounter in 132 and 615, however, the village cannot stop the train from passing through—power and control rest in the hands of the assaulting train. This agency is part of what gives the train its blues-tinged impetus in Wright's haiku; rather than locating loss and pain onto those who have ostensibly created that suffering, it is personified in the scream of a train whistle that shatters the silence of the night. Connecting this image of the train back to the repressive violence presented in Schettler's essay, the intrusion of the train carries with it the menace of social control implied by the nighttime visit of Southern patrollers or the threat of violence implied by Southern lynch law.

In connecting loss and suffering to the agency of trains, Wright also embodies economic, social, and political forces that, while having no direct human agents, impose limitations and exert influence on disenfranchised subjects. Haiku 601 presents the pain of separation through the power the train has over the speaker:

The train that took her
Steams into the autumn hills
And becomes silent.

The verb choice of "took" positions the power and authority the train holds over the speaker, in that the speaker is helpless to stop "her" removal. As with the forceful removal of the speaker's identity by nature in haiku 1, the use of "took" implies a lack of choice and even force in creating the rupture between the speaker the woman who departs. The burgeoning silence of the last line imparts a sense of loneliness and sorrow; the speaker watches the train's departure until it is no longer visible, its sound lost among the "autumn hills." In this sense, the haiku foregrounds the train's ability to literally take away the speaker's happiness. The train's agency and authority is further indicated by its being the subject of all three verbs in the haiku—"took," "steams," and "becomes"—reciprocally emphasizing the speaker's motionlessness and inability to act. A second haiku, 635, gives the train a similar power, although in this case it is in relation to the passage of time:

> An empty seashore:
> Taking a long summer with it,
> A departing train.

The link between the passage of seasons and the passing of time is predicated on the train's departure, giving the train the agency to control the passage of time in the schedule it keeps. As with haiku 1 and 601, the variant verb form of to take—here "taking"—carries with it a lack of choice for those who are experiencing the passage in time. Embodied in the image of the train, human loss and the passage of time portray the human condition as a blues-inflected lament based on a collective lack of control.

Ultimately, Wright's train haiku provide him the space to connect his revisions of the haiku moment with his larger beliefs about the function of art, linking isolation with the mobility and agency that exist outside the speaker. In haiku 636, the speaker observes,

> How lonely it is:
> A rattling freight train has left
> Fields of croaking frogs.

The speaker's feeling of loneliness and isolation are perceived in relation to the absence of mobility and reduction in noise represented by the departing train. The train's authority is represented by what it "has left" behind: a scene of nature. While the "croaking frogs" undoubtedly existed prior to and during the passage of the train, the train's actions are presented as creating the scene. In a slight variation on the "human-centered"[50] haiku examined earlier, the speaker's assumed authority over nature has been supplanted by the train's; the train's ability to leave behind a cargo of already existing croaking frogs mirrors the privileging of the speaker's perspective in haiku 721, where the choice of "ebbs" to describe the speaker's anger allows the stars to "grow bright again." Here, the train's departure leaves the speaker alone to contemplate nature although his contemplation creates no unity or connection to nature. While the speaker's isolation is not a direct product of nature, as with haiku 1, it is produced by the train's passage through and transformation of the scene. In invoking a sense of sadness in the speaker via conveying what she/he does not have—community and companionship—the train provides the speaker with an awareness of the importance and necessity of humanity that was not present before the train's passage. The speaker's blues-induced reflection provides an understanding of the importance of connecting with others—fingering the jagged grain of isolation and estrangement gives the speaker the perspective needed to embrace the necessity of a collective humanity.

The significance of Richard Wright's inversion of the haiku moment comes when readers are able to recognize the relationship that exists between the function of social forces and the experience of alienation in the construction of identity. The separation from nature that Wright articulates in his haiku gives him the space to foreground the unconscious privilege that is at the heart of the exploitation of others and that exists as part of the social fabric. As noted previously, when the haiku moment "deals with man's life, that life must be viewed in the context of nature rather than society."[51] Wright's collective inversion of the haiku moment positions the operation of social forces at the forefront of his haiku, along with the social connections that mediate and perpetuate alienation and estrangement. Making readers aware of the similarities in the hopes and dreams, feelings and experiences that exist between themselves and others gives Wright the space to argue for a common humanity that can transcend notions of difference imposed by the social hierarchies that mediate reality. Further, as Wright's revision of the aesthetic contemplation of poverty found in *wabi* indicates, ignoring the material conditions of those being represented foregrounds the needs of the speaker at the expense of those being represented. The consolation found in contemplating poverty ignores inequality, exposing again the unconscious privilege enjoyed by the speaker. As Wright reveals, in order to transform perceived assumptions concerning difference, readers must locate the connections that unify and unite, not the ones that leave established social barriers intact. When difference governs human interaction, or when the desire to aestheticize inequality is normative, then a haiku is no longer merely a haiku. The potential exclusion implied in the simplest verbal act can have long-ranging repercussions, especially when a speaker remains unaware of the violence being perpetuated on others. Thus, no matter how pretty an utterance is made to sound, it can still cause damage. And while anyone can experience the effects of estrangement and isolation, not everyone recognizes the need to affirm the existence of others. Although alienation may be the closest thing to a common universal human experience, as Wright's haiku indicate, an awareness of the self in relation to others can create the understanding required to make respect and dignity a practical reality.

Notes

1. Yoshinobu Hakutani and Robert L. Tener, afterword to *Haiku: This Other World* (New York: Arcade, 1998), 273.

2. Ibid., 275.

3. Eugene E. Miller, *Voice of a Native Son* (Jackson: University Press of Mississippi, 1990), 246.

4. Richard A. Iadonisi, "'I Am Nobody': The Haiku of Richard Wright," *MELUS* 30, no. 3 (2005): 179.

5. Richard Wright, "Blueprint for Negro Writing," in *Within the Circle*, ed. Angelyn Mitchell (Durham: Duke University Press, 1995), 103.

6. Ibid., 103–4.

7. Ibid., 103.

8. Richard Wright, "Richard Wright: I Curse the Day When for the First Time I Heard the Word 'Politics,'" in *Conversations With Richard Wright*, ed. Keneth Kinnamon and Michel Fabre (Jackson: University Press of Mississippi, 1993), 163.

9. Richard Wright, *Uncle Tom's Children*, in *Early Works*, ed. Arnold Rampersad (New York: Library of America, 1991), 352.

10. Ibid.

11. Ralph Ellison, "Richard Wright's Blues," in *Shadow and Act* (New York: Quality Paperback Book Club, 1994), 89. It is also worth noting that Ellison observes in this essay that Wright's "dual role" is to "discover and depict the meaning of

Negro experience; and to reveal to both Negroes and whites those problems of a psychological and emotional nature which arise between them when they strive for mutual understanding" (77), which is rather portentous when considering Wright's comments in relation to the 1955 interview with *L'Express* quoted above.

12. Wright, "Curse," 163.

13. Zora Neale Hurston, "What White Publishers Won't Print," in *Within the Circle*, ed. Angelyn Mitchell (Durham: Duke University Press, 1995), 119.

14. Wright, "Curse," 163.

15. Floyd Ogburn Jr., "Richard Wright's Unpublished Haiku: A World Elsewhere," *MELUS* 23, no. 3 (1998): 59.

16. Hakutani and Tener, afterword to *Haiku: This Other World*, 254.

17. Ibid., 251.

18. See, for example, Michel Fabre, "The Poetry of Richard Wright," in *Critical Essays on Richard Wright*, ed. Yoshinobu Hakutani (Boston: G. K. Hall, 1992), 252–72, and also Hakutani and Tener, afterword to *Haiku: This Other World*, 274, among others.

19. Miller, *Voice*, 246–47.

20. Meta Schettler, "'The rifle bullet': African-American History in Richard Wright's Unpublished Haiku," *Valley Voices* 8, no. 2 (2008): 67.

21. While I am indebted to Richard A. Iadonisi's essay, my argument plays out in slightly different terms. To clarify, my interest in pursuing Wright's intentional inversion of the haiku moment focuses on combining the formal logic of the haiku moment with Wright's aesthetic manipulation of the haiku; this operates differently than Iadonisi's argument, which examines Wright's structural divergence from haiku aesthetics in order to argue for the "anti-colonial position" (179) articulated in his haiku. Nonetheless, I do see this essay as extending Iadonisi's ideas, particularly in regards to examining those haiku that "foreground materiality and the subjectivity of the impoverished and oppressed [which] form an important and largely unexplored strain in Wright's collection" (192).

22. Iadonisi, "Nobody," 179.

23. Ibid., 184.

24. Yoshinobu Hakutani, "Nature, Haiku, and 'This Other World,'" in *Richard Wright and Racial Discourse* (Columbia: University of Missouri Press, 1996), 280.

25. Hakutani and Tener, afterword to *Haiku: This Other World*, 281.

26. Iadonisi, "Nobody," 187.

27. Quoted in Ogburn, "Unpublished," 70–71.

28. Seasonal words are described by R. H. Blyth as follows: "This word may give the atmospheric background, it may be a kind of seed, a trigger which releases a whole world of emotion, of sounds and scents and colors." See R. H. Blyth, *Haiku*, vol. 1 (Tokyo: Hokuseido, 1962), 335.

29. Iadonisi, "Nobody," 184.

30. Robert L. Tener, "The Where, the When, the What: A Study of Richard Wright's

Haiku," in *Critical Essays on Richard Wright*, ed. Yoshinobu Hakutani (Boston: G. K. Hall, 1982), 287.

31. Ogburn, "Unpublished," 73.

32. Hakutani, *Racial Discourse*, 280.

33. Wright, "Blueprint," 104.

34. Hakutani, *Racial Discourse*, 281.

35. Ibid.

36. Iadonisi, "Nobody," 189–91.

37. Wright's use of floods and flooding in his other works, most notably "Down by the Riverside" from *Uncle Tom's Children* and "The Man Who Saw the Flood" from *Eight Men*, should also give readers insights into the conditions that the refugees in this haiku face.

38. Hakutani, *Racial Discourse*, 281.

39. Iadonisi, "Nobody," 192.

40. Schettler, "History," 70–71.

41. Iadonisi, "Nobody," 192.

42. Wright, *Children*, 225.

43. Ibid., 262.

44. Wright, *Native Son*, 10.

45. Ellison, "Blues," 79.

46. Richard Wright, "The Man Who Was Almost a Man," in *Eight Men* (New York: HarperPerennial, 1996), 18.

47. Ellison, "Blues," 78.

48. Wright, "Curse," 163.

49. Ibid., 82–83.

50. Iadonisi, "Nobody," 184.

51. Hakutani and Tener, afterword to *Haiku: This Other World*, 251.

Japanese Influence on Richard Wright in His Last Years

English Haiku as a New Genre

— SANEHIDE KODAMA —

It may seem strange that Richard Wright, primarily known as an African American novelist with his *Uncle Tom's Children*, *Native Son*, *Black Boy*, and other novels and short stories, should write haiku; but, among his unpublished papers were found several thousand short poems in the form of haiku written shortly before his death in Paris. Since then, twenty-three of these last poetical works were published in *Richard Wright Reader* in 1978.[1] Twenty years later, Wright's selection of 817 haiku was finally published under the title *Haiku: This Other World*. Many of them are excellent pieces of literature. For example:

Standing in the field,
I hear the whispering of
Snowflake to snowflake. (489)

There is in this poem the delicate, subtle, and sensitive response to nature similar to that in many good Japanese haiku. A feeling for affinity with

An earlier version of this essay appeared in *Tamkang Review* 15, no. 1–4 (1985). Reprinted with permission of the author.

nature is shown through the speaker's hearing of the whispering of snowflakes. Wright wrote this kind of short poem on a variety of subjects. Read the following haiku:

With a twitching nose
A dog reads a telegram
On a wet tree trunk. (22)

Here is the kind of humor often found in the early Japanese haiku through personification of a domestic animal. It lies in the twitching nose of the dog that shows its curiosity about a telegram on a wet tree trunk. Between "twitching" and "telegram" is an interaction of visual and olfactory senses. Sometimes the humor in Wright's haiku is grotesquely reminiscent of his early sympathy with the Naturalists. The following poem is closer in its sensibility to senryu.

The dog's violent sneeze
Fails to rouse a single fly
On his mangy back. (20)

The humor of this poem is that the frustrated dog's violent sneeze, which could be loud to the observer, does not bother the tiny fly at all.

Some of Wright's haiku show the "deeply personal" tones.[2] During the summer of 1959, Wright fell ill from amoebic dysentery picked up during his visit to Africa and was hospitalized in the American Hospital in Neuilly, a western suburb of Paris, where he started writing haiku.[3] For example,

An empty sickbed:
An indented white pillow
In weak winter sun. (425)

Hidden under the seemingly indifferent description of cleanliness of the white pillow, in the "weak winter sun," we catch some of the enfeebled, *febrile*, helpless, and lonesome feeling of the patient weakened by fever.

However, the majority of Wright's haiku describe the beauty of nature or the human feeling about peace in nature. The following haiku is a good example:

I would like a bell
Tolling in this soft twilight
Over willow trees. (13)

In this beautiful poem, watching the colorful twilight over the willow trees, the speaker wishes that he could hear a bell toll. But again the poem seems to reflect something deeper in the poet's mind. Peaceful twilight toward the end of the day suggests calmness and silence close to an end. The weeping willow is the symbol of accepting one's fate. It cannot easily be denied that the poem has an overtone of the poet's wish for peace of mind at the time of bell's knell for him.

Some haiku have what may be called "reverberation," not only auditory but olfactory and tactile:

From across the lake,
Past the black winter trees,
Faint sounds of a flute. (571)

The spring lingers on
In the scent of a damp log
Rotting in the sun. (47)

A freezing morning:
I left a bit of my skin
On the broomstick handle. (288)

The sound of the flute, the scent of the damp log, and the coldness of the broomstick handle seem to last for some time in the ear, the nose, and the hand of the reader. This lingering sensory effect may be said to be close to what Bashō called *hibiki*, or reverberation.

In all these short poems by Wright, written on a variety of subjects, are some common denominators. Each line in every poem presents an image with a new sense of mild surprise, arousing in the mind of the reader a fresh sensation of calmness and beauty. And there is nothing at all of that sense of fear or "the terror of white men" that had dominated his earlier novels and novellas. Nor do we find "that thirst for violence that was in me, for intrigue, for plotting, for secrecy, for bloody murders" or "the white threat . . . hovering near again," as recollected in his autobiographical novel, *Black Boy*.[4] Each poem is endowed with subtlety, freshness, suggestiveness, delicacy, and a sense of contentment, quite close to Japanese sensibility.

One may wonder why Richard Wright persistently wrote so many of the short poems belonging to a totally different culture. He read R. H. Blyth's *Haiku* in 1959 and discovered in it something he had been unconsciously seeking to ease his mind. Just as he "hungered for the sharp, frightening, breathtaking, almost painful excitement" of the novel when he had been told by a schoolteacher, Ella,[5] a part of the story of *Bluebeard and His Seven Wives*, Wright seemed to have "hungered" for the world of Oriental poetry when he read the book on haiku. The editors of the *Richard Wright Reader* write: "In 1959, Wright discovered the Japanese haiku. He was entranced by the 17-syllable form and jotted down several thousands of the brief poems, mostly during his treatment at the hospital. 'Maybe I'm fooling around with these tiny little poems, but I could not let them go. I was possessed by them,' he wrote a friend in May 1960, just six months before his death."[6] He may have read some haiku in French translation; he may have been familiar with the form through Imagism; he may have read Harold G. Henderson's *Introduction to Haiku* or Kenneth Yasuda's *Japanese Haiku*, but I would guess that for Wright his encounter with Blyth's *Haiku* was a great event. He borrowed the four volumes from a friend, read them, and attempted to write haiku himself.[7] It is evident that Wright followed very closely what Blyth had written about the haiku: "This 5, 7, 5 had a wave-like character of flow, suspense and ebb, it is symmetrical, yet in odd numbers. Further, there is a kind of syllogistic nature about the form which gives it the utmost clarity while actually containing no logical elements, often no intellectual connections between the parts."[8] Wright observes the syllable count of 5, 7, 5 fairly strictly. He sets down the three lines not in logical, syllogistic order, but in what may be called a "syllogism" of images by presenting, step by step in each line, an independent but related image.

Concerning the *kigo*, or the seasonal reference word, Blyth writes: "There is almost always a season word in haiku. This word may give the atmospheric background, it may be a kind of seed, a trigger which releases a whole world of emotion, of sounds and scents and colours."[9] There are some liberals in Japan who decline to follow the book of collected season words, who insist on being freed from their conventional associations, but many haiku poets follow the tradition in order to render their specific emotion in the poem still more specifically and poignantly in terms of the season. Wright was probably unaware of the existence in Japan of the old, voluminous lists of season words, but there is almost always a seasonal reference word in his haiku. Most of the time, however, his unorthodox use of the season words, with Western connotations and association, accompanies fresh and unexpected beauty connected with specific seasonal feelings.

Blyth makes a further comment in relation to the classification by seasons: "*Haiku* have been for long classified according to the seasons and the subjects of the verse. There are, as it were, five seasons: the New Year, Spring, Summer, Autumn and Winter; there are also a few verses that will not go into any particular season."[10] Before his death Wright arranged the copies of his typescript "*haikus*," dividing them into four sections—Spring, Summer, Autumn, and Winter. In his letter to Margit de Sablonière, his Dutch translator, on March 19, 1960, Wright writes: "During my illness I experimented with the Japanese form of poetry called haiku; I wrote some 4,000 of them and am now sifting them out to see if they are any good."[11] From the material he left, one can gather that, probably after "sifting them out" in March 1960, Wright classified his "*haikus*" into seasons. He wrote some more of them in the spring, summer, and fall of 1960, and before he died in November 1960, he had sifted again and classified them into four seasons, obviously in preparation for publication under the title "This Other World." Division by seasons was suggested by Blyth's similar pattern in his books.

Blyth spends about a hundred pages on the Buddhist influence on haiku in the section, "Zen, the State of Mind for Haiku," explaining such terms as "selflessness," "loneliness," "grateful acceptance," "contradiction," "humor," and "simplicity," immanent in the works of the representative Japanese haiku poets. It is apparent that Wright read this section very carefully and was greatly influenced by the thought underlying it. "It is a condition of selflessness," Blyth writes, "in which things are seen without reference to profit or loss, even of some remote, spiritual kind."[12] He continues: "This losing of one's life, when attained in the will, is a state of rest and ease . . . . When we are in this condition, we can look at anything and everything and see with its eyes, hear with its ears, fly with its wings."[13] "Selflessness" and the sense of "rest and ease" prevail in Wright's haiku. His strong and uneasy consciousness at being an African American in his early years is gone. The figure of the poet abstracted from the personae speaking in his haiku is thin in character and almost as transparent as air. To be "selfless" is often compared to being like air. But "selflessness" in Buddhism is "selffulness,"[14] and the "selfless" but "selfful" state of mind is often symbolized by the wind. Though probably unconsciously, Wright often adopts the image of wind in his poems. Read the following three:

A soft wind at dawn
Lifts one dry leaf and lays it
Upon another. (39)

A leaf chases wind
Across an autumn river
And shakes a pine tree. (669)

Having appointed
All the stars to their places
The summer wind sleeps. (696)

"Loneliness" is likewise "lonelilessness." Wright exquisitely expresses the paradox in the image of a soaring, stately mountain peak:

In the afterglow
A snow-covered mountain peak
Sings of loneliness. (723)

It is difficult to calculate how much influence Blyth had on Wright. But the haiku seems to have provided Wright with an important outlet for peace of mind as an enlightened man accepting and transcending his fate while the novel was the outlet for his violent, African American consciousness. The change in his attitude toward life is so remarkable as to seem almost a religious awakening. Indeed, some of his haiku suggest his spiritual rebirth, as in haiku 219:

Enough of dawn light
To show pearly pear blossoms
Burning from within.

By presenting the image of the pear blossoms glowing and burning "from within" at the first sunlight from the east, Wright might be subtly suggesting his mind glowing and changing within him. Read another one:

Coming from the woods
A bull has a lilac sprig
Dangling from a horn. (175)

This seeming pastoral and pagan poem may also be taken as suggestive of the joy of spiritual rebirth or, at least, a spiritual change of the poet. The same change is suggested too in haiku 1:

I am nobody:
A red sinking autumn sun
Took my name away.

Though echoing the *Invisible Man* by Wright's friend Ralph Ellison, the poem can be taken as an expression of his realization of the importance of a "selfless" attitude to life, suggesting also the rejection of his previous way of life.

However, I am not suggesting that Richard Wright was converted to Buddhism, but rather that he deeply understood the teachings of Zen through Blyth's volumes of *Haiku*, and derived comfort from it. Sick in the hospital, toward the end of his life he was certainly tired of fighting racism. He had been trying to escape it since he left Natchez for Memphis and then for Chicago and New York. Finally, he left the United States in 1947 to live in Paris. Perhaps the last spiritual resting place he discovered there was the world of the haiku. But still he was unable to cast away all his past, as suggested in the following haiku:

The crow flew so fast
That he left his lonely caw
Behind in the field. (117)

On the surface, the poet's position in the poem seems close to that of the speaker who watches a lonely crow passing him, leaving a caw behind. But the poet may be identifying with the crow. The poem seems an indirect expression of the poet's awareness of his still being a "Jim Crow," as he used to call himself, as in "The Ethics of Living Jim Crow," who is now fading away into an unknown world, leaving his voice behind. Wright never forgot that he was black, of which he was rightly proud.

His attempts to attain selflessness and his wish for escape and self-denial seem to have been mixed with his sense of loss at the death of his mother in 1960.[15] The image of death haunts his last pieces:

The oaken coffin,
Between the porch and the car,
Was christened by snow. (764)

A sick cat seeks out
A stiff and frozen willow
Under which to die. (591)

Glittering with frost,
A dead frog squats livingly
In the garden path. (815)

However, the more Wright was obsessed by the idea of death and self-denial, the more his imagination would "blaze"[16] again and again till the very last moment:

Keep straight down this block,
Then turn right where you will find
A peach tree blooming. (3)

In fact, Richard Wright was not the only American who wrote haiku in the late 1950s. Even earlier, Allen Ginsberg had read Blyth's books on haiku in Berkeley and written twenty-one examples of haiku, as he had recorded in his journal in 1955.[17] Still earlier, Gary Snyder had written a haiku with a haiga on Crater Mountain while working as a fire lookout in the summer of 1952.

A butterfly
Scared up from its flower
Caught by the wind and swept over the cliffs[18]

Indeed the American interest in haiku can be traced back to the early part of the twentieth century when the Imagist poets tried short poems based on Ezra Pound's "theory of superposition" which he thought he discovered in the Japanese haiku. A number of poets wrote like Pound's "In a Station of the Metro" during the last decade of "Japonisme": Carl Sandburg, William Carlos Williams, Amy Lowell, Wallace Stevens, Arthur Davison Ficke, John Gould Fletcher, Hilda Doolittle, and Yvor Winters, to name some of them.

But the interest in haiku after World War II in America, especially since 1960, was remarkable. Schoolchildren were taught to write haiku in primary schools, and in many towns haiku clubs were organized. In 1963, a magazine called *American Haiku* was started by those who were more seriously devoted to haiku in English. Though it ceased publication in 1968, such magazines as *Haiku, Haiku West, Modern Haiku,* and *Dragonfly* have appeared. The Haiku Society of America was founded in New York in 1968 under the auspices of the Japan Society.

The Haiku Anthology, first published with an introduction by Cor van den Heuvel in 1974 and now in its third edition, gives a brief history and a bird's-eye view of the American haiku after World War II. Certainly some of the works by the American haiku poets show that they "see the spiritual depth haiku embodies."[19] Read Nicholas Virgilio's haiku:

The vacuum cleaner
drowning out mother's grieving:
my dead brother's room[20]

The poet Virgilio has been writing poems on his brother killed in the war in Vietnam. The poem presents a domestic image, suggesting that humanity suffocates in the highly mechanized society. In the next poem by Marjory Bates Pratt the speaker's direct contact with nature leads her to the realization of its religious implication:

Mountain brook water:
to drink it in my cupped hands
I kneel on the earth.[21]

The act becomes symbolic as in the ritual. The following poems may also show how the Americans are breaking away from traditional Japanese images such as those listed in the *Saijiki*. Take Michael McClintock's haiku as an example:

glimmering morning
silence unfolds all
the yucca[22]

And Robert Spiess's:

Blue jays in the pines;
the northern river's ledges
cased with melting ice[23]

These explorations into the new field of "American haiku," including that of Richard Wright, are characterized by a spectrum of ideas about the nature of that type of poetry. Some of the poets insist on holding to the orthodox 5-7-5 syllable count while most others count far less strictly and a few of the most experimental poets attempt "concrete" haiku, or "eye-ku." Some try to express religious depth, and some are overtly a-religious. Some try humorous poems, closer to senryu, a witty, often ironical, verse in the same 5-7-5 form as haiku without particular reference to nature.

Yet, there are factors common to those American haiku poets: (1) Though some write in four lines and some in one or two lines, most of them write in three. (2) They present concrete images in utmost concentration. (3) They are likely to be suggestive and pithy. These common factors are not to be wondered at because, as they confess in their biographical notes, these

American haiku poets in *The Haiku Anthology* have mostly been inspired by books such as those by Blyth, Yasuda, and Henderson.[24]

Surely there is a strong lyric impulse among modern American poets toward compact gem-like minimalism in poetry even as they are attracted to the Whitmanesque, all-inclusive poetry. If more Americans continue to produce as many good haiku as they have in recent years, and if they continue to be guided by those books that refer to classical examples of haiku, it is possible that some day the haiku may become as well established a genre in the English language as the sonnet.

Notes

1. Ellen Wright and Michel Fabre, eds. *Richard Wright Reader* (New York: Harper and Row, 1978).

2. Ibid., 243. The editors of the book write that "Wright was able to inject a deeply personal tone to these pieces."

3. Ibid., 875.

4. Richard Wright, *Black Boy* (New York: HarperPerennial, 1998), 40, 66.

5. Ibid., 40.

6. Wright and Fabre, eds., *Richard Wright Reader*, 243.

7. According to Fabre, Wright "borrowed the four volumes by R. H. Blyth on the art of haiku in order to systematically learn the complex rules of its composition." Michel Fabre, *The Unfinished Quest of Richard Wright*, trans. from French by Isabel Barzun (New York: William Morrow, 1973), 505.

8. R. H. Blyth, *Haiku* (Tokyo: Hokuseido, 1949), I:373.

9. Ibid., I:382.

10. Ibid., I:384.

11. Fabre, *The Unfinished Quest of Richard Wright*, 505.

12. Blyth, *Haiku*, 163.

13. Ibid., 164.

14. Ibid., 172.

15. David Bakish, *Richard Wright* (New York: Frederick Ungar, 1973), 96.

16. "She [Ella] told how Bluebeard had duped and married his seven wives, how he had loved and slain them, how he had hanged them up by their hair in a dark closet. The tale made the world around me be, throb, live . . . . My imagination blazed." Wright, *Black Boy*, 39.

17. Allen Ginsberg, *Journals: Early Fifties, Early Sixties*, ed. Gordon Ball (New York: Grove Press, 1977), 92–95.

18. Gary Snyder, *Earth House Hold* (New York: New Directions, 1969), 8.

19. Cor van den Heuvel, ed., *The Haiku Anthology* (New York: Norton, 1999), lx.

20. Quoted from the typescript haiku of Nicholas Virgilio. His brother was killed in the war in Vietnam.

21. Marjory Bates Pratt, *The Light on the Snow* (Pennington, NJ: Private Edition, 1979), 7.

22. Cor van den Heuvel, ed. *The Haiku Anthology*, 119.

23. Ibid., 196.

24. R. H. Blyth, *Haiku* (Tokyo: Hokuseido, 1949–1952), 4 vols. Harold G. Henderson, *An Introduction to Haiku* (New York: Doubleday, 1958). Kenneth Yasuda, *The Japanese Haiku: Its Essential Nature, History, and Possibilities in English* (Rutland, VT: Charles E. Tuttle, 1957).

From *Japonisme* to Modernism

Richard Wright's African American Haiku

— SACHI NAKACHI —

I

Japonisme is an aesthetic movement that started in Europe in the middle of the nineteenth century. As soon as Japan changed its policy of isolation and opened its ports to foreign countries in 1865, Japanese woodblock prints, potteries, and paintings flowed into European markets and created a fever for Japan. European impressionist painters such as Manet, Monet, Duret, Degas, Gaugin, Toulouse-Lautrec, Van Gogh, and American painters such as James McNeill Whistler and Mary Cassatt borrowed both subjects and techniques from Japanese art.[1] Writers also showed their interest in Japan. In French literature, writers like Emile Zola, the Goncourt brothers, and Juliet Gautier were considered as ones who were fascinated by Japanese culture. Pierre Loti and Paul Claudel went to Japan and wrote their experience in Japan.[2] English Victorian writers such as Oscar Wilde, Rudyard Kipling, and Sir Edwin Arnold also showed their interest in Japan and Japanese art. According to Earl Miner, "Japan had become a special subject or reality for the mixed Victorian temper."[3]

There was a Japan boom period in theater, too. W. S. Gilbert and Sir Arthur Sullivan's operetta, *The Mikado,* attracted British audiences from its first performance in London in 1885. In the United States, it was performed in theaters in New York such as the Fifth Avenue Theater, American Theater, and Madison Square Roof Garden.[4] Sidney Jones's *The Geisha*

(1886), which is said to be "a missing link between *The Mikado* by Gilbert and Sullivan and *The Madam Butterfly* by Puccini,"[5] was also a phenomenal production. By 1898, it ran 760 performances in London.[6] *The Darling of the Gods* (1902), a play by John Luther Long and David Belasco, was also a great hit in the United States as well as in Britain.[7] In its first season, *The Darling of the Gods* ran 186 performances, whereas *Madame Butterfly* ran only 24 performances.[8]

It is in this period, too, that writers began to show their interest in Japanese literary forms—especially tanka and haiku. Leon de Rosny's *Anthologie Japonaise*, published in 1871, is said to be the first translation of Japanese tanka into French.[9] As for haiku translation, Basil Hall Chamberlain's *The Classical Poetry of the Japanese*, published in 1880, is considered to be the first translation of Japanese haiku into English.[10] In 1905, Paul-Louis Couchoud started a French haiku movement; in America, Ezra Pound was one of the first poets who adopted haiku form into his poetry. Yoshinobu Hakutani speculates that Pound was given information on Japanese poetry by Yone Noguchi.[11] Noguchi introduced Japanese haiku and tanka to the English world during the early decades of the twentieth century. He published *The Spirit of Japanese Poetry* in 1914.

Thus, the history of *Japonisme* is generally traced back to the nineteenth century and considered to be terminated in the 1920s. However, we should not neglect the fact that African Americans played an important role in turning *Japonisme* into another stage in the beginning of the twentieth century. At the end of the 1930s, there were interesting theatrical performances in New York. They were *The Swing Mikado* and *The Hot Mikado*. Both musicals used African Americans as the performers. *The Swing Mikado,* which opened on September 25, 1938, at Chicago's Great Northern Theater, was a great success.[12] On March 1, 1939, it opened at the New Yorker Theatre on 54th Avenue.[13] *The Hot Mikado,* which was produced by Michael Todd and also performed in 1939, was highly praised. However, it is difficult to call these performances as productions of African American *Japonisme* because the directors and the audiences were non–African American, but these performances can be regarded as an African American version of *The Mikado*. Shannon Steen says that *The Hot Mikado* depicts "a swinging Japan colonized by African Americans and overrun by Cotton Club aesthetics."[14]

The 1930s was also a period when African American writers experienced their first visit to Japan. James Weldon Johnson came to Japan to participate in the National Interracial Conference in Kyoto in October 1929. He was warmly welcomed by Japanese journalists and citizens.[15] Langston Hughes visited Japan in 1933 on the way to Shanghai, China, though he was soon forced out by the Japanese government suspecting that he was a Communist.[16] W. E. B. Du Bois visited Japan in 1936. Du Bois's trip to Japan was helped by a Japanese named Yasuichi Hikita, who was educated in Colombia University and associated with people of the Harlem Renaissance such as Du Bois, Alain Locke, James Weldon Johnson, and Arthur Schomburg.[17] Hikita is said to have helped shape Du Bois's opinions of the Imperial Japan.

In many cases, African American interest in Japan seems to have been different from Euro-American interest in Japan at the turn of the century. African Americans did not regard Japan as just an exotic country in the Far East; they were interested in Japan because it was a colored nation that could compete with the Western countries. Du Bois admired Japan as a colored empire standing against the European imperialism. He "championed Japan as the best hope for saving the nonwhite world from enslavement to Europe."[18] Commenting on Japanese victory in the Russo-Japanese War in 1905, Du Bois wrote: "The Russo-Japanese war has marked an epoch. The magic of the word 'white' is already broken, and the Color Line in civilization has been crossed in modern times as it was in the great past. The awakening of the yellow race is certain. The awakening of the brown and black races will follow in time, no unprejudiced student of history can doubt."[19] Du Bois regarded Japan as a model for African Americans. He kept this view until the mid-1930s when relations between Japan and China got worse.[20]

African American writers' response to Japan and Japanese culture was relatively affirmative even in the wartime. Richard Wright writes in *12 Million Black Voices*, published in 1941, as follows: "There are others of us who feel the need of the protection of a strong nation so keenly that we admire the harsh and imperialistic policies of Japan and ardently hope that Japanese will assume the leadership of the 'darker races.'"[21] Wright tells us that African Americans continued to have sympathy for Japan in the period when Anglo-Americans became antagonistic to Japan. They still regarded

Japan as their colored brother country that could be their model. Wright himself was interested in Japan in and after the war period. When he was asked about the historical date most charged with significance to him in an interview in 1955, Wright answered without hesitation, "The 1905 victory of the Japanese over Russia. That date marked the beginning of the termination of the Godlike role which the Western white man had been playing to mankind. That date marked the beginning of the de-Occidentalization of the world."[22] As Wright's words suggest, African American interest in Japan was political rather than artistic. Still, there is no doubt that African Americans played a significant role in keeping Japanese boom at the turn of the century in modern American culture. African American fascination with karate in the 1950s and 1960s[23] was not a sudden outbreak but a phenomenon continuing from the prewar period. In this sense, African Americans contributed to turning *Japonisme* into another stage after World War II.

II

To examine *Japonisme* after the 1930s, the ethnic minority's contribution to the Western late-modernist writing cannot be ignored. Modernism is often regarded as an Anglo-American literary movement represented by writers such as T. S. Eliot, James Joyce, Samuel Beckett, Virginia Woolf, Gertrude Stein, Ezra Pound, William Faulkner, and Ernest Hemingway, but it was actually a complex cultural movement involving minority writers as well as immigrant and foreign writers. Although the late nineteenth century was a period of unquestionable Western dominance, it was also a time for the emergence of Asian modernity.

In the late nineteenth century, what is called as a new Buddhism movement started in Japan. This was also the period when the worldwide revival of Buddhism started. Among the Buddhists who were involved in the revival movement of Buddhism, D. T. Suzuki can be regarded as the most important person because of his enormous influence in the field of American literature. Suzuki was born in 1870 in Japan. While he studied at Tokyo University, he also attended Zen practices in a temple at Kamura and there he met Shoen Shaku.[24] Shaku took Suzuki to the United States as an interpreter when he was invited to speak at the World Parliament of Religions held in Chicago in 1893.[25] Thus Suzuki's career started as an interpreter and a translator. He also helped Paul Carus translate Eastern spiritual literature into English.[26] While working as a translator, he started writing his own books and published *Essays in Zen Buddhism* in 1927 in the United States. Since then he published many Zen books in English, which gave a great impact on the Western intellectuals. Carl Jung, who was interested in the Eastern philosophy, also read Suzuki's books. In a foreword to Suzuki's *An Introduction to Zen Buddhism*, Jung writes: "We cannot be sufficiently grateful to the author, first for the fact of his having brought Zen closer to Western understanding, and secondly for the manner in which he has achieved this task."[27] As Jung points out, Suzuki explained Zen in the frame of Western philosophical logic. Suzuki's books had such a great appeal to the Western intellectuals because of his Western rhetoric. According to David L. McMahan, "Much in Suzuki's writing on Zen derives from Romanticism, Transcendentalism, and their successors . . . [Suzuki] amalgamated Buddhist and German idealist and American Transcendentalist cosmological concepts with Buddhist one and presented the Japanese poets as deeply and religiously attentive to nature like the English Romantics and Transcendentalists—yet, he insisted, superior."[28] Actually, Suzuki employed the Transcendentalist terms such as "Man" and "Nature" to explain the philosophy of Zen. The notion of "simplicity" in Zen also echoes that of Wordsworth.

R. H. Blyth, a translator of haiku, was also much influenced by Suzuki's books, and he interpreted haiku in terms of Zen. Blyth's motivation of using Zen in his translation of haiku was different from Suzuki's, for Blyth's attitude was more like that of Orientalists in the nineteenth century who longed to keep Japan unmodernized for their own nostalgia of good old days. Blyth's haiku books, which often compare Japanese haiku to English Romantic poetry, were motivated by his Romantic inclination, but he also defined Japanese haiku as the philosophical product of Zen. Thus, Blyth's translation of haiku became a stimulus for the American haiku movement led by the late-modernist poets.

Richard Wright came to be familiar with Japanese haiku poetry in 1959 by reading Blyth's four volumes of *Haiku*.[29] By March 1960, he wrote more than 4,000 haiku. This extraordinary number shows his obsession with haiku, a traditional Japanese poetry consisting of seventeen syllables.

Although some critics think that Wright reserved haiku only for his personal and sentimental expression, it is important to note that they were written in the period when Wright had become interested in postcolonial struggles of the Third World. Already in 1947, Wright said in an interview: "The voice of [the] American Negro is no longer a lone voice. You hear echoing voices in the people of Burma, China, South Africa. Three-quarters of the world's population is colored. The attitude toward the Negro problem is entering a new phase."[30] His international concerns, especially about the Third World, were intensified in the 1950s. From June to August 1953, Wright traveled in the Gold Coast. Then in April 1955, Wright went to Bandung, Indonesia, to attend the first Afro-Asian Conference in the world. He came to Bandung from Madrid via Rome, Cairo, Baghdad, Calcutta, and Bankoku. His journey itself proves that he was eager to broaden his international point of view and establish human connections beyond nations. Wright's adoption of haiku, a non-Western form of poetry, can thus be regarded as his literary challenge to bridge the colored countries under the Western oppression.

According to Margaret Walker, Wright began to think he would like to visit Japan in the 1950s.[31] Just like Van Gogh's view of Japan as his ideal country, Wright seemed to have projected his ideal to Japan, a small mysterious country of the Far East that changed the history of the Western domination over the world by winning over Russia in 1905. Wright's *Japonisme*, however, is different from Van Gogh's. It is true that Wright used the Japanese haiku form for his own sake just as early Japonists/Orientalists did, but his motivation of employing haiku as his poetic expression came from his resistance against the Western art form as well as his desire for the political alliance with Asian culture. By composing haiku, Wright developed *Japonisme* into a new modernist form, with which he looked for a new possibility of transnational literature by combining the elements of the East and the West.

III

Although Wright's haiku seem to reflect his inclination for Japan, we should note that they are completely different from Japanese haiku.

Referring to Wright's haiku, Michel Fabre says, "At the final stage of his evolution, at a moment when nature and the individual played an increasingly important part in his thinking, the poet developed a taste for these intimate tercets in which he could condense the quintessence of his art."[32] Robert L. Tener also says, "Like the Japanese poet Bashō, Wright had achieved in many of these haiku, which he selected himself for publication, the sense of sad oneness in nature, coupled with an ironic smile of joy and compassion. At his best, Wright was clearly capable of perceiving the peaceful and temperate aspects of nature and of avoiding the confused and violent elements both in man and in nature. He could create, as it were, his own Wordsworthian 'sports of time,' seeing into the life of things."[33] Yoshinobu Hakutani also sees love of nature as an essential characteristic of Wright's haiku. He states, "Another major characteristic of haiku Wright learned is a love of nature that is inseparable from ordinary."[34] Critics thus tend to see that Wright's haiku represent his love of nature, which he could not express in his protest novels. These opinions, however, could be problematic because Wright had a complicated relation to nature as an African American writer. From his lyrical description of the landscape in *Black Boy*, we know that Wright had a delicate sensitivity of loving nature, but we should also note that he often claimed the fact that African Americans were deprived of their right of loving nature.

From the beginning of his career, Wright wrote how racism entered every aspect of African Americans in the South and prevented them from enjoying nature. Hakutani considers that "Big Boy Leaves Home," a short story in *Uncle Tom's Children*, can be an evidence of Wright's identification with nature, but we should note that it is a work protesting against the white society that deprives African American boys of their joy in nature. On a hot summer day, boys decide to swim in a creek. They are excited, joking about a hippopotamus by sinking themselves down under the water. Their enjoyable moment in nature, however, turns into a nightmare when a white woman looks at their naked bodies and screams. Wright's attention turns more to the disruption of the peaceful moment in the natural world than to the beauty of nature itself. Although Wright describes the beauty of nature in his works, it is clear that he does not regard nature as benevolent. In "Down by the Riverside," another short story in *Uncle Tom's*

Children, the flood changes the peaceful life of Mann and leads him into a tragic life. From this story, we know that Wright considers a natural phenomenon as a cause leading African Americans into destruction. Nature is often cruel to African Americans.

In fact, Wright's appreciation of natural life is different from that in Japanese haiku. As Hakutani and Tener write in the afterword to *This Other World*, "[Japanese] haiku traditionally avoided such subjects as earthquakes, floods, illnesses, and eroticism—ugly aspects of nature."[35] Wright, however, often chooses ugly things in the world. Vermin (rats, mice, flies, cockroaches, and lice) and disgusting small animals and insects (serpents, snakes, crows, snails, spiders, and moths) are often depicted in his haiku. Also, the dead bodies of small animals are often the subjects of Wright's haiku. The following four haiku are about the dead animals:

At the water's edge,
Amid drifting brown leaves,
A dead bloated fish. (70)

A dead mouse floating
Atop a bucket of cream
In the dawn spring light. (408)

With solemnity
The magpies are dissecting
A cat's dead body. (711)

In a full zinc tub,
Winter rain pelting a rat,
Floating and bloated. (801)

In these haiku, the grotesque bodies of dead animals are under Wright's objective gaze. Death could be the ultimate unity with nature, but it is hard to see the sense of unity with nature in these haiku because these small animals do not seem to have natural death. Moreover, these small animals' bodies are dirty and ugly, implying that the world Wright describes is full of cruelties and mercilessness.

Moreover, as the dead woman's body in *Native Son* shows, Wright was obsessed with the dead bodies throughout his life as a writer. When we discuss Wright's haiku, it is rather reasonable to see continuities with his earlier works than discontinuities. For example, Wright's haiku have something in common with "Between the World and Me," his early poem on a lynched body, which starts with the pastoral prose lines that remind us of the poems by Robert Frost:

> And one morning while in the woods I stumbled suddenly upon the thing,
> Stumbled upon it in a grassy clearing guarded by scaly oaks and elms.
> And the sooty details of the scene rose, thrusting themselves between the world and me . . .[36]

The poem then moves from a pastoral scene to a grotesque one in the next line that presents the remains of a burned body of a lynched African American man. The poem is structured carefully. In the first part of the poem, the persona who stumbled onto the site of a lynching in the woods is the observer. But in the second half, the persona's identity merges into the dead and experiences lynching happening to the dead. Occurring in the second part of the poem is what JanMohamed calls "intransitive identification."[37] The last stanza finalizes the persona's complete identification with the lynched body: "Now I am dry bones and my face a stony skull starting in yellow surprise at the sun . . ."[38]

In Wright's haiku, the moment of "intransitive identity"—a moment "to overcome inter-subjective boundaries and understand the predicament and the capabilities of the death-bound subjects"[39]—is not clearly described, but we can still say that there are moments in which boundaries between the object and the writer become ambiguous in some of his haiku. His haiku about scarecrows are good examples:

> Scarecrow, who starved you,
> Set you in that icy wind,
> And then forgot you? (577)

Late one winter night
I saw a skinny scarecrow
Gobbling slabs of meat. (150)

Wright's feeling to the scarecrow is sympathetic. Scarecrows are often funny and comical in Japanese haiku, but Wright's scarecrows are always miserable and tragic. They are often "skinny," "lonely," "frozen," and "starved." Evidently, Wright's scarecrows are the embodiments of African American grudge against the Jim Crow society. In haiku 577 the scarecrow is starved and left in cold wind without being given attention to by anybody. Haiku 150 also develops the same theme; a scarecrow turns into a more grotesque figure because of hunger. Just like Zombie coming back from the grave, a scarecrow wakes up in the midnight and devours slabs of meat. It should be remembered that "hunger" was a key word for Wright to speak about his childhood and adolescence in *Black Boy*. Although Wright sees scarecrows from a point outside, his sympathy to scarecrows allows readers to see them from inside perspectives.

Thematically speaking, Wright's haiku is not very different from his other works including his protest novels. Although some critics see aspects of Zen philosophy in Wright's haiku, it is difficult to say how much Wright was influenced by Zen Buddhism because he, who hated his grandmother's fanatic religious tendency, was always dubious of religion and had a negative view of anything irrational. Hakutani, who claims that Wright was influenced by Zen philosophy, cites haiku 1 as an example of Wright's interest in Zen state of void[40]:

I am nobody:
A red sinking autumn sun
Took my name away.

In Hakutani's interpretation, Wright achieves the state of nothingness, which allows him to experience enlightenment. But this can also be read as a reflection of Wright's historical gaze on the African Americans whose ancestors were deprived of their property and names. In the 1950s, Wright was already famous as an American intellectual, and he was no longer a "nobody." He was an "established writer" with international readers and called a Parisian intellectual,[41] but he was not just satisfied with his success. In the 1950s, Wright gave more attention to Africans' colonial experience in the past. By manifesting himself "nobody," Wright tried to achieve the "intransitive identification" with one of a thousand of nameless Africans who might have died looking at the red sinking sun on the slave ships.

Hakutani also claims that Wright tries to "suppress egoism and attain a state of nothingness"[42] in haiku 721:

As my anger ebbs,
The spring stars grow bright again
And the wind returns.

Hakutani says, "Only when he reaches a state of nothingness and what he calls in *Black Power* 'a total attitude toward life' is he able to perceive nature with his enlightened sense."[43] From a point of view that Wright was trying to embody Zen philosophy in his haiku, this interpretation is reasonable. But it is a haste conclusion if we think that Wright was influenced by Zen only because he read the books by Blyth and Suzuki and started to compose haiku. I think this haiku can be interpreted differently. I would like to interpret it in terms of Wright's interest in blues rather than in Zen because he rekindled his interest in blues in the 1950s.

Wright was a "blues man" throughout his life. As Ralph Ellison finds aspects of the blues in Wright's *Black Boy,* blues is a key to understand Wright's literary work.[44] In the 1930s Wright wrote several blues poems such as "Red Clay Blues" and "The FB Eye Blues."[45] He devoted much time to the study of the blues in the late 1930s and the early 1940s.[46] In his late years, Wright came to be interested in the blues again because he found that blues was not only an African American artistic heritage born out of the history of colonialism and black Diaspora but also a universal art which appealed beyond nations. Moreover, Wright was attracted to the blues because of its cathartic power. In 1959 Wright was asked to write the foreword to Paul Oliver's *Blues Fell This Morning.* In it, he writes as follows, "Yet the most astonishing aspect of the blues is that, though replete with a sense of defeat and down-heartedness, they are not intrinsically pessimistic; their burden of woe and melancholy is dialectically redeemed through sheer force of sensuality, into an almost exultant affirmation of life, of love, of sex, of movement, of hope. No matter how repressive was the American environment, the Negro never lost faith in or doubted his deeply endemic capacity to live."[47] In blues, Wright saw the power to overcome woe and melancholy. When he wrote "As my anger ebbs, / The spring stars grow bright again / And the wind returns," the spirit of blues could be with him, for the "spring stars" and "wind" seem to represent something more sensual and romantic than Zen enlightenment.

In his final years, Wright was fascinated with composing haiku, but we should not regard his haiku just as an imitation of Japanese poetry. Rather, it should be regarded as a new hybrid form of art, through which Wright tried to transcend his nationality. After Wright, African American writers such as Robert Hayden, Julius Lester, Etheridge Knight, and Sonia Sanchez have contributed to composing haiku and inventing a new form of modern African American literature. Considering how *Japonisme* started and developed in the Western countries, African American relation with *Japonisme* and Asian art should be given special attention because it has played an important role in cultivating the field of African Asian art, which could challenge the Western hegemony in literature.

Notes

1. Earl Miner, *The Japanese Tradition in British and American Literature* (Princeton, NJ: Princeton University Press, 1958), 69.

2. Ibid., 74.

3. Ibid., 273.

4. IBDB (Internet Broadway Database), *The Mikado*. http://www.ibdb.com (accessed March 16, 2008).

5. Yorimitsu Hashimoto, "Japanese Tea Party: Representations of Victorian Paradise and Playground in The Geisha (1896)," *Histories of Tourism: Representation, Identity and Conflict*, ed. John K. Walton (Clevedon: Channel View Publications, 2005), 104.

6. Andrew Lamb, "The Geisha," in *The Geisha: A Japanese Musical Play* by Sidney Jones (London: Hyperion Records, 1998), 5.

7. William Winter, *The Life of David Belasco* (New York: Mofatt, Yard, and Company, 1918), 109–11.

8. David Belasco, *Six Plays: Madame Butterfly, Du Barry, the Darling of the Gods, Adrea, the Girl of the Golden West, the Return of Peter Grimm*, ed. Montrose J. Moses (Boston: Little Brown, 1928), 142.

9. Bertrand Agostini, "The Development of French Haiku in the First Half of the 20th Century: Historical Perspectives," *Modern Haiku* 32, no. 2 (2001): 46–60. http://www.modernhaiku.org/essays/frenchhaiku.html (accessed March 16, 2008).

10. Charles Trumbull, "The American Haiku Movement Part I: Haiku in English," *Modern Haiku* 36, no. 3 (2005): 33–73. http://www.modernhaiku.org./essays/AmHaikuMovement1.html (accessed March 16, 2008).

11. Yoshinobu Hakutani, "Ezra Pound, Yone Noguchi, and Imagism," in *Modernity in East-West Literary Criticism*, ed. Yoshinobu Hakutani (Madison, NJ: Fairleigh Dickinson University Press, 2001), 67.

12. Stephen M. Vallillo, "The Battle of the Black Mikados," *Black American Literature Forum* 16 (1982): 153–54.

13. Ibid., 155.

14. Shannon Steen, "Racing American Modernity: Black Atlantic Negotiations of Asia and the 'Swing' Mikado," in *Afro Asian Encounter: Culture, History, Politics*, ed. Heike Raphael-Hernandez and Shannon Steen (New York: New York University Press, 2006), 170–71.

15. Toru Kiuchi, Robert J. Butler, and Yoshinobu Hakutani, eds., *The Critical Response in Japan to African American Writers* (New York: Peter Lang, 2003), ix.

16. Ibid.

17. David Levering Lewis, *When Harlem Was in Vogue* (New York: Penguin, 1979), 302.

18. Reginald Kearney, *African American Views of the Japanese: Solidarity or Sedition?* (New York: State University of New York Press, 1998), 19.

19. W. E. B. Du Bois, "The World Problem of the Color Line," in *W. E. B. Du Bois on Asia: Crossing the World Color Line*, ed. Bill V. Mullen and Cathryn Watson (Jackson: University Press of Mississippi, 2005), 33.

20. Bill V. Mullen, *Afro-Orientalism* (Minneapolis: University of Minnesota Press, 2004), 25–26.

21. Richard Wright, *12 Million Black Voices* (New York: Thunder's Mouth Press, 1988), 143.

22. Keneth Kinnamon and Michel Fabre, eds., *Conversation with Richard Wright* (Jackson: University Press of Mississippi, 1993), 165.

23. Vijay Prashad, *Everybody Was Kung Fu Fighting: Afro-Asian Connections and the Myth of Cultural Purity* (Boston: Beacon, 2001), 133.

24. Rick Fields, *How the Swans Came to the Lake: A Narrative History of Buddhism in America*, 3rd ed. (Boston: Shambhala, 1992), 136–37.

25. John R. McRae, "Oriental Verities on the American Frontier: The 1893 World's Parliament of Religions and the Thoughts of Masao Abe," *Buddhist-Christian Studies* 11 (1991): 26.

26. Fields, *How the Swans Came to the Lake,* 138–39.

27. Carl Jung, foreword to *An Introduction to Zen Buddhism* by D. T. Suzuki (New York: Grove Press, 1964), ix.

28. David L. McMahan, *The Making of Buddhist Modernism* (Oxford: Oxford University Press, 2008), 122.

29. Michel Fabre, *The Unfinished Quest of Richard Wright* (Urbana: University of Illinois Press, 1993), 238.

30. "Why Richard Wright Came Back from France," in *Conversations with Richard Wright,* ed. Keneth Kinnamon and Michel Fabre (Jackson: University Press of Mississippi, 1993), 124.

31. Margaret Walker, *Richard Wright: Demonic Genius* (New York: Amistad, 1988), 314.

32. Michel Fabre, "The Poetry of Richard Wright," in *Critical Essays on Richard Wright,* ed. Yoshinobu Hakutani (Boston: G. K. Hall, 1982), 270.

33. Robert L. Tener, "The Where, the When, the What: A Study of Richard Wright's Haiku," in *Critical Essays on Richard Wright,* 296.

34. Yoshinobu Hakutani, *Cross Cultural Visions in African American Modernism: From Spatial Narrative to Jazz Haiku* (Columbus: The Ohio State University Press, 2006), 155.

35. Yoshinobu Hakutani and Robert L. Tener, afterword to *Haiku: This Other World* by Richard Wright (New York: Arcade, 1998), 245.

36. Richard Wright, "Between the World and Me," *Richard Wright Reader,* ed. Ellen Wright and Michel Fabre (New York: Harper and Row, 1978), 246.

37. Abdul JanMohamed, *The Death-Bound Subject: Richard Wright's Archaeology of Death* (Durham: Duke University Press, 2005), 29.

38. Wright, "Between the World and Me," 247.

39. JanMohamed, *The Death-Bound Subject,* 29.

40. Hakutani, *Cross-Cultural Visions in African American Modernism,* 160.

41. Fabre, *The Unfinished Quest of Richard Wright,* 382.

42. Hakutani, *Cross-Cultural Visions in African American Modernism,* 160.

43. Ibid.

44. Ralph Ellison, "Richard Wright's Blues," *The Antioch Review* 5 (1945): 198–211.

45. Wright, *Richard Wright Reader,* 242–43.

46. Fabre, *The Unfinished Quest of Richard Wright,* 238.

47. Richard Wright, foreword to *Blues Fell This Morning* by Paul Oliver (New York: Cambridge University Press, 1990), xv.

Nature, the South, and Spain in *Haiku: This Other World*

— JIANQING ZHENG —

Richard Wright's *Haiku: This Other World,* published posthumously in 1998, is a record of his momentary joy, haunting ailments, wistful humor, dreamed return, exiled life, and loneliness. In contrast to his novels such as *Native Son* and *Black Boy,* this collection of 817 haiku received little attention from the public. The neglect could be that Wright was little known as a poet in the literary world even though he was "widely recognized as the father of the contemporary Afro-American novel"[1] or that there were "misunderstandings about haiku as a form of poetry. Perhaps most spring from certain misconceptions about why the novelist and essayist began to write haiku in 1959."[2] It could also be that Wright's haiku had waited too long for publication, thirty-eight years after his death in 1960.

Wright discovered haiku at a friend's house. There he met Sinclair Beiles, a young poet from South Africa, who introduced him to R. H. Blyth's four-volume *Haiku.* He was immediately enchanted with this Japanese poetic form and started writing his haiku when he was sick from amoebic dysentery in 1959.[3] Later he asked his wife to purchase a set of Blyth's *Haiku* in London.[4] Wright's boundless enthusiasm led eventually to a production of some 4,000 haiku. In a letter of September 23, 1960, to his friend Margrit de Sablonière, Wright wrote about his fascination: "I've finished nothing

---

Parts of the essay were previously published in *Southern Quarterly* 46, no. 2 (2009), *Frogpond* 30, no. 1 (2007), *and Notes on Contemporary Literature* 37, no. 2 (2007). Reprinted with permission of the author.

this year but those damned haikus, and I've not even looked at them since my friends in New York looked at them. I'll sit down one of these days and go over them, that is, reread them and see how they sound."[5] This large quantity of haiku shows the world that, in looking to nature for poetic and spiritual inspiration, Wright found a way to reveal his true self for a harmonious union with nature and to enjoy through this harmony the aesthetic faculties of natural beauty.

Technically, a haiku presents the occurrence of an event at present time. It emphasizes the spiritual fusion of human beings with nature. Because of its characteristics such as terse pattern, concrete expression, and present time, haiku has a strong tendency to be "intuitive rather than intellectual or allusive."[6] As a haiku poet and, more important, a humanist, Wright knew how to transform his sensibility to nature into vivid images so as to reflect his view of both nature and human nature. In most of his fiction, Wright used his pen as a loudspeaker to cry out the pain and suffering of African American people in a segregated country and as a weapon to accuse the social injustice he had witnessed and experienced. But, in his haiku, he used his pen as a brush to paint his tender feelings of nature and human nature. When we read Richard Wright in the twenty-first century, it is of perennial significance to examine the poetic values of his haiku that show his true self as a human being and that reflect a change in his writing.

There is no doubt that his haiku collection shows a change in his writing. In talking about the change in Wright's writing after he left America, Margaret Walker, who befriended Wright in their early years in Chicago, comments that Wright "suffered a kind of sea-change in Paris. His daemonic powers lessened. His imaginative writing was no longer frenetic, neither electric nor as freely mercurial. If the voice within him was not still, it was at least less vociferous . . . . Mind and body he wandered over the earth seeking always a common ground of humanity . . . . But despite his constant fight against dehumanizing forces of racism, anti-Semitism, imperialism, including colonialism and neocolonialism, he never found that common ground of humanity."[7] Walker may be right in saying that Wright's power in his writings has lessened, but she may not be right in saying that Wright has never found his common ground of humanity. In fact, Paris guaranteed "a certain social and aesthetic freedom" for Wright.[8] It is doubtless that Wright's writings experienced a sea-change in Paris, but this was a change that helped him switch his focus from America to other parts of the world, from the human society to nature where he could find calmness, balance, and harmony, especially during his period of illness, and view the world from a new angle.

When he was a black boy in the Deep South, Wright suffered very much from his miserable life and racial discrimination. When he became a writer, he felt it was his responsibility to "battle the ignorance, violence, starvation, misery, bigotry and hopelessness that surrounded his childhood until he had beaten them for himself, and then turn around and try to beat them for all American Negroes."[9] Believing that people in the United States should be integrated, Wright said in an interview in May 1945, "As I see it, integration—complete equality—is the only solution, and as an artist I want to bring out the oneness of human life."[10] When he was invited by the French government to visit Paris in 1946, he saw a different world where he had "not detected the least iota of racial tension against the Negroes."[11] A year later, Wright went back to Paris as an expatriated American writer. He decided to leave his own country because he loved freedom and needed more of it. To him, "freedom . . . is equated to concrete reality, to life; it is not something abstract, something to be won or hoped for; it is life itself, each day, each hour, each moment . . . ."[12]

Another reason was his "desire to escape the racial pressure of the United States."[13] Wright was probably despaired in his struggle with the racial dilemma in his native land where he spent his life "fighting for the rights of the Negro people.[14] He says, "I knew that that fight was, morally and legally, a correct one; that it was supported by our democratic traditions and our Constitution. Yet, deep down, during all of those years, I felt that there was something organically wrong with a nation that could so cynically violate its own laws in meting out cruelties upon a helpless minority."[15] When asked in an interview why he felt more at home in Paris, Wright answered that he was an American and would live and die an American, but personally he leant to the European world-feeling. He emphasized that "this was not a matter of intellectual processes, but of feeling."[16] However, whether or not Wright really found "freedom" in Paris is discussable. Jerry W. Ward notes that "what [Wright] found was relative freedom from racial oppression rather than a paradise of racial freedom!"[17]

This geographical and emotional change for living and feeling played an important part in the second half of Wright's writing career. He no longer focused his writing solely on the African American life in America; instead, he began to turn his attention to Africa, Europe, and Asia. His worldview helped broaden his vision of human values and urged him to write such books as *Black Power, Pagan Spain*, and *The Color Curtain*. This change of feeling and attitude became greater when Wright discovered Japanese haiku. He was completely attracted by its minimal form. Ollie W. Harrington, his friend and also an American expatriate in Paris at the time, remembers that "when Dick wasn't tramping in the woods or sitting with the voluble Norman peasants in a café "down the road," he was engrossed in his newest obsession. One uses the term obsession because Dick admitted that since he'd discovered it he was completely incapable of stopping. . . . Wright found in them a remarkable control of words and symbols and plunged into one of his characteristically meticulous and exhaustive studies."[18]

Unfortunately, Wright's health was declining from recurring amoebic attacks while he was engrossed in haiku practice. He had also suffered from exhaustion, fever, and weight loss. Julia Wright says that her father's haiku "were self-developed antidotes against illness, and that breaking down words into syllables matched the shortness of his breath, especially on the bad days when his inability to sit up at the typewriter restricted the very breadth of writing."[19] She says that haiku 647 speaks especially well for her father's legacy:[20]

> Burning out its time,
> And timing its own burning,
> One lonely candle.

However, this lonely candle burned out its time with the prolific production of 4,000 haiku. It was likely that Wright wrote haiku against illness, out of loneliness, and for oneness with nature and that writing haiku had a healing power on him. Yet, to a great extent, his haiku writing was a search for beauty either in nature or in human nature. To achieve this, he presented a colorful world of his spiritual union with nature through images of the sun, the moon, the low of a cow, the flowers, the bell, the rain, and the butterfly. Read haiku 45 with an image of the sun:

As though for always
Each petal lit by the sun,—
Apple blossoms!

This haiku, in its minimal scope, encompasses the infinity of nature through the speaker's exclamation about the transient beauty of sun-lit apple petals. The interaction between the apple blossoms and the sun offers an ecstatic moment of celebration of beauty. Haiku 62 is also about the sun:

A lance of spring sun
Falls upon the moldy oats
In a musty barn.

There is a contrast between the spring sun and the moldy oats in a musty barn. The former image extols beauty of spring while the latter one suggests decay in the human world, but the juxtaposition of the first two visual images along with the olfactory image of the musty barn creates a sense of coexistence of birth and decay in the recycling process of nature and the human world.

Haiku writing requires poets to present beauty of nature through images. In Wright's haiku celebrating beauty is prevailing, and one of the most important characteristics of his haiku is the presentation of beauty with a sad, controlled tone. This sad beauty can be perceived especially through the image of the moon. Read haiku 145:

A bright glowing moon
Pouring out its radiance
Upon tall tombstones.

The theme of this haiku is death. The humanized moon pouring its serene light on the dead brings out sad beauty of nature and controlled mourning of the speaker. The third line evokes a poignant sensibility that Wright might have experienced. Julia Wright feels that her father's haiku "attempted to bring closure to the numerous mournings he experienced during the same period" when he was obsessed with haiku writing.[21] In 1958 and 1959, news of death after death of his friends and of his beloved mother brought grief to Wright. Ed Aswell, who was Wright's favorite editor, died. Then the death of his mother, Ella, hit Wright deeply. To add to his grief was the accidental death of Albert Camus, a French writer Wright befriended and highly admired. Then George Padmore, a close friend and co-traveler with Wright to Africa, died unexpectedly in London where Wright planned to move the family after he sold his farmhouse in Ailly, Normandy.

Although the moon conveys sad feelings in haiku 145, it also brings out in contrast a pleasant, sensational surprise, as in haiku 469:

> The spring flood waters
> Lap slowly at the doorsteps,—
> A radiant moon.

This haiku shows that Wright is irrevocably an artist with keen sensibility to nature. The two parts of the poem, spring waters and radiant moon, are well juxtaposed to allow for internal comparison. Both literal images interact to each other through visual and auditory senses to create a synesthetic effect. Such concurrence of sensations appeals deceptively to more than one sense so that a reader either hears the radiance of the moonlight or sees the lapping of the spring waters.

One prominent part of Wright's haiku is the use of the image of the sun or the moon to present the landscape of the South. Haiku 38 is a good example:

> That abandoned house,
> With its yard of fallen leaves,
> In the setting sun.

This haiku presents a desolate picture of the South. Instead of telling us directly, Wright conveys the meaning through the combination of images that make a reader feel intuitively. Further, the montage of the close-up of the abandoned house and fallen leaves followed by the long shot of the setting sun creates a perspective that Wright is not unfamiliar with when he was a black boy living in the villages and small towns in Mississippi and

Arkansas. Although the sun functions as an intensifier of desolation in this haiku, in other haiku of his, it functions as a soothing power that brings warmth to a person's poor life, as in haiku 60:

> Sun is glinting on
> A washerwoman's black arms
> In cold creek water.

"Black arms in cold creek water" may suggest the washerwoman cannot receive warmth from the human society, but ironically, she can have it, though momentarily, from nature. Haiku 345 is another haiku that shows Wright's memory of the South:

> The sad sound of hymns
> Flooding on to autumn fields
> In hazy moonlight.

This is certainly a blues haiku that reminds a reader of the sad, old days on the plantations in the Deep South. Through his haiku Wright re-familiarizes himself and the reader with the cultural landscape of the South.

The South keeps pulling a chord in Wright's haiku, as shown in haiku 725:

> From a cotton field
> To magnolia trees,
> A bridge of swallows.

This haiku presents a visual picture of the South with mainly two Southern images: cotton field and magnolia trees. The static, slumberous picture is touched alive with a bridge of swallows. In Wright's haiku, South is a place full of dreams, memories, beautiful scenes, and loneliness as well. His vivid description of the South in *12 Million Black Voices* seems represented in his haiku: "In summer the magnolia trees fill the countryside with sweet scent for long miles. Days are slumberous, and the skies are high and thronged with clouds that ride fast. At midday the sun blazes and bleaches the soil. Butterflies flit through the heat; wasps sing their sharp, straight lines; birds fluff and flounce. . . . The throaty boast of frogs momentarily drowns out the call and counter-call of crickets."[22]

To Wright, memory of the South can also mean sadness and homesickness, as described in the following three haiku:

Is this tiny pond
The great big lake in which
I swam as a boy? (559)

A bloody knife blade
Is being licked by a cat
At hog-killing time. (30)

Don't they make you sad,
Those wild geese winging southward,
O lonely scarecrow? (581)

Memory seems a sad loss in haiku 559. Time has changed; ecology has changed; and man has changed as well. This haiku reveals Wright's sadness when he sees the lake, now a small pond, in which he swam. Haiku 30 and 581, which express Wright's memory of the South, may be the echoes of nostalgia in *12 Million Black Voices* in which he says, "In autumn the land is afire with color. . . . hogs are slaughtered and cured in lingering smoke; corn is husked and ground into meal. At twilight the sky is full of wild geese winging ever southward . . ."[23] Meaningfully, Wright's haiku on the South display valuable cultural treasure and heritage; they also convey the poet's memories of the lost days in the South.

Another image that appears in Wright's haiku on the South is the rain. For example, in haiku 565, Wright writes emotionally of his mother:

A slow autumn rain:
The sad eyes of my mother
Fill a lonely night.

This is one of the best haiku by Wright because he uses the technique of internal comparison to juxtapose rain and his mother's sad eyes. This juxtaposition intensifies his remembrance and lonely feeling in an autumn night. Writing this haiku, Wright must have recalled the old days of poverty and his mother's suffering. When they lived in a tenement in Memphis, he told his mother one afternoon that he was hungry, she paused her ironing and looked at him with tears in her eyes. In *Black Boy*, Wright talks emotionally:

> My mother's suffering grew into a symbol in my mind, gathering to itself all the poverty, the ignorance, the helplessness; the painful, baffling, hunger-ridden days and hours; the restless moving, the futile seeking, the uncertainty, the fear, the dread; the meaningless pain and the endless suffering. Her life set the emotional tone of my life. . . . A somberness of spirit that I was never to lose settled over me during the slow years of my mother's unrelieved suffering, a somberness that was to make me stand apart and look upon excessive joy with suspicion, that was to make me self-conscious, that was to make me keep forever on the move, as though to escape a nameless fate seeking to overtake me.[24]

Wright presents in haiku 565 a moment of seeing sad beauty in the South. However, in other rain haiku of his, he offers us a chance to see natural beauty and his joy with nature. See how the raindrops bring out aesthetic pleasure in haiku 76:

> The path in the woods
> Is barred by spider webs
> Beaded with spring rain.

A haiku is usually fragmentary with two parts of literal images linked by a caesura to suggest an implicit contrast or a metaphorical montage. Because of its conciseness and presentness, haiku uses images to describe an intuitive feeling for an intellectual or aesthetic appreciation. Although haiku 76 is a complete sentence that may not allow for imagination or for the effect of juxtaposition, it is still a good one for it shows that natural beauty exists in things simple and inter-dependable; it also shows that

Wright relates his sensibility to every simple thing in nature that gives him a pleasant surprise. To him, things in nature reflect the inscapes of his spiritual oneness with the natural world. Here is another haiku that depicts rain and spider:

> Escaping spring rain,
> Scuttling over a door sill,
> A fuzzy spider. (796)

Because of its concrete brevity, a haiku refuses abstract ideas and detailed description, but its incompleteness challenges the reader to fill his correspondence through the spontaneous effect of seeing and feeling. This haiku shows the keen perception of the speaker who sees a fuzzy spider escaping the spring rain. It may also suggest that the speaker cannot escape his loneliness or desperation implied in the image of the scuttling spider.

Traditionally, haiku is a poetic form that requires the use of *kigo*, a season indicator. In Wright's haiku, lauding the arrival of spring is a favorite theme, as in haiku 3:

> Keep straight down this block,
> Then turn right where you will find
> A peach tree blooming.

On the surface, the speaker gives direction to a person who is eager to see a blooming peach tree, a true beauty of nature in spring, but in a deeper sense, he wants to find his joy and symbolic union with nature in every moment he can catch. In turn, his joy becomes a curiosity about the outside world, as shown also in haiku 80:

> After the rainstorm,
> A tendril of Wisteria
> Peeps over the wall.

or a pleasant surprise when realizing his affinity with nature, as in haiku 110:

I laid down my book:
A tendril of Wisteria
Encircling my leg.

Wright is a lover of nature in most of his haiku. Through the transience of a peeping or encircling tendril of wisteria, he catches a glimpse of beauty that can be easily overlooked in the mundane world.

As discussed earlier, beauty relies on interaction not only between nature and human nature but between natural images as well, whether they are transient or infinite. In haiku 82, Wright presents beauty of nature through the visual images of the sunshine and the fluttering wings of a butterfly:

A butterfly makes
The sunshine even brighter
With fluttering wings.

The sunshine becomes brighter and kinetic through the fluttering of the wings. In the same way, the butterfly looks more beautiful when it flutters against the sunshine. The interaction between light and motion intensifies natural beauty. Haiku 597 is another butterfly poem that describes a scene in which both the butterfly and the blind man form an inseparable part of a lovely picture:

A slow encircling,
Inquisitive butterfly
Follows the blindman.

Wright's love of nature is also depicted in his haiku about farm life, which is an organic component of Wright's haiku world. In his heart, Wright always wanted to live on a farm where he could feel closer to nature. When he was a teenager in Mississippi, he had the desire to run away from the plantation farm since he could not tolerate the suffering of hunger and racial discrimination, but when he became an exile in Paris in his middle age, he had the desire to live on a farm where there was no struggle for freedom except peace and farming. In 1957, he purchased an old farmhouse in Ailly, Normandy, where he could devote his time to writing and thinking without any disturbance. While settling down there, Wright "suddenly realized that above all he was a man of the country. He needed the smoky, dawn-shrouded fields, the ever-busy birds and the cattle lowing in the mist."[25] His desire for a lonely, peaceful farm life is obvious in haiku 352:

Why do I listen
To each low of the cow
This still autumn night?

Through his listening, Wright yearns to identify with nature. We can feel the implicit loneliness of the speaker through his listening. This haiku conveys a sense of *sabi*, a haiku term that is traditionally related to beauty with loneliness.

In Japanese haiku tradition, autumn night always implies the sense of loneliness; for example, in Matsuo Bashō's famous crow poem:

On the dead limb
squats a crow—
autumn night[26]

A resonance of loneliness is at once created through the superposition of a lonely crow on a dead limb upon the autumn night. Bashō's haiku is also a good example that uses *sabi*, which means "a sense of beauty and spiritual depth in loneliness and tranquility, especially in natural images, generating a subtle sentiment that emerges quietly in the overtones of the poem."[27] Wright's haiku 442 is another poem with an image of the cow that shows his feeling with the use of *sabi*:

Over yellow corn,
As muted as the sunset,
The low of a cow.

This haiku also conveys a sense of loneliness in tranquility. The second line indicates that quiet beauty is intensified by the low of a cow that deepens the speaker's feeling of loneliness.

The sensibility of *sabi* is also visualized in haiku 501:

Autumn moonlight is
Deepening the emptiness
Of a country road.

The beauty of this haiku is that it uses the technique of narrowing focus that starts with a contrast between the sky and the earth: the wide-angle lens on the autumn moonlight switches to a close-up of an empty or down-hearted country road. Eugene E. Miller mentions in *Voice of a Native Son* that "Wright was aware of a functional similarity between the haiku form and the lyrics of folk blues, both of which work by juxtaposing or superimposing disparate elements."[28] Maybe blues played a tune in Wright's creative thinking when he wrote haiku 501. In *Blues Fell This Morning: Meaning in the Blues,* to which Wright wrote a foreword in 1959, there is a blues song on a lonely road that may reverberate with haiku 501:

Look down that long old lonesome road,
My poor feet is tired but still I've got to go.

There's no train to my home town, there ain't but the one way to,
There's mile after mile, stepping down that long old muddy road.

There ain't but one thing that worries me both night and day,
That's the place they call Death Valley, and it's just half-way.

I've been tramping this lonely road, night after night and day after day,
If your prayers don't help me, you know I'll die trying to make my way.[29]

About the astonishing aspect of blues, Wright says that "though replete with a sense of defeat and down-heartedness, they are not intrinsically pessimistic; their burden of woe and melancholy is dialectically redeemed through sheer force of sensuality, into an almost exultant affirmation of life. . . . All blues are a lusty, lyrical realism charged with taut sensibility."[30] His words should add a footnote to his country road haiku.

If haiku 442 and 501 stress a sense of loneliness in nature, the following haiku, which also uses *sabi,* transcends human loneliness to nature:

An old blindman
Playing a black violin
Amid fallen leaves. (367)

Here loneliness drifts along with the sound of the violin played by the old blind man, and it is intensified with the color of the violin, the blindness, and the fallen leaves. Another poem that shows transcendence is haiku 671:

A pale winter moon,
Pitying a lonely doll,
Lent it a shadow.

This is a well-crafted haiku because the poet does not express his emotion but detach himself from it. Loneliness is intensified through the interaction between the winter moon and the doll. The doll, a man-made object, alludes indirectly to human loneliness. Wright dissolves the speaker's personal loneliness into the impersonal object through the doll. This depersonalized feeling becomes stronger with the shadow of the winter moon on the doll. Even though the speaker can seek consolation in nature, it is ironic that the pale winter moon itself is an image of loneliness.

Moreover, Wright's haiku on the South also present an atmosphere of *sabi*, for instance, the persona's loneliness expressed in haiku 636:

How lonely it is:
A rattling freight train has left
Fields of croaking frogs.

After the train rattles past, perhaps with the speaker's dream, what has left with him are the fields of croaking frogs. This haiku echoes one of Bashō's:

Loneliness—
Standing amid the blossoms,
A cypress tree.

Makoto Ueda notes that loneliness in Bashō's haiku does not refer to "a man's personal emotion; it is describing an impersonal atmosphere, a mood created by a natural landscape."[31] In the same way, Wright's haiku 636 presents a lonely atmosphere, but it is the loneliness of the freight train. In a sense, nature, represented by the croaking frogs, shows no emotion but provides a backstage for loneliness. Wright's haiku resembles Bashō's in the expression of an impersonal attitude toward life. Further, it reflects the Zen philosophy of lonelilessness beyond loneliness.

However, music and bell are the two beautiful thematic parts of Wright's haiku world. In the following haiku, the interaction of natural images in the first two lines and the human creation of flute in the third creates a harmonious picture of imagination that involves the working of the senses:

From across the lake,
Past the black winter trees,
Faint sounds of a flute. (571)

Haiku 339 is about the bell:

A cathedral bell
Dimming the river water
In the autumn dusk.

This one displays the transference from the auditory image of the bell to the visual one of the dim river water and builds up an immediate connection between human beings and nature.

Travel is also a significant theme in Wright's haiku. While living as an American intellectual in Paris in the 1950s, Wright made three trips to Spain, from August 15 to September 10, 1954; from November 8 to December 17, 1954; and from February 20 to early April 1955. These trips provided valuable resources not only for *Pagan Spain* but also for his haiku writing. *Pagan Spain*, says Wright in an interview by Barry Learned, is a descriptive account of three automobile trips he "made in Spain, the Spanish people [he] met, the fiestas, flamencos, bullfights, the feeling of the country, the warmth of the people and the incredible poverty."[32]

It seems that Wright made his initial trip to Spain as if to pay his indebtedness to Gertrude Stein, another American expatriate in Paris. In the second paragraph of *Pagan Spain,* Wright remembers that in his chat with Stein a few days before her death in 1946, she encouraged him to go to see Spain: "You'll see the past there. You'll see what the Western world is made of. Spain is primitive, but lovely. And the people! There are no people such as the Spanish anywhere. I've spent days in Spain that I'll never forget. See those bullfights, see the wonderful landscape."[33] So Wright made his Spanish trip. He was alone in his car near the border, and this vision of loneliness was intensified when he posed himself in the vast silence of the bleak landscape: "I was under the blue skies of the Midi, just a few hours from the Spanish frontier. To my right stretched the flat, green fields of southern France; to my left lay a sweep of sand beyond which the Mediterranean heaved and sparkled. I was alone. I had no commitments. Seated in my car, I held the steering wheel in my hands. I wanted to go to Spain."[34] This statement indicates that Wright was a careful observer at the crossroads. It presents him immediately in "a cosmic moment of destiny."[35] Swinging his car southward, Wright was on his way to Spain with an uneasy question in his mind: "How did one live after the death of the hope for freedom?"[36]

Having lived in France for a few years, Wright thought he had freedom, but he felt uneasy when he witnessed that the Spanish people lived without the hope of freedom. His witness should provoke him to ponder upon the real meaning of freedom and the human values in a totalitarian country in civilized Europe, the continent where "the individual is placed at the top of a carefully graded scale of values."[37] The first Spanish village Wright saw was "in a pall of heat and dust. Scrawny black goats nibbled at starved grass; stunted, barefoot boys minded dreamy sheep. . . . The irregular paving stones made my car do a nervous dance. The walls of the whitewashed houses held lurid bullfight posters. This village was conspicuous for the prevalence of dogs in it."[38] Wright presents here a picture of poverty and suffering in human life. The prevalence of dogs reinforces his vision of the desolation of the Spanish village. However, in contrast, Wright presents a different picture of the Spanish village in haiku 396:

A Spanish village:
Flowers and gurgling water,—
How silent it is!

This haiku shows that although Spain was under Franco's dictatorship and its people lived in poverty, Wright could still catch its beauty through the images of flowers and gurgling water that flesh out peace and tranquility in this Spanish village. When we compare the descriptions of the two villages, we can feel that the beauty of silence through flowers and water tones down the suffering and poverty in the Spanish country life.

One thing that is prominent in *Pagan Spain* is Wright's description of the bullfight. While visiting Barcelona, Wright went to see one. Seated on the bare slab of concrete and jammed between two other people, Wright awaited the bull to thunder out the gate: "A wild, black, horned beast, his eyes ablaze, his nostrils quivering, his mouth open and flinging foam, his throat emitting a bellow. He halted for a second, amazed, it seemed, at the spectacle confronting him, then he settled squarely and fearlessly on his four hoofs, ready to lower his head and charge at the least sign of movement, his sharp horns carrying the threat of death, his furious tenacity swollen with a will that would brook no turning aside until all movement about him had been struck down, stilled, and he alone was left lord and master of the bloody field."[39] The sight of this black bull made Wright feel that it was "a complement of a subjective part of almost everybody in the stadium" and "a creature of our common fantasy."[40] He was interested "not only in the emotional but the psychological, cultural, and even spiritual dimensions of the spectacle."[41] In fact, Wright wanted to see into the inner being of human nature through the bullfight. The killing of the bull is like a religious ritual because "death must serve as a secular baptism of emotion to wash the heart clean of its illegal dirt."[42] Wright saw in the killing, which is "beautiful and awful and horrible and glorious," a fusion of man and bull into "one plastic, slow-moving, terrible, delicate waltz of death."[43] Finally the bull was cruelly slaughtered to satisfy the emotional and psychological needs of human beings to kill: "He slid slowly forward, resting on his stomach in the sand, his legs stretching straight out. He rolled over on his back, his four legs already stiffening in death, shot up into the air."[44] The scene of the slaughtering of the bull is evoked in haiku 68:

A chill Spanish dawn:
Vapor from the blood of a
Freshly slaughtered bull.

Wright realizes in *Pagan Spain* that "in Spain, all things were Spanish,"[45] not only the bullfight, but the dawn as well. Here, in haiku 68, death becomes equivalent to birth and mystically symbolizes the cycle in nature. As a writer traveling in Spain and watching the bullfights, Wright can easily juxtapose the red dawn to the blood of a freshly killed bull.

Wright was a lone traveler. One morning when the sky was still black he got up at five o'clock and drove toward Madrid. On a mountain along the way he paused in awe as "a brutal sun burst forth from behind jagged, fantastically sculptured rocks and painted the wildest and most savage landscape . . . . Naked promontories of rubble jutted up into a pale, flat, blue sky that refused to bend at the horizon. An uneasy loneliness settled upon me, for I drove hour after hour and failed to see a single other car. The highway was an empty path stretching through an empty world, belonging only to me, the desolate peak, the sun-filled sky, and the whirling birds."[46] The sight of the Spanish landscape, though it was magnificent and aesthetically enjoyable, aroused a feeling of loneliness in Wright. He "could not conceive of its sustaining human life."[47] The above passage is reminiscent of haiku 787:

This autumn evening
Is full of an empty sky
And one empty road.

This haiku is wonderful in that it conveys the traveler's loneliness but depersonalizes his emotion. The poet delineates an outline for the reader to complete: a fullness of emptiness or loneliness expands and takes the world. Wright's expression of loneliness in this haiku is again based on *sabi* that suggests "a sense of beauty and spiritual depth in loneliness and tranquility, especially in natural images"[48] that help the poet and the reader to empathize with nature. In Wright's haiku the juxtaposition of the autumn evening and the empty sky and road intensifies and deepens the sense of loneliness.

Faith Berry has noted in his introduction to *Pagan Spain* that "the 1950s marked a profound change in the literary and intellectual life of Richard Wright. . . . During his fourteen-year residence abroad, he produced, beside several new novels, a sequence of important nonfiction books that established him internationally. In those publications, a new and liberated Richard Wright emerged: one whose identity was not that of a second-class American citizen but a citizen of the world."[49] But I think this change should also include some 4,000 haiku Wright wrote. These haiku indicate that Wright had set his writing in a new direction: digging out his long latent sensibility to nature rather than keeping his focus only on the dark aspects of the human world and racial intolerance that he had dealt with for almost all his life. As we have discussed so far, Wright's haiku world should mainly be an integral combination of nature and human nature. Through these haiku, a reader sees an artist in Wright who showed his desire for spiritual oneness with nature and created a colorful world of haiku moments.

While living in France, Wright expected to find "serenity and harmony."[50] Fortunately, he found both in his haiku. However, a reader needs to know that the majority of Wright's haiku lack the quality of a good haiku composed of two parts to allow for internal comparison. In other words, most of his haiku "work perfectly well as short Western poems"[51] rather than as haiku. Luckily, however, the merits of his haiku lie in that nature fulfilled him and made him an integrated part of it. This is where his great achievement exists in the change of his writing. Reading Wright's haiku, a reader can feel that he sees nature through Wright's eyes, walks to nature in Wright's footsteps, and experiences nature through Wright's sensibility. In a sense, the Wright that emerged from his haiku is indeed a pleasure to read.

Notes

1. Michel Fabre, *The World of Richard Wright* (Jackson: University Press of Mississippi, 1985), 34.

2. Robert L. Tener, "Richard Wright's *Haiku: This Other World*," in *Modernity in East-West Literary Criticism*, ed. Yoshinobu Hakutani (Madison, NJ: Fairleigh Dickinson University Press, 2001), 137.

3. "After visiting Africa, during the summer Wright falls ill from amoebic dysentery and is hospitalized in the American Hospital in Neuilly where he starts writing his haiku poetry." Ellen Wright and Michel Fabre, eds., *Richard Wright Reader* (New York: Harper and Row, 1978), 875.

4. Fabre, *Richard Wright Books and Writers* (Jackson: University Press of Mississippi, 1990), 14.

5. Fabre, *The World of Richard Wright*, 54. According to Constance Webb, Wright completed 4,000 haiku within a few months. See Webb's *Richard Wright: A Biography* (New York: Putnam, 1968), 393. See also Wright's letter to Margrit de Sablonière on March 19, 1960, that says: "During my illness I experimented with the Japanese form of poetry called haiku; I wrote some 4,000 of them and am now sifting them out to see if they are any good." Quoted from Michel Fabre's *The Unfinished Quest of Richard Wright* (Urbana: University of Illinois Press, 1993), 505.

6. Haruo Shirane, *Traces of Dreams* (Stanford: Stanford University Press, 1998), 21.

7. Margaret Walker, *Richard Wright: Daemonic Genius* (New York: Amistad Press, 1988), 212.

8. M. Lynn Weiss, *Gertrude Stein and Richard Wright: The Poetics and Politics of Modernism* (Jackson: University Press of Mississippi, 1998), 4.

9. Mary Braggiotti, "Misery Begets Genius," in *Conversations with Richard Wright*, ed. Keneth Kinnamon and Michel Fabre (Jackson: University Press of Mississippi, 1993), 57–58.

10. Charles J. Rolo, "This, Too, Is America," in *Conversations with Richard Wright*, 70.

11. Anne Perlman, "Richard Wright, Negro Author, Is Here to Make Home in Paris," in *Conversations with Richard Wright*, 91.

12. Richard Wright, "I Choose Exile," in *The Writer's Presence*, ed. Donald McQuade and Robert Atwan (Boston: Bedford/St. Martin's, 2003), 289.

13. Ibid.

14. Ibid., 290.

15. Ibid.

16. Allan Temko, "An Interview with Expatriate Richard Wright in Paris," in *Conversations with Richard Wright*, 151.

17. Jerry W. Ward, letter to author, July 20, 2010.

18. Ollie W. Harrington, *Why I Left America and Other Essays* (Jackson: University Press of Mississippi, 1993), 14–15.

19. Julia Wright, introduction to *Haiku: This Other World* by Richard Wright, ed. Yoshinobu Hakutani and Robert L. Tener (New York: Arcade, 1998), viii.

20. According to Constance Webb, "Later, in her father's empty study, Julia sat with his haikus. Finally, she picked up a pen and wrote: 'This is Daddy.'" Constance Webb, *Richard Wright: A Biography* (New York: Putnam, 1968), 400.

21. Julia Wright, ibid., viii.

22. Richard Wright, *12 Million Black Voices* (New York: Thunder's Mouth Press, 1988), 32.

23. Ibid.

24. Richard Wright, *Black Boy* (New York: Perennial, 1998), 100.

25. Harrington, *Why I Left America and Other Essays*, 9.

26. Bashō, *On Love and Barley: Haiku of Bashō*, trans. Lucien Stryk (New York: Penguin, 1985), 35.

27. Shirane, *Traces of Dreams*, 297.

28. Eugene E. Miller, *Voice of a Native Son: The Poetics of Richard Wright* (Jackson: University Press of Mississippi, 1990), 239.

29. Paul Oliver, *Blues Fell This Morning: Meaning in the Blues* (Cambridge: Cambridge University Press, 1960), 54–55.

30. Richard Wright, foreword to *Blues Fell This Morning*, xv.

31. Makoto Ueda, *Literacy and Art Theories in Japan* (Cleveland: Press of Western Reserve University, 1967), 149.

32. Barry Learned, "U.S. Lets Negro Explain Race Ills, Wright Declares," in *Conversations with Richard Wright*, 185.

33. Richard Wright, *Pagan Spain* (Jackson: University Press of Mississippi, 1995), 4.

34. Ibid., 3.

35. John Lowe, "Richard Wright as Traveler / Ethnographer," in *Richard Wright's Travel Writings*, ed. Virginia Whatley Smith (Jackson: University Press of Mississippi, 2001), 120.

36. Wright, *Pagan Spain*, 4.

37. Wright, "I Choose Exile," 290.

38. Wright, *Pagan Spain*, 9.

39. Ibid., 111.

40. Ibid., 112.

41. Keneth Kinnamon, "Wright, Hemingway, and the Bullfight," in *Richard Wright's Travel Writings*, ed. Virginia Whatley Smith (Jackson: University Press of Mississippi, 2001), 162.

42. Wright, *Pagan Spain*, 114.

43. Ibid., 126.

44. Ibid., 129.

45. Ibid., 114.

46. Ibid., 136.

47. Ibid.

48. Shirane, *Traces of Dreams*, 297.

49. Faith Berry, introduction to *Pagan Spain*, ix.

50. Michel Fabre, *From Harlem to Paris* (Urbana: University of Illinois Press, 1991), 176.

51. Lee Gurga, "Richard Wright's Place in American Haiku," *Valley Voices: A Literary Review* 8, no. 2 (2008): 41.

Richard Wright's Place in American Haiku

— LEE GURGA —

Richard Wright's haiku are a subject of perennial interest. Their charm and simplicity have universal appeal. Their contrast, in tone and subject, to his other writings makes them stand apart, especially in the context of the poverty, racial hatred, and governmental harassment to which he was subjected. Ultimately, however, Wright's haiku must stand or fall on their own merits in this poetic genre. To judge them in any other way would be a disservice both to Wright's achievements and to the unique beauty of haiku.

To assess Wright's poems, however, we need to answer several questions. What, in fact, is haiku? How do his haiku measure up against well-recognized aesthetic principles of haiku? How do his haiku stand up against the best of English-language haiku? While the examination of Wright's haiku in relation to these questions may not enable us to praise his haiku uncritically, it will enable us to see what makes his good haiku succeed and give us an idea of his true place in American haiku.

To evaluate Wright's poems, one must first be able to answer the question, "What is haiku?" With the limited resources Wright had available, his answer might have been something like "a poem, originally Japanese, with five, seven, and five syllables in three lines." As Julia Wright quotes her father, "It's always five and seven and five like math. So you can't go wrong."[1] One can judge Wright's haiku by the standard that any poem in this 5-7-5 pattern is haiku, but this superficial understanding of haiku as haiku form does not communicate what is unique about the haiku genre.

In his book *Haiku in English,* Harold Henderson described what he considered the four general rules of Japanese haiku and proposed that writers of English-language haiku would have to explore each of them and adapt them to our language.[2] These rules are form, nature reference, reference to a particular event, and the presentation of this event in the present rather than the past tense. In addition, he discussed the use of the fundamental haiku technique of internal comparison, in which a haiku is made up of two images that interact imaginatively with each other.[3] I will discuss each of these guidelines briefly in relation to Wright's haiku. I will also discuss the use of literal images and figurative language.

First is form. Taking the understanding that Japanese haiku is composed of seventeen syllables, some people somehow get the idea that anything written in seventeen syllables in English constitutes a haiku even though the nature of syllables differs greatly between Japanese and English. What seems most difficult for some people to understand is that haiku is a genre of poetry, not merely a form.

Indeed, the great majority of haiku now published in English does not follow a set syllabic form, but pay greater attention to another aspect of haiku form, its internal structure. Haiku are generally composed of two parts with a caesura or pause between them. When the images comprising the two parts are well chosen, this pause allows for internal comparison between the images. When the poem is written in three lines, the pause usually occurs at the end of either the first or the second line. This produces two parts of unequal length, which preserves the asymmetry that is an important characteristic of Japanese haiku form. Kôji Kawamoto has named these two parts the "base" and the "superposed part"[4] According to Kawamoto, the base of the poem provides interest while the superposed part provides significance.

Seasonal references were originally included in haiku to evoke the time of the year in which the poem was composed. But some poets, beginning with the great Japanese haiku master Bashō, recognized that the seasonal reference contained within it the seeds of something much more powerful. By connecting the experience of a single moment to the universal forces of change and renewal, the seasonal reference has developed into haiku's most powerful tool to engage the reader: it enables the poet to invoke the whole of the natural world with a single image, and thus suggest the infinite with the finite. The effort to maintain the seasonal reference while remaining true to contemporary experience is one of the greatest challenges of haiku today.

Haiku tries to record a singular experience in the present tense, the so-called haiku moment. James Joyce called moments like these "epiphanies." Czeslaw Milosz remarks, "Epiphany is an unveiling of reality . . . when we intuitively grasp a deeper, more essential reality hidden in things or persons."[5] These are the kinds of moments the best haiku present.

The primary technique for conveying significance in haiku is internal comparison, brought about by carefully juxtaposing two or more images. The interaction between the juxtaposed images creates an imaginative space in which the reader's emotions can grow.

What sets haiku apart from other genres of poetry is its use of literal images that can be interpreted figuratively rather than of overtly figurative language. This is perhaps one of the most misunderstood aspects of haiku in the West, and a failure to appreciate this fundamental characteristic has led to much of the tension that has developed between poets in the academic/poetic mainstream and American haiku poets.

While simile, metaphor, and personification enhance the expressive range of poetry in general, in the tiny haiku they more often limit the range of the poem rather than expand it. Although the Japanese masters did occasionally use deliberately figurative language, their finest haiku use literal images. The role of figurative language in haiku is replaced by the juxtaposition of literal images. For example, consider one of Bashō's most famous haiku:

on a withered bough
a crow is perched—
autumn evening.

Bashō does not tell us that the crow is the grim reaper and that the closing of the day represents the waning of our lives. Instead, the extraordinary combination of an autumn evening, the bare branch, and the crow tells us as much about mortality as we need to know without the poet having to spoon-feed us with literary tropes. Certainly we are free to make any of these associations ourselves and others if we please. We are free to choose them, but they are not forced upon us by the poet. That these interpretations are not forced enables these haiku to be read on two levels, literal and symbolic, creating a richness that is lost with the use of purely figurative language.

Now let us take a look at the poems in Richard Wright's *Haiku: This Other World* in relation to these five elements of haiku. The form that Wright chose to use, a three-line form of five, seven, and five syllables, was apparently based on his understanding that Japanese haiku traditionally has seventeen syllables. He chose this form in spite of the fact that R. H. Blyth's translations of Japanese haiku, with which he was familiar, were not in seventeen syllables. While the seventeen-syllable form seems for the most part to have worked well for Wright, there are poems such as haiku 703 and 782:

In tense dry panic,
A fallen leaf goes flying
Over other leaves.

From the dark still pines,
Not a breath of autumn wind
To ripple the lake.

in which he appears to have padded out the poem with unnecessary adjectives, or with extraneous phrases, as in haiku 205 and 209, to achieve this form:

As my delegate,
With joints stiff with winter cold,
The first ant of spring.

As my delegate,
The spring wind has its fingers
In a young girl's hair.

In other cases, as in haiku 622, what seem to be inappropriate verb choices have been made apparently in the interest of achieving this form:

Pen me a letter
From where plum trees are blooming,
Pilgrimaging geese!

While the consistent use of 5-7-5 does give this collection a sort of integrity, it does also pose certain disadvantages, the most striking of which is a loss of immediacy in many of the poems. Take, for example, number 209. In this poem, the unnecessary metaphorical commentary in the first line has been added to pad out a touching image, and what could have been the base of a fine haiku, into seventeen syllables. That the commentary is unnecessary can be demonstrated by comparing it to haiku 479:

Head bent in spring sun,
A dog whimpers now and then,
Licking his penis.

In this effective poem, the reader is allowed to experience a moving spring scene as well as to interpret the symbolic nature of the images for him or herself.

Wright appears to have been unaware of the internal structure of haiku. This is evidenced by the large number of poems in *This Other World* that are composed of single images. In spite of this, some of Wright's poems do have the two-part structure described by Kawamoto and others (for example, see Robert Spiess's "A Certain Open Secret about Haiku"),[6] with the base contributing interest and the superposed part providing significance. An example of this structure is haiku 198:

The first day of spring:
A servant's hips shake as she
Wipes a mirror clean.

Here, the second and third lines act as the base, and the first line acts as the superposed section. In this poem, an intuitive relationship between the seasonal image and the sensual image of the servant creates an effect that is both subtle and profound. A large number of the poems in *This Other World*, however, are just single-image poems of the type that are often referred to as "nature sketches," that is, poems that contain a simple image of nature without any real significance. Haiku 542 is a typical example:

The dazzling spring sun
Dwindles the glittering sea
And shrinks the ships.

While it is true that not every one of Wright's poems contains a reference to the season, they do all have some reference to nonhuman nature. In this regard, Wright has more closely followed the Japanese model than haiku attempts by most Western poets.

With few exceptions, most of Wright's haiku were written in the present tense, so it appears that Wright was at least intuitively aware of this important element of haiku aesthetics. The power of the present, as opposed to the past tense in haiku, can be seen by comparing two of Wright's haiku, haiku 50 and 39. Here is haiku 50:

One magnolia
Landed upon another
In the dew-wet grass.

And haiku 39:

A soft wind at dawn
Lifts one dry leaf and lays it
Upon another.

In the first haiku, the use of the past tense produces a closure that makes it little more than a statement. In the second poem, however, the use of the present tense creates a lightness that lifts us along with the leaf and creates an unresolved tension. Will the leaf lift again? It is exactly the lack of finality that makes this a fine haiku. Wright's universal incorporation of nature, if not the seasons, and his frequent presentation of a single event in the present tense could be seen as the most successful part of Wright's exploration of haiku.

Whether or not Wright understood the use of the caesura to create a cut in the haiku, most of Wright's better haiku make use of the technique of internal comparison through the juxtaposition of images. For example, the very first haiku of the book uses a cut very effectively:

I am nobody:
A red sinking autumn sun
Took my name away.

However, one has to go a long way into the book to find as effective a cut as this. In fact, in *This Other World*'s first 200 poems, there are only a few, such as numbers 1, 39, 74, 130, 158, and 198, that have a true caesura. Some of the other poems do contain subtle syntactical cuts, but often these are only slight pauses contained within single-image poems. A consequence is that many of Wright's haiku lack the internal comparison (present in numbers 39, 198, and 479 quoted above) that is vital to haiku.

It is Wright's repeated use of personification, overt metaphor, and simile—hallmarks of Western poetics—that diminishes so many of these poems as haiku. Take haiku 236 as an example:

The dusty petals
Of ferocious sunflowers
Hold the rain at bay.

In fact, the sunflowers do no such thing. They are ferocious only in the poet's conceptual mind, so in this case Wright has replaced insight with fancy. The genius of haiku is in finding the seemingly hidden places where the spiritual world seeps through into the material world. In this haiku, and many others like it, the world of the spirit is obscured rather than revealed by the poet's imagined response.

On the contrary, in Wright's strongest haiku, he presents us with vivid literal images as in this justly famous haiku, number 31:

In the falling snow
A laughing boy holds out his palms
Until they are white.

He does not clutter this poem with figurative language—if he were to do so, it would considerably reduce the poem's impact. When he trusts to the reader and trusts the haiku to do its work, Wright is capable of the most delicate effects, as in the startling haiku 203:

Did somebody call?
Looking over my shoulder:
Massive spring mountains.

Unlike many of the other poems that contain fanciful rhetorical questions, this poem reverberates in the reader's mind with a haunting sense of mystery.

The best haiku deliver what Robert Bly has called "news of the universe."[7] While the best of Wright's poems in *This Other World* do bring this sort of news, most only bring news of the poet's mind and fancy. This brings us to an important question: Are these poems all haiku, or are many of them Western poems written in haiku form? While Wright can certainly be considered an important pioneer of haiku in English, his categorization of the poems in earlier drafts of the manuscript in sections with names like "Projection," "Personification," "Pathos," and the like[8] indicates that in many cases he was attempting to explore standard Western poetics within what he understood to be the haiku form, rather than attempting to delve deeply into the poetics of haiku itself. His original subtitle for the collection, "projections in the haiku manner," indicates that even he did not view them completely as haiku at a time when it was still being debated whether haiku could be written in English at all. His remark about counting to seventeen adds credence to this speculation since it indicates that he was exploring haiku as a form rather than as a genre of poetry. Since much of what Wright wrote in *This Other World* proves to have missed important elements of haiku aesthetics, it seems to be too much to ask that most of his haiku will be remembered as true haiku. In spite of this, however, a surprising number of his poems do work as haiku and will always be an important part of the Wright canon. But will they become a part of the canon of American haiku?

Cor van den Heuvel, editor of three editions of *The Haiku Anthology* (most recently from Norton in 1999), is a poet who was himself writing haiku of striking originality in the late 1950s and early 1960s. Van den Heuvel says of Wright's haiku, "I think it highly likely that if Wright had had the benefit of the give and take of advice and criticism with other poets . . . and more time in his life, he would have become a major haiku poet. As it turned out he is only a minor figure in haiku."[9]

William J. Higginson, author of the three books on haiku, *The Haiku Handbook, Haiku Seasons,* and *Haiku World,* writes, "The bottom line, for me, is that Wright's better haiku, the one to two hundred or so, would have knocked the socks off anyone in our nascent haiku community at that time." However, he goes on to say, "I'm afraid that the poor quality of the majority of the poems in *This Other World* dooms the book to ultimate dustbins, however popular it may be with academics today. If some major entity would put out a slim volume of just the cream of the R[ichard] W[right] crop, his haiku would become well-remembered. But the tome of *This Other World* is daunting, and [a reader] of real poetic sensibility soon tires of searching so hard for the gems among the dross. . . . In retrospect, *This Other World* is only a footnote to the development of haiku in English."[10] This assessment is consistent with that of publisher William Targ, who wrote to Wright of a manuscript of *This Other World* that "a fine little book could be produced from a careful selection."[11] As Higginson's remarks indicate, Wright might have had a major impact on the development of English-language haiku, but the unfortunate delay in their publication has reduced Wright's potential legacy.

I don't think that anyone questions the fact that Bashō was Japan's greatest haiku poet. Yet the excellence of some of his poems led to a veneration of all of his poems for two hundred years after his death. As a result of Masaoka Shiki's reappraisal of Bashō's haiku in the 1890s, it is now recognized that not all of his haiku are great. Some of Bashō's haiku are excellent, but a significant number of them are not. I believe that if we apply the established standards of haiku to Richard Wright's poems, we will come to a similar conclusion. Some of his poems are excellent, especially considering how little information about haiku was available to him. But many of his haiku are not. As Anthony Walton wrote in his review of *This Other World* for *The Oxford American,* "Many could be student work, and some are utter failures."[12] Learning to differentiate the quality of Wright's haiku not only increases our knowledge and appreciation of the haiku genre but also helps us to understand what made his best haiku successful. It is in this context that I propose that some of his poems are excellent and will become part of the English-language haiku canon whereas many will not.

To return to the question posed earlier, are they haiku or are they Western poems in haiku form? I believe the answer is both. Some do work as haiku with the seasonal reference, present tense, caesura, and internal comparison that are characteristics of the genre, but very few of the 817. However, many of the remaining poems work perfectly well as short Western poems. In other words, what have been viewed in the past by haiku critics as failed haiku can now be seen as successful non-haiku poems in haiku form. Whatever they may be called, the poems in *This Other World* show Wright's poetic abilities and are a valuable window into his life. My recommendation to the editors of *This Other World* is that they restore the subtitle, "projections in the haiku manner," to future editions in order to avoid confusion over this matter.

Let us celebrate Wright's work in haiku for what it is, sometimes seriously flawed, but the best of it among the best haiku that was being written in English at the time. Let us preserve the very best of Wright's haiku and give it its proper place in the English-language haiku canon. Two hundred years after Bashō's death, Masaoka Shiki stunned the Japanese haiku world by suggesting that not every one of Bashō's haiku was a masterpiece. Once Japanese haiku had recovered from the shock, it exploded with creative energy in a way it had not in centuries. Wright is hardly comparable to Bashō in terms of English-language haiku, but let us not wait so long to shed the baggage of Wright's poorer haiku. As both Higginson and Targ point out, Wright's stature in American haiku could be considerably enhanced by the appearance of a more selective volume of his haiku.

We know Wright was familiar, through the translations of R. H. Blyth, with the haiku of Bashō, Buson, and Issa, the greatest Japanese haiku poets of the seventeenth, eighteenth, and nineteenth centuries. Bashō is known for his great philosophical depth, Buson for his painterly skill in creating vivid visual images, and Issa for his sympathetic treatment of small creatures and for his use of haiku to deal with the loneliness of his life as a homeless orphan driven away by a wicked stepmother. As a result of the similarities of his experiences of loneliness and exile to those of Issa, many of Wright's haiku tend to fall in the third category. As an exile himself, he seems to have found in haiku a way to express deep sympathy for those creatures whose lives, like his own, were subject to the whims of chance. And in these haiku, he seems also to be searching for the sympathy and fellow feeling he himself needed to carry on.

Bashō is considered the greatest haiku poet. Issa, perhaps because of his accessibility and sympathy, is the most popular with the general public. Wright's haiku seem closer to Issa's than to Bashō's, which should lead us to predict a similar fate for Wright's reputation as a haiku poet. While I don't believe that Wright will ever be recognized as the greatest American haiku poet, he will, like other poets such as Allen Ginsberg and Jack Kerouac, be remembered for his pioneering work in haiku, if not for the quality of the haiku themselves. I do believe that his work will always have a wide audience because in his haiku he faces directly the very human problems of loneliness and exile and helps to give each of us the hope needed to go on in this world for another day.

Because of Wright's simplicity and accessibility and the widespread availability of *This Other World*, he will be the door through which many people will enter American haiku, and for that reason it is doubly unfortunate that this book was not available sooner. Blyth calls haiku "an open door which looks shut."[13] I believe Wright will open that door for many people. That Wright clearly understood that it was not the door to our ordinary world is indicated by the title he chose for his collection, *This Other World*. As this haiku by the twentieth-century Japanese haiku master Yatsuka Ishihara shows, this is a magical world recognized by all haiku poets:

pulling light
from the other world . . .
the Milky Way[14]

Wright's "projections in the haiku manner" are a window that gives us a vision of that other world.

Notes

1. Julia Wright, introduction to *Haiku: This Other World* by Richard Wright (New York: Arcade, 1998), viii.

2. Harold G. Henderson, *Haiku in English* (Rutland, VT: Charles E. Tuttle, 1967), 14–17.

3. Ibid., 18.

4. Kôji Kawamoto, *The Poetics of Japanese Verse* (Tokyo: University of Tokyo Press, 2000), 73–74.

5. Czeslaw Milosz, *A Book of Luminous Things* (New York: Harcourt Brace, 1998), 3.

6. Robert Spiess, "A Certain Open Secret about Haiku," *Modern Haiku* 32, no. 1 (2001): 59.

7. Robert Bly, *News of the Universe: Poems of Twofold Consciousness* (San Francisco: Sierra Club Books, 1980).

8. Floyd Ogburn Jr., "Richard Wright's Unpublished Haiku: A World Elsewhere," *MELUS* 23 no. 3 (1998): 69.

9. Cor van den Heuvel, personal correspondence to author, December 12, 2000.

10. William J. Higginson, personal correspondence to author, December 1, 2000.

11. Ogburn, "Richard Wright's Unpublished Haiku: A World Elsewhere," 57.

12. Anthony Walton, "Richard Wright, Haiku Poet," *Oxford American* (November/December 1999). https://www.utne.com/2000-03-01/RichardWrightHaikuPoet.aspx (accessed December 4, 2000).

13. Cor van den Heuvel, *The Haiku Anthology* (New York: Norton, 1999), lxiv.

14. Yatsuka Ishihara, *Red Fuji: Selected Haiku of Yatsuka Ishihara*, ed. William J. Higginson, Tadashi Kondo, and Kristen Deming (Santa Fe, NM: From Here Press, 1997), 73.

Works Cited

Agostini, Bertrand. "The Development of French Haiku in the First Half of the 20th Century: Historical Perspectives." *Modern Haiku* 32, no. 2 (2001). 46–60. http://www.modernhaiku.org/essays/frenchhaiku.html.

Austin, J. L. *How to Do Things with Words*. Cambridge, MA: Harvard University Press, 1962.

Bakish, David. *Richard Wright*. New York: Frederick Ungar, 1973.

Bashō. *On Love and Barley: Haiku of Bashō*. Trans. and intro. Lucien Stryk. New York: Penguin, 1985.

Belasco, David. *Six Plays: Madame Butterfly, Du Barry, the Darling of the Gods, Adrea, the Girl of the Golden West, the Return of Peter Grimm*. Ed. Montrose J. Moses. Boston: Little Brown, 1928.

Berry, Faith. Introduction to *Pagan Spain* by Richard Wright. Jackson: University Press of Mississippi, 1995.

Bhabha, Homi. *The Location of Culture*. New York: Routledge, 1994.

Bielenson, Peter, ed. and trans. *The Four Seasons*. Mt. Vernon, NY: Peter Pauper Press, 1958.

———. *Japanese Haiku*. Mt. Vernon, NY: Peter Pauper Press, 1955.

Bly, Robert. *News of the Universe: Poems of Twofold Consciousness*. San Francisco: Sierra Club Books, 1980.

Blyth, Reginald H. *Haiku*. 4 vols. Tokyo: Hokuseido Press, 1949–1952.

———. *A History of Haiku*. 2 vols. Tokyo: Hokuseido Press, 1963.

Cummiskey, Gary. "Interview with Sinclair Beiles, Yeoville, 1994." http://realitystudio.org/interviews/who-was-sinclair-beiles.

Danquah, J. B. *The Akan Doctrine of God: A Fragment of Gold Coast Ethics and Religion*. London: Frank Cass, 1944.

Du Bois, W. E. B. "Color Line Belts the World." *W. E. B. Du Bois on Asia: Crossing the World Color Line*. Ed. Bill V. Mullen and Cathryn Watson. Jackson: University Press of Mississippi, 2005.

Ellison, Ralph. "Richard Wright's Blues." *The Antioch Review* 5 (1945): 198–211.

———. "Richard Wright's Blues." *Shadow and Act*. 77–94. New York, Quality Paperback Book Club, 1994.

Fabre, Michel. *From Harlem to Paris*. Urbana: University of Illinois Press, 1991.

———. "The Poetry of Richard Wright." *Critical Essays on Richard Wright*. Ed. Yoshinobu Hakutani. Boston: G. K. Hall, 1982. 252–72.

———. *Richard Wright Books and Writers*. Jackson: University Press of Mississippi, 1990.

———. *The Unfinished Quest of Richard Wright*. New York: William Morrow, 1973.

———. *The Unfinished Quest of Richard Wright*. 2nd ed. Urbana: University of Illinois Press, 1993.

———. *The World of Richard Wright*. Jackson: University Press of Mississippi, 1985.

Fields, Rick. *How the Swans Came to the Lake: A Narrative History of Buddhism in America*. 3rd ed. Boston: Shambhala, 1992.

Fisher, Dexter, and Robert Stepto. *Afro-American Literature: The Reconstruction of Instruction*. New York: Modern Language Association, 1979.

Gillan, Maria Mazziotti, and Jennifer Gillan, eds. *Unsettling America: An Anthology of Contemporary Multicultural Poetry*. New York: Penguin, 1994.

Gilroy, Paul. *The Black Atlantic: Modernity and Double Consciousness*. Cambridge, MA: Harvard University Press, 1993.

Ginsberg, Allen. *Journals: Early Fifties, Early Sixties*. Ed. Gordon Ball. New York: Grove Press, 1977.

Giroux, Joan. *The Haiku Form*. Rutland, VT: Charles E. Tuttle, 1974.

Gounard, Jean-Franfois. *The Racial Problem in the Works of Richard Wright and James Baldwin*. Trans. Joseph J. Rodgers Jr. Westport, CT: Greenwood, 1992.

Gurga, Lee. "Richard Wright's Place in American Haiku." *Valley Voices: A Literary Review* 8, no. 2 (2008): 34–43.

Hakutani, Yoshinobu, ed. *Critical Essays on Richard Wright*. Boston: G. K. Hall, 1982.

———. *Cross-Cultural Visions in African American Modernism: From Spatial Narrative to Jazz Haiku*. Columbus: The Ohio State University Press, 2006.

———, ed. *Modernity in East-West Literary Criticism*. Madison, NJ: Fairleigh Dickinson University Press / London: Associated University Press, 2001.

———. *Richard Wright and Racial Discourse*. Columbia: University of Missouri Press, 1996.

———, and Robert L. Tener. Afterword to *Haiku: This Other World* by Richard Wright. New York: Arcade, 1998. 245–300.

Harrington, Ollie W. *Why I Left America and Other Essays*. Jackson: University Press of Mississippi, 1993.

Hashimoto, Yorimitsu. "Japanese Tea Party: Representations of Victorian Paradise and Playground in *The Geisha* (1896)." *Histories of Tourism: Representation, Identity and Conflict*. Ed. John K. Walton. Clevedon: Channel View Publications, 2005.

Henderson, Harold G. *An Introduction to Haiku*. New York: Doubleday, 1958.

———. *Haiku in English*. Rutland, VT: Charles E. Tuttle, 1967.

Higginson, William J. Personal Correspondence to Lee Gurga, December 1, 2000.

Hill, Patricia Liggins, ed. *Call & Response: The Riverside Anthology of the African American Literary Tradition*. Boston: Houghton Mifflin, 1997.

hooks, bell. *Killing Rage: Ending Racism*. New York: Henry Holt, 1995.

Humphreys, Christmas. *Zen Buddhism*. London: Allen & Unwin, 1957.

Hurston, Zora Neale. "What White Publishers Won't Print." *Within the Circle*. Ed. Angelyn Mitchell. Durham: Duke University Press, 1995. 116–21.

Iadonisi, Richard A. "'I Am Nobody': The Haiku of Richard Wright." *MELUS* 30, no. 3 (Fall 2005): 179–200.

Ishihara, Yatsuka. *Red Fuji: Selected Haiku of Yatsuka Ishihara*. Ed. William J. Higginson, Tadashi Kondo, and Kristen Deming. Santa Fe, NM: From Here Press, 1997.

JanMohamed, Abdul R. *The Death-Bound Subject: Richard Wright's Archaeology of Death*. Durham: Duke University Press, 2005.

———. "Negating the Negation as a Form of Affirmation in Minority Discourse: The Construction of Richard Wright as Subject." *The Nature and Context of Minority Discourse*. Ed. Abdul R. JanMohamed and David Lloyd. New York: Oxford University Press, 1990. 102–23.

Japanese Classics Translation Committee. *Haikai and Haiku*. Tokyo: Nippon Gakujutsu Shinkokai, 1958.

Kawamoto, Kôji. *The Poetics of Japanese Verse*. Tokyo: University of Tokyo Press, 2000.

Kearney, Reginald. *African American Views of the Japanese: Solidarity or Sedition?* New York: State University of New York Press, 1998.

Keene, Donald. *Japanese Literature: An Introduction for Western Readers*. New York: Grove Press, 1955.

Kinnamon, Keneth. "Wright, Hemingway, and the Bullfight." *Richard Wright's Travel Writings*. Ed. Virginia Whatley Smith. Jackson: University Press of Mississippi, 2001. 157–64.

———, and Michel Fabre. *Conversations with Richard Wright*. Jackson: University Press of Mississippi, 1993.

Kiuchi, Toru. Letter to Yoshinobu Hakutani, August 7, 2005.

———, Robert J. Butler, and Yoshinobu Hakutani, eds. *The Critical Response in Japan to African American Writers*. New York: Peter Lang, 2003.

Kodama, Sanehide. *American Poetry and Japanese Culture*. Hamden, CT: Archon, 1984.

———. "Japanese Influence on Richard Wright in His Last Years: English Haiku as a New Genre." *Tamkang Review* 15, no. 1–4 (Autumn 1984–Summer 1985): 63–73.

Lacan, Jacques. *The Four Fundamental Concepts of Psychoanalysis*. Ed. Jacques-Alain Miller, trans. Alan Sheridan. New York: Norton, 1981.

———. *The Seminar of Jacques Lacan*, bk. 2, *The Ego in Freud's Theory and in the Techniques of Psychoanalysis, 1954–1955*. Ed. Jacques-Alain Miller, trans. Sylvana Tomaselli. New York: Norton, 1988.

Lamb, Andrew. "The Geisha." *The Geisha: A Japanese Musical Play by Sidney Jones*. London: Hyperion Records, 1998. 3–7.

Lewis, David Levering, ed. *The Portable Harlem Renaissance Reader*. New York: Viking, 1994.

———. *When Harlem Was in Vogue*. New York: Penguin, 1979.

Lowe, John. "Richard Wright as Traveler / Ethnographer." *Richard Wright's Travel Writings*. Ed. Virginia Whatley Smith. Jackson: University Press of Mississippi, 2001. 119–47.

Miller, Eugene E. *Voice of a Native Son: The Poetics of Richard Wright*. Jackson: University Press of Mississippi, 1990.

Milosz, Czeslaw. *A Book of Luminous Things*. New York: Harcourt Brace, 1998.

Miner, Earl. *The Japanese Tradition in British and American Literature*. Princeton, NJ: Princeton University Press, 1958.

Miyamori, Asataro. *An Anthology of Haiku: Ancient and Modern*. Westport, CT: Greenwood, 1970.

Morrison, Toni. *Beloved*. New York: Vintage International, 2004.

Mullen, Bill V. *Afro-Orientalism*. Minneapolis: University of Minnesota Press, 2004.

———, and Cathryn Watson. *W. E. B. Du Bois on Asia: Crossing the World Color Line*. Jackson: University Press of Mississippi, 2005.

Nichols, Charles H., ed. *Arna Bontemps—Langston Hughes Letters, 1925–1967*. New York: Paragon, 1990.

Noguchi, Yone. *Selected English Writings of Yone Noguchi: An East-West Literary Assimilation*. Ed. Yoshinobu Hakutani, 2 vols. London: Associated University Presses, 1992.

Ogburn, Floyd, Jr. "Richard Wright's Unpublished Haiku: A World Elsewhere." *MELUS* 23, no. 3 (1998): 57–81.

Pound, Ezra. "As for Imagisme." *New Age* 16, no. 13 (1915): 349–50.

———. *Ezra Pound: Selected Poems*. New York: New Directions, 1957.

———. "Vorticism." *Fortnightly Review* 96, no. 573 (September 1, 1914): 461–71.

Prashad, Vijay. *Everybody was Kung Fu Fighting: Afro-Asian Connections and the Myth of Cultural Purity*. Boston: Beacon, 2001.

Pratt, Marjory Bates. *The Light on the Snow*. Pennington, NJ: Private Edition, 1979.

Reich, Wilhelm. *Character-Analysis*. New York: Orgone Institute Press, 1949.

———. *The Function of the Orgasm*. New York: Orgone Institute Press, 1942.

———. *The Mass Psychology of Fascism*. New York: Orgone Institute Press, 1946.

———. *The Sexual Revolution*. New York: Orgone Institute Press, 1945.

Rexroth, Kenneth. "The Influence of Classical Japanese Poetry." *The Elastic Retort*. New York: Seabury Press, 1973. 149–57.

Rowley, Hazel. *Richard Wright: The Life and Times*. New York: Henry Holt, 2001.

Schettler, Meta L. "'The rifle bullet': African-American History in Richard Wright's Unpublished Haiku." *Valley Voices: A Literary Review* 8, no. 2 (2008): 66–80.

Sharpe, E. A. *William Sharp: A Memoir*. London: Heinemann, 1910.

Shirane, Haruo. *Traces of Dreams*. Stanford: Stanford University Press, 1998.

"Sinclair Beiles and the Beat Hotel," January 24, 1997. http://www.111.co.za/beathotel.

Smith, Virginia Whatley, ed. *Richard Wright's Travel Writings: New Reflections*. Jackson: University Press of Mississippi, 2001.

Snyder, Gary. *Earth House Hold*. New York: New Directions, 1969.

Spiess, Robert. "A Certain Open Secret about Haiku." *Modern Haiku* 32, no. 1 (2001): 57–64.

Steen, Shannon. "Racing American Modernity: Black Atlantic Negotiations of Asia and the 'Swing' Mikado." *Afro Asian Encounter: Culture, History, Politics*. Ed. Heike Raphael-Hernandez and Shannon Steen. New York: New York University Press, 2006. 167–87.

Suzuki, Daisetz T. *Essays in Zen Buddhism*. The Third Series. London, New York: Rider, 1960.

———. *An Introduction to Zen Buddhism*. Ed. Christmas Humphreys. London: Arrow, 1959.

———. *Zen and Japanese Culture*. Bollingen Ser. 64. Princeton, NJ: Princeton University Press, 1959.

Syndicate of Czeck Authors. Letter to Richard Wright. January 9, 1949. Box 106, Folder 1630. JWJ Collection, Beinecke Library, Yale University.

Tener, Robert L. "Richard Wright's Haiku: *This Other World*." *Modernity in East-West Literary Criticism*. Ed. Yoshinobu Hakutani. Madison, NJ: Fairleigh Dickinson University Press, 2001. 137–57.

———. "Union with Nature: Richard Wright and the Art of Haiku." *Chiba Review* 10 (1988): 19–34.

———. "The Where, the When, the What: A Study of Richard Wright's Haiku." *Critical Essays on Richard Wright*. Ed. Yoshinobu Hakutani. Boston: G. K. Hall, 1982. 273–98.

Trumbull, Charles. "The American Haiku Movement Part I: Haiku in English." *Modern Haiku* 36, no. 3 (2005). http://www.modernhaiku.org/essays/AmHaikuMovement1.html.

Ueda, Kansho, and Mihoko Okamura, eds. *Suzuki Daisetz towa Dareka* [*Who Is Daisetz Suzuki?*]. Tokyo: Iwanami Shoten, 2002.

Vallillo, Stephen M. "The Battle of the Black Mikados." *Black American Literature Forum* 16 (1982): 153–57.

Van den Heuvel, Cor, ed. *The Haiku Anthology*. New York: Norton, 1999.

———. Personal Correspondence to Lee Gurga, December 12, 2000.

Walker, Margaret. *Richard Wright: Daemonic Genius*. New York: Amistad Press, 1988.

Walton, Anthony. "Richard Wright, Haiku Poet." *Oxford American*. November/December 1999. https://www.utne.com/2000-03-01/RichardWrightHaikuPoet.aspx.

Ward, Jerry W. Letter to Zheng. July 20, 2010.

Warren, Nagueyalti. "Black Girls and Native Son: Female Images in Selected Works by Richard Wright." *Richard Wright Myths and Realities*. Ed. C. James Trotman. New York: Garland Publishing, 1988. 59–77.

Webb, Constance. *Richard Wright: A Biography*. New York: Putnam, 1968.

Weiss, M. Lynn. *Gertrude Stein and Richard Wright: The Poetics and Politics of Modernism*. Jackson: University Press of Mississippi, 1998.

Williams, Diane, and Jerry W. Ward. "A Conversation on Richard Wright." *Valley Voices: A Literary Review* 8, no. 2 (2008): 99–112.

Winter, William. *The Life of David Belasco*. New York: Mofatt, Yard, and Company, 1918.

Wright, Julia. Introduction to *Haiku: This Other World* by Richard Wright. New York: Arcade, 1998. vii–xii.

Wright, Richard. *Uncle Tom's Children*. New York: Harper, 1938.

———. *Black Boy*. 1945 (*American Hunger*). *Richard Wright: Later Works*. Ed. Arnold Rampersad. New York: Library of America, 1991.

———. *Black Boy (American Hunger)*. New York: HarperPerennial, 1998.

———. *Black Power: A Record of Reactions in the Land of Pathos*. New York: Harper & Brothers, 1954.

———. *Black Power*. New York: HarperPerrennial, 2008.

———. "Blueprint for Negro Writing." *New Challenge* 2, no. 1 (Fall 1937): 53–65.

———. "Blueprint for Negro Writing." *Within the Circle*. Ed. Angelyn Mitchell, 97–106. Durham: Duke University Press, 1995.

———. *The Color Curtain: A Report on the Bandung Conference*. New York: World Publishing, 1956.

———. *Eight Men*. New York: HarperPerennial, 1996.

———. Foreword to *Blues Fell This Morning* by Paul Oliver. New York: Cambridge University Press, 1990. xiii–xvi.

———. *Haiku: This Other World*. Ed. Yoshinobu Hakutani and Robert L. Tener. New York: Arcade, 1998.

———. "I Choose Exile." *The Writer's Presence*. Ed. Donald McQuade and Robert Atwan. Boston: Bedford/St. Martin's, 2003. 288–95.

———. "Journal." January 14, 1945. Box 117, Folder 1860, JWJ Collection, Beinecke Library, Yale University.

———. Letters to Hornung. January 12, 1960; January 19, 1960; February 5, 1960; March 16, 1960. Michel Fabre Private Collection.

———. Letters to Margrit de Sablonière. April 8, 1960; April 20, 1960; May 22, 1960. Michel Fabre Private Collection.

———. *The Long Dream*. Garden City, NY: Doubleday, 1958.

———. *Native Son*. 1940. New York: Perennial Classics, 1998.

———. *Pagan Spain*. Jackson: University Press of Mississippi, 1995.

———. "Richard Wright Describes the Birth of Black Boy: An Autobiography Destined to Disturb White Egotism." *New York Post*, November 30, 1944, B6.

———. *Richard Wright Reader*. Ed. Ellen Wright and Michel Fabre. New York: Harper & Row, 1978.

———. "This Other World: Projections in the Haiku Manner." Box 70, Folders 832 and 833, JWJ Collection, Beinecke Library, Yale University.

———. "Travel Journal." Box 22, Folder 344, JWJ Collection, Beinecke Library, Yale University.

———. *12 Million Black Voices*. New York: Thunder's Mouth Press, 1988.

———. *Uncle Tom's Children*. In *Early Works*, ed. Arnold Rampersad. New York: Library of America, 1991. 221–441.

———. *White Man, Listen!* Garden City, NY: Doubleday, 1957.

Yasuda, Kenneth. *The Japanese Haiku: Its Essential Nature, History, and Possibilities in English*. Rutland, VT: Charles E. Tuttle, 1957.

Zheng, Jianqing. "Richard Wright's Haiku." *Southern Quarterly* 46, no. 2 (2009): 61–70.

———. "The South in Richard Wright's Haiku." *Notes on Contemporary Literature* 37, no. 2 (2007): 6–9.

Bibliography on Richard Wright's Haiku

Articles in Journals, Anthologies, and Books

Brown, Bridgette. "Light and Dark Images in Richard Wright's Haiku." *Valley Voices: A Literary Review* 9, no. 2 (2009): 8–10.

Fabre, Michel. "From Revolutionary Poetry to Haiku." *The World of Richard Wright.* Jackson: University Press of Mississippi, 1985. 34–55.

———. "Richard Wright, Poète." *Presence Africaine* 135 (1985): 39–55.

Gurga, Lee. "Richard Wright's Place in American Haiku." *Valley Voices: A Literary Review* 8, no. 2 (2008): 34–43.

Hakutani, Yoshinobu. "Nature, Africa, and Richard Wright's Haiku." *Modern Haiku* 31, no. 2 (2000): 69–81.

———. "Nature, Haiku, and 'This Other World.'" *Richard Wright and Racial Discourse.* Columbia: University of Missouri Press, 1996. 261–91.

———. "The Poetics of Nature: Wright's Haiku, Zen, and Lacan." *Cross-Cultural Visions in African American Modernism: From Spatial Narrative to Jazz Haiku.* Columbus: The Ohio State University Press, 2006. 153–69.

———. "Richard Wright's Haiku, Zen, and the African 'Primal Outlook.'" *Modern Philology* 104, no. 4 (2007): 510–28.

Iadonisi, Richard A. "'I Am Nobody': The Haiku of Richard Wright." *MELUS* 30, no. 3 (2005): 179–200.

Inouchi, Yushiro. "Richard Wright's Encounter with Haiku." *Waseda University English Literature* 79 (2000): 131–45.

Kiuchi, Toru. "Japan." *The Richard Wright Encyclopedia.* Ed. Jerry W. Ward Jr. and Robert J. Butler. Boston: Greenwood, 2008. 206–8.

———. "The Japanese Translation of English Haiku: The Case of Richard Wright." *Sable: A Haiku Magazine* 23 (1986): 24–25.

———. "Nature in Richard Wright's Haiku." *Waseda Review* 21 (1982): 64–73.

———. "Teaching Richard Wright's Haiku in Japan." *Black Scholar* 39, no. 1–2 (2009): 59–62.

———. "Zen Buddhism in Richard Wright's Haiku." *Journal of College of Industrial Technology* (Nihon University) 39 (2006): 1–9.

———. "Zen Buddhism in Richard Wright's Haiku." *Valley Voices: A Literary Review* 8, no. 2 (2008): 18–33.

Kodama, Sanehide. "Japanese Influence on Richard Wright in His Last Years: English Haiku as a New Genre." *Tamkang Review* 15, no. 1–4 (Autumn 1984–Summer 1985): 63–73.

———. "Richard Wright and His Haiku." *American Poetry and Japanese Culture.* Hamden, CT: Archon, 1984. 156–62.

Kurosu, Kishiko. "The World of Richard Wright's Haiku." *Annual Proceedings of Saitama Junior College* 9 (2000): 31–38.

Li, Yi. "On the Intergradation of Richard Wright's Poetry and Black Aesthetics." *Proceedings of the International Conference on the 20th Century American Poetry* (2009): 211–17.

Miller, Eugene E. "The Cosmos: Uses of Orgone and Haiku." *Voice of a Native Son.* Jackson: University Press of Mississippi, 1990. 212–52.

Miller, Shawnrece D. "Female Images in Richard Wright's *Haiku: This Other World.*" *Modern Haiku* 32, no. 3 (2001): 54–57.

Minagawa, Soichi. "Richard Wright and Haiku." *New Japanese Literature* 29 (1974): 101–5.

Missias, A. C. "Wright Redux." *Frogpond* 24, no. 1 (2001): 63–65.

Ogburn, Floyd, Jr. "Richard Wright's Unpublished Haiku: A World Elsewhere." *MELUS* 23, no. 3 (1998): 57–81.

Sato, Kazuo. "Richard Wright's Haiku." *From Japanese Haiku to English Haiku: The Reception of Haiku in America and Britain.* Tokyo: Nanundo, 1987. 156–59.

Schettler, Meta L. "'The rifle bullet': African American History in Richard Wright's Unpublished Haiku." *Valley Voices: A Literary Review* 8, no. 2 (2008): 66–80.

Tener, Robert L. "Richard Wright's Haiku: This Other World." *Modernity in East-West Literary Criticism: New Readings.* Ed. Yoshinobu Hakutani. Madison, NJ: Fairleigh Dickinson University Press, 2001. 137–57.

———. "Union with Nature: Wright and the Art of Haiku." *Chiba Review* 10 (1988): 19–34.

———. "The Where, the When, the What: A Study of Richard Wright's Haiku." *Critical Essays on Richard Wright.* Ed. Yoshinobu Hakutani. Boston: G. K. Hall, 1982. 273–98.

Watson, Pamela. "Richard Wright's Haiku on Loneliness." *Valley Voices: A Literary Review* 9, no. 2 (2009): 11–12.

Zheng, Jianqing. "Richard Wright's Haiku." *Southern Quarterly: A Journal of the Arts in the South* 46, no. 2 (2009): 61–70.

———. "Richard Wright's Travel to Spain." *Frogpond* 30, no. 1 (2007): 53–57.

———. "Sensibility to Nature in Richard Wright's Haiku." *Modern Haiku* 38, no. 1 (2007): 54–61.

———. "Sensibility to Nature in Richard Wright's Haiku." *Dust of Summers Anthology.* Winchester, VA: Red Moon Press, 2008. 155–63.

———. "The South in Richard Wright's Haiku." *Notes on Contemporary Literature* 37, no. 2 (2007): 6–9.

———. "Tangible Imagination in Richard Wright's Haiku." *Frogpond* 25, no. 2 (2002): 61–62.

———. "Tangible Imagination in Richard Wright's Haiku." *Pegging the Wind Anthology.* Winchester, VA: Red Moon Press, 2003. 50–52.

———. "Zen in Richard Wright's I AM NOBODY." *The Explicator* 68, no. 2 (2010): 127–30.

Introduction, Notes, and Afterword

Hakutani, Yoshinobu, and Robert L. Tener. Afterword to *Haiku: This Other World.* New York: Arcade, 1998. 245–304.

———. "Notes on the Haiku." *Haiku: This Other World.* New York: Arcade, 1998. 207–44.

Wright, Julia. Introduction to *Haiku: This Other World.* New York: Arcade, 1998. vii–xiv.

Book Reviews

Brainard, Dulcy. "*Haiku: This Other World.*" *Publisher's Weekly* 245 (1998): 71.

Brevard, Lisa Pertillar. "'Branches without Roots'—But Full of Flowers." *Black Issues in Higher Education* 16 (1999): 74.

Clarence, Judy. "Wright, Richard. *Haiku: This Other World.*" *Library Journal* 123 (1998): 84.

Glenn, Karen. "Richard Wright's Surprising Secret." *Literary Cavalcade* 51, no. 5 (1999): 20–21.

Hamill, Sam. "The Unlikeliest Haiku Master." *Seattle Weekly*, September 30, 1998. http://www.seattleweekly.com/1998-09-30/food/the-unlikeliest-haiku-master.php.

Hass, Robert. "Five Haikus by Richard Wright." *Washington Post*, April 11, 1999. http://www.washingtonpost.com/wp-srv/style/books/features/19990413.htm.

Olson, Ray. "Wright, Richard. *Haiku: This Other World.*" *Booklist* 95 (1998): 58.

Pinson, Hermine. "*Haiku: This Other World* by Richard Wright." *Richard Wright Newsletter* 7 (2000): 4–6.

Walton, Anthony. "Richard Wright, Haiku Poet." *Oxford American.* November/December 1999. https://www.utne.com/2000-03-01/RichardWrightHaikuPoet.aspx.

Brief Discussions

Gurga, Lee. *Haiku: A Poet's Guide.* Lincoln, IL: Modern Haiku Press, 2003. 86.

Harrington, Ollie W. *Why I Left America and Other Essays.* Jackson: University Press of Mississippi, 1993. 14–15.

Higginson, William J. *The Haiku Handbook.* New York: McGraw-Hill, 1985. 65, 88–89.

Osborne, Mamie. "An Analysis of 'In the Falling Snow.'" *Haiku Page* 1, no. 1 (2008): 2.

Person, Precious. "My Favorite Haiku by Richard Wright." *Valley Voices: A Literary Review* 9, no. 2 (2009): 13.

Ziliak, Stephen T. "Haiku Economics: Little Teaching Aids for Big Economic Pluralists." *International Journal of Pluralism and Economics Education* 1, no. 1–2 (2009): 108–29.

Contributors

Shawnrece D. Campbell directs the Africana Studies Program and is a tenured assistant professor at Stetson University. Her research interests and presentations center on the collective power of females of all ages and the life and works of Toni Morrison. Her publications include articles and reviews in *International Journal of Africana Studies, Journal of Pan African Studies, Journal of Black Studies, African American Review*, and *Modern Haiku*. She is working on a book project entitled *The Power of the Red Dress* that examines the connection between womanism, the spiritual synergistic power created through childhood games, and the communal power of females of all ages.

Lee Gurga is an award-winning haiku poet. He is past president of the Haiku Society of America and former editor of *Modern Haiku*. He is currently editor of Modern Haiku Press. His book, *Haiku: A Poet's Guide*, was awarded the Best Book of Criticism by Haiku Society of America in 2004. The Japan-America Society of Chicago gave him their Cultural Achievement Award in 2006.

Yoshinobu Hakutani is professor of English and University Distinguished Scholar at Kent State University, Ohio. He is the author or editor of many books including *The City in African American Literature* (with Robert Butler); *Richard Wright and Racial Discourse*; *Cross-Cultural Visions in African American Modernism: From Spatial Narrative to Jazz Haiku*; *Haiku and Modernist Poetics*; *Wright's Haiku: This Other World* (with Robert L. Tener); and *Theodore Dreiser's Art, Music, and Literature, 1897–1902*.

Richard A. Iadonisi teaches at Grand Valley State University. He is the author of "Amy Lowell and the Gendered Aesthetics of Haiku" and "Writing the (Revolutionary) Body: The Haiku of Sonia Sanchez." He has also published articles on Robert Frost's "Snow" and Art Spiegelman's *Maus.*

Toru Kiuchi, professor of English at Nihon University in Japan, is an editor of *The Critical Response in Japan to African American Writers* (New York: Peter Lang, 2003) and translator of Richard Wright's *Haiku: This Other World.* He is the leading translator and scholar of Richard Wright's work in Japan.

Sanehide Kodama is professor emeritus of English and former president of Doshisha Women's College of Liberal Arts in Japan, but he remains chairman of the Council of the Doshisha Corporation. He is the author or editor of books including *American Poetry and Japanese Culture* and *Ezra Pound and Japan: Letters and Essays.* He lectures widely throughout Japan on everything from American literature to Japanese gardens and published his seventh book on American poetry in 2004.

Thomas L. Morgan is an assistant professor of English at the University of Dayton in Dayton, Ohio. His research examines the politics of narrative form in late-nineteenth-century periodical culture, analyzing the relationships between authors, editors, and readers in regards to the aesthetic categories of literary production. He has published on Paul Laurence Dunbar and James Weldon Johnson in *African American Review*, has edited, with Gene Jarrett, *The Complete Stories of Paul Laurence Dunbar* (published by Ohio University Press), and has a forthcoming essay on the production values of periodical culture in *American Literary Realism.*

Sachi Nakachi is a professor of English at Tsuru University in Japan. She received her Ph.D. in 2001 from Ohio University. She was a visiting Fulbright scholar in New York University and University of California, Berkeley, from 2009 to 2010. She has published many articles on African American literature as well as American *Japonisme* literature in the Japanese *Journal of Black Studies*, the *Journal of Japonisme Studies,* and elsewhere.

Meta L. Schettler is an associate professor of Africana Studies at California State University, Fresno. Her research interests include twentieth-century African American poetry as well as twentieth-century South African culture and politics grounded in the theoretical frameworks of postcolonialism, feminism, and multiculturalism. She has published essays in the *International Journal of Africana Studies, Valley Voices, Obsidian, Abafazi,* and *Safundi: The Journal of South African and American Comparative Studies.*

Jianqing Zheng, chair and professor of English at Mississippi Valley State University, is author of *The Landscape of Mind*, editor of *Valley Voices* and *Poetry South*, and coeditor of *Essays on African American Literature*. He was a Fulbright Scholar in 2009 and a recipient of the NEH grant on Richard Wright and of the Mississippi Arts Commission Fellowship in Poetry.

Index